Places of Our People

Ozarks
White River Valley

The Vanishing Ozarks
Volume 2

nature and culture . org

Freda Cruse Phillips, PhD

ISBN: 978-0-9842111-1-1

Library of Congress Control Number: 2011905637

Printed in the United States by Morris Publishing®
3212 East Highway 30
Kearney, NE 68847
1-800-650-7888

TABLE OF CONTENTS

DEDICATION

Ima Loveta Fulks 1926-2004 Lonnie Edward Cruse 1925-1992

Places of Our People is dedicated to my Momma & Daddy. I particularly love this photo of them sitting in our living room, the pictures of us three kids seen clearly in the bookshelf behind them. My momma's table always had room for another plate and the furniture in the living room could be moved to accommodate musicians and dancers, later blankets on the floor for sleeping. Daddy could always find work for anyone that was willing to work hard, something we all understood. Mrs. Bennett told me about the time Johnny didn't have work. He went down to the saw mill and asked for a job. "Your daddy told him pointing to your Momma, 'if you can keep up with her. You're hired." When he got home that night I asked him if he got hired. "I'm not sure I kept up with that woman, but he paid me a day's wages and told me to come back tomorrow."" Children of the Great Depression, they both knew hunger. Having a roof over our heads, food on our table and clothes on our backs told us how much they loved us. Music and stories were a large part of our lives. I love you Momma. I love you Daddy. Words that can never be said enough. – "Fritzi"

ACKNOWLEDGEMENTS

Selecting individuals and stories for inclusion in this effort remained, being born, raised or currently living in Stone County, Arkansas as it did for *Voices of Our People* (2009) and continues for the ongoing photographic exhibit Mountain Music Project at Country Time, in Mountain View. As I became deeper involved in "Places" I realized that the area along the White River between Talburt's Ferry where Chief Benge crossed on the Trail of Tears and south to Batesville, the oldest surviving city in Arkansas, was really what I was writing about. The rivers were the roads and the settlements established themselves there. I had a lot of help and a lot of fun on *Places*.

EIC Crew – For all our great adventures, from escaping snake bites in cemeteries, enduring the heat of summer for the first ever Civil War re-enactment at Lunenburg, to glorious waterfalls, cleaning up the historic cemetery of Jane Mason Jeffery, venturing into what is likely the slave auction house of the Dillard family and exploring the Buckhorn with Sam Younger. The first land patent applied for in this region, for all of Izard, Independence and Stone County, was at the Buckhorn in 1810 by John and Sarah Lafferty. Stone County is "old Izard County". Visit the website ExploringIzardCounty.com for more photos, videos and stories of our adventurers exploring, discovering and sharing our heritage in "old Izard County." And I must thank every family or individual who has given them and me permission to be on their land to document the history of the White River Valley.

Dennis & Ellen Brannon, Mountain View, Arkansas, owners and publishers of the Stone County Citizen, newspaper, for their continued support and recognition of the significance the history of the White River Valley holds in our nation's history.

White River Current newspaper staff and owners Calico Rock, Arkansas for their continued support of the ICHS and writers such as myself and Susan Vargo promoting and enhancing efforts to preserve the history of the White River Valley (especially Cindy Stewart who keeps me on target).

The Izard County Historical Society for its dedication and commitment to the region and the willingness and eagerness of its members to support EIC and *Places of Our People.* I encourage everyone to stop by the restored Trimble House in Calico Rock, visit the new museum next to the rail road tracks in historic downtown and tour "Peppersauce Alley."

Bob Fleming (1946-2010), my partner for the last 5 years photographing, traveling and discovering people and places at every turn, always ready to shoot pictures or 'carry my bags'. With very little input from me, Bob wrote, "Mountain Meadows Massacre" featuring Kenneth Rorie an extra-ordinary piece with much information privy only to the LDS. Bob died unexpectedly on May 23, 2010 the morning after having completed the article. It is the only one in this book solely credited to another person. Not everyone gets their prayers answered. Bob did not want to die alone and he wanted to go fast. Although it took them a day to pronounce him brain dead, he died in less than a minute and I was there with him. He answered my prayers as well. He gave me a renewed sense of living, of not wasting a single moment and never letting someone leave you in anger, or without knowing you love them. His last words to me were "Thank You." I remain indebted to him and will forever hold him close to my heart.

Kenneth Rorie for his invaluable assistance in explaining family relationships and providing photographs of not only the Rorie family but of numerous other extended family members, and always being at the other end of a question, with an answer.

Richard Decker, Laudis Brewer, Ches Beckham, Dwain Nesbitt, Neva Petty Foll and according to them "that young whipper snapper Edwin Luther" – I could write the history of Stone County without having ever talked to another person other than these extra-ordinary people. I have had incredible experiences venturing into new places with Mister Richard as we explored the remains of Riggsville and with Mister Ches as we drove the Civil War route of Baumer's troops including fording a swollen Rocky Bayou Creek, to spending hours pouring over pictures and documents with Laudis in his home and Edwin at the SCHS that ended up with Bob asleep on the floor. I owe them all an immense debt of gratitude for the time they shared with me. My understanding of the history of our people is so much greater because of them. I am particularly indebted to Ches Beckham for having shared so much with me about the Civil War that in his words "no body ever ask about before." All of these men have been willing to talk to me at any time of the day or night, load up in the vehicle with me and go places, "a grown man knows better" to go, as Miss Libby (Decker) said, "Proof an old man will still do things he shouldn't if a young woman's involved." She delighted in whispering to me a day later that she'd really enjoyed getting to "pick ticks off" Mister Richard after our trip to Riggsville.

L.C. Sutterfield for sharing his rich knowledge of our family history and the Sylamore Valley and for providing invaluable photographs and documents but most of all for sharing the medical bag of Grandpa Crews with both me and my grandson Denali.

Bud Cooper who has researched and written about the Civil War in the White River Valley most of his life, assisted in numerous ways in all Civil War related pieces, from his willingness to trek through Round Bottom, poke around in cemeteries to editing and working on individual pieces with me. His knowledge of the people and places of Mt. Olive, Boswell and Round Bottom was critical to capturing the history of those places. He and his sisters, Mary Cooper Miller and Linda Cooper, members of the ICHS, have provided clarifications, photographs and documents that are invaluable to the over all efforts of the entire book.

Carol Jeffery Cooper not only let the EIC crew bring a large group of people through her home, the A.C. Jeffery House, she willingly spent another day with Bob and I dragging out documents and photographs which provided an insight into the relationships of the early settlers that otherwise would have been almost impossible to understand.

Bill Wallace, the last ferryman on the White River, for his endless hours of listening to me talk and ask questions about his family, taking me to places I'd only heard about and ultimately for making sure I didn't get eaten by a bear. The photographs, stories and documents compiled by his late sister, Mary Ann Wallace Whitaker proved to be a resource that I turned to over and over in completing this book. Although I have known Bill since he was the ferryman at Guion where I grew up, I didn't get to really know him until we worked on this project. His life as the last ferryman on the White River is worthy of a book all by itself.

Dale Hanks for his first hand knowledge of the Jeffery family history and the inter-relationships between the hundreds of descendants. The wealth of information that he has yet to get on paper himself would fill volumes. I was most honored when I learned that he had been with the National Guard Unit that walked the Little Rock 9 into Central High during the 1957 riots. I spent 10 glorious days traveling with Dale beginning in Memphis, TN where we attended church with Rev. Al Green, driving through Tennessee, Kentucky, North Carolina and Virginia with incredible stops along the way to museums and battlefields in Fredicksburg, Chancellorville, Walker Plantation. From research and lectures at Randolph Macon College to digging through photos and documents, Dale's knowledge and love of history surpasses my own. Coming on the heels of Bob's death, most importantly, during those 10 days, Dale helped me understand what love and friendship really mean.

Jesse Beal and the entire Beal family for sharing the history of the Mingo Swamp Massacre and for the hours of music that has lifted and inspired me, especially Jesse Beal for the use of the words to Mingo Swamp Massacre; their CD is available locally at Mellon's Country Store.

Buddy Case from Enola, Arkansas, an award-winning singer/songwriter and musician for allowing me to use the words to the haunting historical ballad Ghost of Gettysburg.

Dawn Young Lindsay for her expertise in not only photography but in dealing with me and my "can't do that" attitude. She picked up where Bob left off in so many ways. She's been at the other end of the line when I needed her and was with me when the doctor in Springfield told us that Bob was brain dead. She called my friends, Marsha Teague Henderson and Shelly Stewart Jaynes, held my hand and helped heal my heart, mostly by being like Bob and telling me what I didn't want to hear when I needed to hear it the most. And, for designing the wonderful cover for *Places of Our People*.

So many people have contributed stories, photographs and time, Pauline Mitchell Via, Wilma Teague Wolfe, Omalee Decker Beckham, an entire book could be written on each of them and their families. I encourage them to do so.

Beau Hardison, what can I say, you have seen me at my worst and you are still here. Thank you for your patience, your friendship and love.

And to my friends and family who have incessantly had to listen to me talk for hours affirming, I have become my mother.

INTRODUCTION

Our history in the White River Valley began long before we became counties or even a state, in fact long before white people ever set foot here. The Osage occupied this land for at least 2,500 years before the first whites ventured here. While there is considerable and growing evidence to support that European explorers were here as much as 800 years before Columbus, it would have been a rare contact with someone other than with aother tribe for people inhabiting this valley. Since 1797, there are four distinct groups of people in the White River Valley 1) those before the Civil War, 2) those after the Civil War but before 1903, 3) 1903-1950 and 4) those arriving after 1950 and a 5th is emerging. My area of interest and expertise is in the first 50 years, 1797-1847 when the birth of the Ozark culture occurred through a blending of Indians, whites and blacks. It didn't begin here, but defined itself into what those of us whose families go back before the Civil War understand and take for granted, and those that come after recognize but can't identify.

For Native Americans' when you became one of theirs, by choice or capture, you were Shawnee, or Cherokee, or whatever clan or tribe in which you ended up. Therefore maintaining specific knowledge of bloodlines was a critical issue for the groups. But it also led to much misunderstanding of the Native Americans in their practice of polygamy just as the belief that everyone in the Ozarks marries their cousins. Mimicking the aristocracy of Europe, the sons and daughters of tribes were married to each other to create alliances, one such alliance was between the Rainmaker, Hop, Moytoy and Cornstalk's. As the presence of Europeans became greater explorers from Spain, France and England reaching further into the mainland had increasing contact and influence on the Native Americans. Most people are unaware that the astounding beadwork of Native Americans' was introduced to them along with weaving through contact with the first Europeans. Skills that have become our own with unique patterns and designs that distinguish locales and tribes. Does anyone mistake a Southwestern tapestry, works of the Pueblos or silverwork of the Navajo? For purposes of the White River Valley it was contact between the Europeans and Okowellos (who was dubbed Cornstalk due to his height and flowing white hair, which was likely due already to white contact) that is of most interest to our culture here in the White River Valley.

In the late 1600's a number of prominent whites are noted in American Indian history – including John Greenwood who migrated from England in 1635, Edmund Ward who brought his sons here and worked to achieve an aristocratic status through uniting England with the Moytoy and Cornstalks in 1730, Thomas Watts 1642, Brewer's, Walker's, Ross, Houston's and others. Their off spring were half white and half Native American, something neither modern day whites or Indians like to discuss suggesting somehow it diminishes the accomplishments of the individuals within their ethnicity or culture. Come on folks, these men were here "without women." Nature took its course and the best and the brightest, the strongest and most ferocious of adventurers and warriors, leaders resulted: among them here in the White River Valley and Arkansas, Chiefs, John Walker, John Ross, John Jolly, Robert Benge, John Benge, Jacob Watts, John Avey, Peter Avey/Adams, Sequoyah, Tecumseh, Robert "Drowning Bear" Brown, John Bowles and Robert Bowles. These men were related to each other and just as the Trail of Tears was not allowed to enter present day Stone County, it was with the same need to survive that they moved here to the Arkansas Territories. In 1730, under King George II the British were allied with the Moytoy and Cornstalks, Leaders of the Shawnee and Cherokee. Children of Edmund Ward were married to children of those leaders in the centuries old tradition of creating alliances through such marriages. Sequoyah is the son of Wurteh Watts and Nathaniel Gist, both who were ½ white. Sequoyah was Cherokee, Metis, Pekowi and Chalakatha, ½ white. He created the Cherokee written language with his aunt Lucy Ward. Wurteh was the mother of Chief Benge who led the Trail of Tears, Chief Bowles who moved to the White River after the 1811 earthquake, John Jolly, Chief of the Arkansas Cherokee and Jacob Watts. Jacob married Emily Ross, daughter of Chief John Ross. The Watts family of the White River Valley and Sylamore can be traced back to Jacob just as the Jeffery family can be traced back to Jehoiada, the Wards to Joseph Ward, descendant of Bryant Ward and Anna Pekowi, the Fulks and Chitwoods to Francis "Chief Fivekiller" Ward and Tame Doe Carpenter and the Brewer's and Avey's to Chief Hokolesqua Cornstalk and Ounacona Moytoy.

Their move here began with the impending loss of the American Revolution to the colonists. Migrating out of the southern states north through Tennessee, Kentucky to the Ohio River Valley, the Ohio and Cumberland Rivers, down through Paducah, Ky and the Cape along the Mississippi into Arkansas. Few entered through the Southern Route along the Arkansas as it was heavily populated by the Caddo, Choctaw and Chickasaw. Along the way, they raided and fought back, including the infamous raids on Fulks Run, Martin and Ruddell Station's where they took over 200 prisoners, many who would live the rest of their lives with the Indians. Although there were white 'traders' before him, captive George Lail was the first white settler of Cape Girardeau, his sister Elizabeth was sold back to the British for a keg of whiskey (of whom many of the Franks are descendants). Captives Abraham Ruddell, 6, and Stephen Ruddell, 12, lived with the Shawnee as brothers to Tecumseh for nearly 20 years. Shortly after returning to the whites, Abe moved to Missouri where he and many others of the aforementioned were signers on the Wilkinson's agreement, an effort to create a new nation which ultimately led to Vice President Aaron Burr being tried for treason. Upon the failure of that agreement, many moved further into the more rugged areas of North Arkansas. Abe would become one of the first settlers of Batesville, Arkansas. Tecumseh's sister is buried north of Mountain Home and likely his mother is buried at St. James (The Buckhorn). The reservation of 1817-1828 eastern boundary began at the White River extended west to the current western boundary of the state of Oklahoma.

While most people believe the Indians just left, moved on, "probably Oklahoma", the truth is, a conscious decision to assimilate into the white culture necessitating denying one's Indian heritage was made. It remained illegal in Arkansas for Indians to own land until 1956. Only in the last 60 years have families been able to discuss that portion of their heritage. People here became inherently suspicious of anyone who moved here. Understanding who their people were and where their sentiments lay was an important if not critical component of survival. By the time the War of 1812 came about, Europeans that had chosen not to go back to England, Scotland or Ireland at the close of the American Revolution could now fight for the new country and therefore no one cared who they were before, they were now "Americans". The Indians that were trying to maintain their heritage and identity such as Chief Jimboy who took 400 warriors to fight in the Seminole Wars under Andrew Jackson, lost his home and 4 of his children died, even though he had been promised that by leading this war party that they and his men's families would be exempt. Timbo, Arkansas is named for Chief Jimboy of the Chalakatha. It was difficult for the Indians to understand the actions of the whites who did not honor their word, verbal or written. Honor was not part of who these new people were, subjugated in Europe without a possibility of ever owning land, they fought for control over the Indians. Here in the White River Valley, a man's handshake, his word, his name, met everything, and still does. The concept of owning the land instead of being stewards of it remains a large part of who we are and we have difficulty adhering to the inability to walk, ride or hunt anywhere we want as lands are fenced and posted. As names of historic places and roads are changed to reflect a family of today and churches success is measured in its size rather than its souls, we shake our heads and pray to God to help these people just as we did 2,000 years ago.

People who have roots here going back 200 years, know who we are, know who the others are and understand these idiosyncrasies that are ours. We have had no need or desire to explain them to outsiders. My effort in writing the stories of our people is not to expose us, or explain us, but to celebrate us. And, in doing so, much will be exposed and answered. Our history may be the key to our future. We are as unique as Jamestown, VA and as rich in our rock walls, homes, springs, music and culture as any place I have ever visited.

As information has become available or proven out to be incorrect it has been changed from the newspaper editions. The information contained herein is as accurate as data, documents and family histories can support. I especially thank Chief Don Greene of the Appalachian Shawnee for his help.

I am proud to be born on Main Street at Dr. Burton's Clinic. I am proud to be from Mountain View, Arkansas, from Stone County. After reading *Places of Our People*, I hope you share that pride with me.

- Freda

Places of Our People

Stories of the People and Places
of the Ozarks
White River Valley

The Vanishing Ozarksî
Volume 2

In every place, there is a story

Freda Cruse Phillips

Richard Decker – Riggsville

I have heard the stories for years about the government bonded whiskey still (1888-1905) in Martin (Still) Holler; stories about drunken pigs and revenuers, in Riggsville, our first settlement. Riggsville, the first settlement of Mountain View, in 1819, was situated at the base of the mountain near the spring (present day location on South Bayou Drive, up the valley towards Cooper Point and Star Gap Road, about 3 miles form the court square on private land.) It had a water mill, tanning yard, blacksmith shop, general store and at least two churches, both Flatwoods and the Methodist Church were started at Riggsville. It was the major trading area for citizens before and during the Civil War and had more slaves than it did white folks. Mister Richard Decker lived in the area as a young boy, now almost 92, his stories of life, lived by his parents and grand parent's, lead me to state and county records, historical archives of marriages, births, deaths, land transactions and census. I learned there was a time you paid for the right to vote with a poll tax, women couldn't vote and slaves were listed along with cattle, hogs and real estate as personal wealth. I have researched enough records that I am confident of what I have written. However, I am not a historian, but rather a folklorist, a cultural historian at best. The expedition and story of Riggsville, begins *Places of Our People*.

Richard Decker, 92, with Hinkle & Nancy Decker and grand son Jesy, 3.

It was an unusually cool August morning in 2009 when I picked up Richard Decker for our trip out to Riggsville. I knew there would be ticks and chiggers, but I didn't anticipate the downed trees we'd have to climb over and under, the boulders and the rocks, the terrain that challenged me, much less,

Richard Decker, about to turn 92, without a doubt the oldest man in Stone County to visit the oldest remains of our beginnings as a town perhaps 50 years before there was Mountain View, before we were a county; there was the settlement of Riggsville. We drove out to his nephew Hinkle Decker's. He and Danny Thomas, had rode out a couple days before, Hinkle on his horse and Danny on his mule, in an unsuccessful effort to locate the Riggsville dam. Hinkle drove us through a couple gates and breaks in the fence, crossed some deep ditches and over fields, the unmarked path, clear in Mister Decker's mind as he pointed the way.

At the far end of the property where the fields gave way to the break of the mountain we parked and climbed over a fence then walked along the uneven and rocky creek bed. The ice storm earlier this year had left a tremendous amount of felled trees which impeded Hinkle and me from realizing that we were at the base of 'old military road'. But not Mister Decker, as Hinkle and I would wander off towards the bigger creek bed, he would boom out, "I don't know where you two think you're going. It's this way." Climbing over and under trees, holding back branches and vines, on all fours I saw a foundation. "Mister Decker, this is a foundation. What was here?"

You could see the smile come over his face, the delight in returning to a place that he knew as a young man. "This is where the spring house was at, the mill. The flume, you see, came down the creek from the dam, to here," he said, pointing to the huge hand hewn rocks that clearly served as a foundation for the building that had once been the mill for the town of Riggsville. "And here, this was the still," he said. "As a boy, I'd come up here digging around, finding the old whiskey bottles and then trade them to the other boys, Buster (Decker) you know, for things I wanted. This was a building here; I'm not sure what it was." "The houses were over there, along the base of the mountain, above the high water line," he said, pointing back to a knoll in the field. Standing where we were at, it was clear that we had driven over what had once been the residential area of the settlement of Riggsville just along the tree line above the high water mark of a flood; a rock wall that lined both sides of the road leading up to the town, virtually intact, still clearly visible. I could see Riggsville, the horses that would ride up the road, children playing, fields being worked, women, children and slaves, young men building homes and businesses, parties in the tavern and worship in the churches. It was there as clear in my vision as it was in Mister Decker's memory, stories his parents and grand parents, lived. Walking along the creek bed, I could see the boulders that were un-naturally out of place, symmetrically lining the edge of the creek, where the flume had traversed the water way from the dam to the mill. Was it the sweat of the brow of slaves, men, white and black working together, who had moved these monstrous boulders into place, 10-15 feet apart along the bed of the creek, foundation supports for the flume that ran from the dam to the spring house, the mill, later the whiskey still? As I crested the high point of the west bank of the creek, I saw it.

Richard Decker – Riggsville Dam

There it was; the Riggsville Dam, crossing from one side of the creek to the other, approximately 50 feet wide, 10 ft tall, almost no damage. I yelled out that I could see it. "I told you it was just over here," I could hear Mister Decker saying to himself. I watched from the creek bed, as he made his way off the hillside to the top of the dam. I was honored, silenced, in the presence of this man returning to this place. I watched as he walked out onto

16

the top of the dam. Hinkle helped him sit, his feet dangling over the side, he was that kid that use to come here fishing, looking for whiskey bottles, with his buddies or his girl. Hinkle and I, we both felt it. The sound of the water spilling over the top of the dam in harmony with the chirping birds, reminders of people who heard these sounds, inhabited this valley nearly 200 years ago silencing us.

I joined Hinkle and Mister Decker at the top of the dam; the rock work was incredible. I knew there would be a date, somewhere. I looked for what my great grandpa had shown me on fences and walls; there it was, 1862 and then 1892. Did work on the dam come to a halt in 1862 when the Civil War (1861-1865) broke out and the slaves escaped to Union territories, or was it completed that year? Did the dam serve as a water and grist mill for 30 years and then another 30 years later in 1892 become part of the legal government still that was allowed until 1905? Mister Decker didn't know the answers, only, this is Martin Holler and the still was government bonded by the Martin family.

How we come to know our history is as much a journey as the history was in its being lived. These lands were settled by frontiersmen who boldly challenged the Native Americans at the encouragement of the U.S. government. Prior to 1803, it had belonged to France. A time when persons traveling more than 20 miles from their declared home place had to apply from France for a passport, thus the term, "You can't get there without a passport," wasn't about the terrain, but rather the distance you were traveling, at least 20 miles. If you were a traveler that had a passport, you were "from off" meaning a distance of greater than 20 miles. In the early 1800's this county didn't exist, it was part of the newly established Arkansaw Territories. Jacob Wolf was appointed the first representative of the new territories in 1819.

In 1822, a young Thomas Augustus Riggs, 20, married Rhoda Casey, 18, in Marion County, Alabama. It is recorded that their son William Carrell was born October 30th, 1822. Thomas Riggs was a hardworking earnest young man who had returned from a trip into the regions west of the Mississippi along the White River near Polk Bayou (present day Batesville); where he lay claim to land for he and his new bride, two days west at the base of a big spring. He reported "use of a new ferry at Polk Bayou to cross the river then traveled two days to reach lands that were abundant with wild life, including turkeys, deer and 'injuns'."

The ferry at Polk Bayou was established in 1819, which places Riggs in the area around 1819 but certainly before his marriage and the birth of his son in 1822. The land on the south side of the White River was the eastern boundary of the Cherokee Reservation. "The U.S. government has just moved the Osage (who had lived here for over a 1,000 years) west to Oklahoma and allowed the Cherokee to move to the Arkansaw;" thus creating the Cherokee Indian reservation which included present day Stone County from 1817-1828. The new government of the Arkansaw Territories General Assembly met for the first time in 1820. Although land west of the White

River was encouraged for settlement land transactions could not be recorded until 1836 when Arkansas became a state. It is recorded that Thomas Augustus Riggs in April 1824, recorded the settlement of land in 1819 that was later sectioned by description near two springs, to be that both of the settlement of Riggsville and near present day Blanchard Springs; 'having been working and improving the hostile environment.' 1824 is when he appears to have made his second trip bringing with him slaves to work the land in his absence. Deputy Surveyor Charles H Pelham began the surveys of Riggsville in 1829 with recordings entered in December 1836, following statehood. The area around Blanchard was not surveyed until 1844 and is recorded as homesteaded by Isaac Teague. Most of the homesteaded land in present day Stone County was not officially recorded until 1855-1862 due to the conflicts rising between the North and the South and the need to establish ownership. Upon the Jan 1, 1863 Act by Lincoln freeing the slaves in the midst of the Civil War, freed slaves were entitled to 80 acres and a mule.

The decision to improve and make a settlement at Riggsville likely lay in the fact that it was less of a trek to the river than Blanchard. One of the earliest maps located shows Syllamo (Allison), Buckhorn (St.James), Riggsville (Mtn View/South Bayou Drive), Richwoods (Mtn View/Dodd Mountain) and Table Rock (City Rock Bluff on Culp Road near Calico Rock). Thus the path of least resistance to the river was likely the deciding factor for the location of Riggsville since both Riggsville and Blanchard Springs continue to have plenty of water for a town.

The recorded births of Riggs children support extended absences which coincide with his being in the Riggsville area. Thomas and Rhody had William, 1822, a girl child, 1824 (d 1825), John, 1825, Brannick, 1828, as reported on the 1830 Free White Persons Census in Pickens, Alabama.

Barney born 1831 and Thomas 1832 were also born in Marion County, Alabama. Mr. Riggs then moved his family to Mississippi (statehood 1817), which provided him less travel distance between the new settlement and his family, Riggsville not yet safe for his young family as Arkansas was engaged in the Indian Wars. Rhoda had James, 1835 and Margarett, 1836 in Mississippi. She and the children arrived in Riggsville, sometime prior to 1839 as the 1840 census records Martha's birth as 1839 in Riggsville. By the 1850 Population and Slave Census, Thomas Riggs reported his occupation as a farmer with real estate around $1,000 and a holding of nine slaves (a single 'young buck' was valued at approximately $600). He and Rhoda had had two additional children born in Riggsville, Rhoda in 1841 and Charles in 1846. Thomas and Rhody's oldest son, William, now 27, had married Nayoma Flannery born in 1830 at Syllamo, Arkansas.

Leaving the dam and the creek, we climbed the hillside to a clearing and there it was, without fallen timber, with the morning sun filtering through the trees, "Old Military Road." Mister Decker, Hinkle and I had walked on part of it at the base of the mountain not realizing due to the downed trees and thickets of vines, it was in fact "the road". But here, on top of the hill under the canopy of the trees, it was as clear that this was the old road, as the hand hewn rocks were the foundations of once thriving businesses along its path.

"Old" Military Road was the first road west of the Mississippi to be granted Federal monies for improvement. Its beginnings started as nothing more than an Indian trail known as the Natchitoches Trail, which was a network of trails, not a single trail. It traversed present day Stone County beginning at the White river near Round Bottom or Herpel, topping the hill just west of where Mountain View School sits, continuing south (near the Shell station) to the Cherokee Tsalagi Indian encampment (farm of Richard

Decker behind Wilson's Town and Country), then south along land presently owned by John Dan Kemp (South Bayou Drive) up the valley and across the mountain on the east side of Cooper Point along Star Gap to present day Misenheimer Road, south to Luber Road, east and south along Hanover towards the Little Red River and the Caddo Indian settlements.

In 1830, President Jackson attached funding to military appropriation bills that provided for improvements to the road which included, cutting trees, pulling stumps, building bridges, dams and in some cases leveling the road and digging ditches. Arkansas has several "military roads," including the well-known Memphis to Little Rock Military Road. The chosen route that parallels the Natchitoches Trail, later called the Southwest Trail, remains the acknowledged "Old Military Road" for the state and does not include these side trails or roads. However it does not diminish the importance of the large number of smaller connecting roads which included Riggsville and likely the building of the Riggsville Dam as well as the road south of Tucker's Ferry, a few miles outside of present day Batesville.

Mister Decker standing on his farm in the aftermath of the 2008 tornado; All remains of the Cherokee Indian Trading Post on this site are now gone.

"Old Military Road" through this part of Arkansas was the project of Sam Houston, first President of the Republic of Texas and brother to John P. Houston, Little Rock lawyer and first clerk of Izard County, at Athens, 1830-1836. The military road project began in St. Louis and crossed the length of Arkansas ending in the Red River Valley of Texas and was a vital part of Sam Houston's military plans in his battles with Mexico. Sam had been living in Arkansas with John Jolly, then Chief of the Cherokee near present day Clarksville (Johnson County). Steve Austin, former territorial legislator in Missouri and lead mining tycoon had moved into Arkansas. Austin's father,

Moses, had received a land grant in Texas of almost 5,000 acres as an incentive to help defend against the Mexicans. It is clear that both Thomas Riggs and Steve Austin knew Sam Houston and each had a vital interest in the installation of Stone County's "Old Military Road", especially Austin who needed to get his lead ore south to Texas. John Houston was enticed to move from Little Rock, to the remote area of Izard County and take the position of clerk. They selected Jehoiada Jeffery, one of the first settlers in 1816 along the White River, just north of Sylamore, at Mt. Olive, as surveyor. His work included that of Batesville and Riggsville along with portions of the now famed "Old Military Road." Austin and Jeffery were friends with Thomas Riggs already one of the largest land and slave owners in the area. It seems clear that Riggs used both his slaves and the Cherokee Tsalagi Indians to build the road and perhaps the Riggsville dam around 1830.

For Riggs, the building of this road not only provided access to the land he had acquired around Stair Gap (so called due to the almost step like conditions of the terrain which is current day Star Gap) and the settlement of Richwoods atop Dodd Mountain, but more importantly helped cement his relationships with prominent persons in Texas which is where the majority of his family moved following the Civil War, including Riggs who died there in 1867. The use of "Old Military Road" during the Civil War by both Union and Confederate soldier's is documented in numerous records, providing both growth and safety to the settlers who resided in Riggsville.

In 1855 with talk of Civil War in the air, Thomas Riggs began recording his homesteaded land which included acreage for his daughters, Rhoda who married William D. "Commodore" Copeland and Margaret who had married Charles Stuart (Stewart); land presently owned for the most part by Danny Stewart at Star Gap. He then began moving the growing town of Riggsville recorded as the largest settlement in the area closer to what had been the Indian encampment on the knolls, where the last remaining buildings, the barn (built by John Cartwright in 1890) and the store still stand. It seems clear that the 1862 date on the Riggsville Dam was an act of ownership due to the 1862 Homestead Act, just prior to Lincoln freeing the slaves Jan 1, 1863 in the midst of the Civil War.

The high expectations and prospects of the Riggs family from 1850-1855 could not have foreseen the misfortune of the late 1850's. The Riggs second son, John, moved his wife, Elizabeth Jane Johnson and their three children, Rhoda, Margarett and William, all born in Riggsville to Texas, where their youngest child, John was born in the summer of 1858. His tale as a 9 month old sitting in a pool of his mother's blood, arrows piercing her body has been depicted in a 1,000 western novels and movies.

Living among Indians was not new to the Riggs family. The Cherokee, Delaware, Shawnee and Creek populated the areas of present day Stone County with two major encampments near the settlement of Riggsville. John and Jane Riggs moved to Nolanville, Texas about 100 miles south of Dallas at the edge of conflict between the Mexicans and the Comanche. Their children were Rhoda 9, Margarett, 7, William, 3, and John nine months old, when on March 16th, 1859 a band of a dozen or more Indians began a murderous rampage. The last recorded Indian massacre in Texas included the deaths of John and Jane Johnson Riggs. They first killed a man by the name of Pierce a few miles from the Riggs home. About 9 o'clock in the morning they came upon John Riggs and Dave Elms returning from town, only 400 yards or so from the Riggs home. Elms, a sixteen year old boy driving the Riggs second wagon loaded with supplies was pulled from the wagon, whipped unmercifully and stripped of his clothes. He wrangled free dashing into a thicket escaping.

John Riggs unarmed, threw rocks at the Indians as they shot arrows through his body. His wife, Jane hearing his screams ran to the aid of her husband who then shot arrows through her body as she ran towards her husband. They both died from multiple arrow wounds. The oldest of the children Rhoda and Margarett, at their mother's instructions, tried to run away but were seen and captured. The Indians fled with them on horseback leaving William and John behind. Perhaps the Indians did not realize there were smaller children, prized boys, inside the cabin when they fled with the girls. Further down the road the Indians encountered a Mr. Cruger and chased after him but he managed to outrun them, making his way to Belton and alerting the townsfolk. By mid afternoon the locals had formed a posse of men to begin pursuit of the Indians but not before there was another attack, killing a man by the name of Peavy.

Richard Decker in front of the old store, Riggsville

The Riggs daughters were still being held captive, riding back side of their capturer's horses. One of the Indians made an effort to pass the younger sister, to another rider while continuing riding and dropped her. Seeing what had happened to her younger sister, Rhoda jumped from her horse to the ground running to her sister's side. The Indians hesitated only briefly then moved on, leaving the young girls behind. Darkness was approaching. Bruised, barefoot and hungry the girls started back from the direction they had come. In the distance they saw a chimney and walked to find a vacant house. It was dark and growing cold so they took shelter in the house with "Rhody" removing most of her clothing, wrapping her younger hurt sister Margarett to keep her warm.

In the darkness, the posse of two dozen or more men camped only a short distance from the house but didn't find it or the children until morning. They took the girls to a nearby home where they were fed and clothed. Word was sent to Arkansas to Thomas Riggs of the massacre and the fate of his grand children. Although the posse continued pursuing the Indians for a hundred or more miles, they were informed some where near Fort Colorado that the soldiers were also in pursuit. They were never captured. Knowing there were children in the Riggs home, local folks arrived to find the nine month old baby boy, John, sitting in his mother's blood, crawling on her in an effort to nurse. Thomas Riggs (Jr) and Walter Clark came from Riggsville, Arkansas, the family homestead of John Riggs' father, to get the four children returning them to Riggsville to the home of their grandparents. John and Jane were buried in the Sugarloaf Mountain Cemetery in Bell County. Their deaths along with the above information are denoted by a Texas historical marker in Comanche Gap, Nolanville, Texas (Bell County) at the intersection of Comanche Gap and FM2410 Road, 2 miles South West of Nolanville.

Thomas Riggs had acquired additional land in 1855 for his sons, increasing the Riggs family holdings of real estate and slaves with every intention of remaining in Riggsville and had begun expanding into the valley closer to present day South Bayou Drive and the home of Judge John Dan Kemp. As the story goes, while up north, John Jacob Kemp heard rumors that war was imminent. He got word to Riggs he was in the market for cattle. Riggs purchased his slaves and Kemp replaced his holdings with cattle. Then Riggs' son John was shot by Indians, his grand daughters held captive and Civil War broke out.

Just before the outbreak of the Civil War, 1861-1865, Riggs reported in the 1860 census, real estate, cattle, hogs and slaves, along with his adult sons to include a combined wealth of over $30,000. Due to the death of his son John and wife in the Comanche Gap Indian Massacre, in Texas, children in the home now included Rhoda Elizabeth, 10, Margarett A., 7, William C. 4, and John Roland, the youngest, now 2, along with their own children Charles, 14, Susan, 10, (b 1850), and Rachel, 9, (b 1851). It is believed, as reported by descendants of the Riggs family, that Susan and Rachel were Riggs' illegitimate children born of another mother in Little Rock, Arkansas while Riggs served office in the Arkansas Legislature. The 1860's town of Riggsville was prosperous and included stores, a livery, two churches, the dam and mill. It served soldiers from both the North and South. In 1867 it is recorded that Thomas Storey ran the tannery in Riggsville.

William Carroll Riggs, his wife Nayoma Flannery and children lived at Sylamore. Brannick "Billy" Riggs had married Mary Elizabeth Robbins and moved to Texas. Barney Kemp Riggs named after Colonel John Jacob "J.J." Kemp, had married Eliza, and had two children. Thomas Riggs (Jr) had married Hannah Felton. James Monroe Riggs lived nearby in the home of his sister Margarett and her husband, Charles Harrison Stuart (Stewart); they had two children both born in Riggsville. Martha Riggs had married J.B. "Mac" Whitehead and lived in Richwoods. Rhoda Riggs, born May 18, 1842, in Riggsville, married William D "Commodore" Copeland Oct 7, 1857 at age 16. Rich Woods situated on top of the mountain was an extension of the Riggsville settlement offering rich soil and areas easier to clear and till.

Richard Gravelly was a young black slave around the age of 25 when the Civil War arrived in the hills of Arkansas. He and several other slaves banded together in a group in the hills between Round Bottom and Sylamore overlooking the river. From this vantage point they could see the river below and the farmland that was being worked by other slaves, friends and family. There was no 'road' as we know it, only a rough mountain trail that lead off the mountain towards the river and streams below. The only improved road in the area, "Old Military Road" served as the mail route which originated in Missouri and slaves didn't venture upon the same road, but instead used the paths through the hills. The slaves joined others hiding out above Kickapoo Bottoms (just north of Jack's boat dock) about two miles up river from Sylamore in the fall of 1861. A group of locals had banned together to help the slaves move north to free states but were stopped cold in their tracks when Governor Rector ordered that the Izard County Investigative Committee to seek out those disloyal to the Confederacy. They arrested 103 members of the Peace Society but reported that most of them were young boys not aware of the consequences of their actions and thus allowed the opportunity to "wipe out the foul stain" by joining the Confederate Army. Three were hang 53 were shot and the other 47 'volunteered.'

The slaves continued to hide out on the hills above Kickapoo Bottoms which is named for the Kickapoo Indians tribe of Chief Peter Cornstalk/85 whose primary emcampment prior to 1830 was in the present day fields of Hale Hayden. An "'uprising' at Sylamore occurred that required the Arkansas Militia to repel an insurrection of 40 or 50 days," from Dec 1861 to Feb 1862 near Kickapoo Bottoms. Batesville, some 35 miles away, fell to the Yankees on May 4, 1862 becoming Union headquarters on the White River. In late May 1862 the slaves encountered another skirmish just above Kickapoo Bottoms that involved "about 150 Union soldiers and a herd of the same number of rebel outlaws (Confederates). Three Confederate men were killed and about 25 captured, along with 40 horses and mules." Following the skirmish, many of these black men joined the Union troops making their way back to Batesville, where they formed one of the first colored troops of the Union Army in June 1862.

Each black man was required to report in oral testimonial his status including ownership upon enlistment. Richard Gravelly joined in 1864, wherein he reported he was born in Riggsville in 1835 and believed himself to be the son of Thomas Riggs. He had been sold at the age of three or four in 1838 or 1839 to William Hill Dillard at Round Bottom. He remained a Dillard slave until Lucy Dillard, "Bill's" sister, married Henry Hill Harris; he then became a Harris slave at Sylamore. While owned by the Harris family he was employed in building homes along the river including around 1850 the construction of the home of Henry Harris and his wife, Lucy Dillard Harris, present day home of Guy and Liz Harris, the two story former Dobbins home (at present day Allison) in the Harris Township of Stone County. Gravelly was a Harris slave residing with the Harris family when the Civil War broke out. The Harris family owned a vast amount of land on the west banks of the White River from Sylamore to Optimus including Kickapoo Bottoms.

Gravelly's mother was from Alabama and had moved first with the Riggs to Mississippi in 1833, then was brought by Mr. Riggs along with two male slaves to Riggsville, where his mother gave birth to him in the summer of 1834 or 1835. Gravelly served in the Union Army out of Batesville until the end of the war in 1865. He then made Batesville his home. Following the war, in 1868, he married Matilda Pinkett. Richard Gravelly is more than likely the first person of record born in Riggsville. No census was taken until 1840, three years after statehood. Hundreds of slaves were reported in the Slave Census' of 1840-1860 in Stone County. A young black boy is listed in the Slave Census of William Hill Dillard, Round Bottom Landing in 1840. It is entirely possible that he is the son of Thomas Riggs as Gravelly was sold at the age of three or four, just prior to the arrival of Mrs. Riggs from Mississippi to Riggsville. The selling of young children was not typical of the day which supports he was sold to hide his paternity. It's possible that Richard Gravelly's mother is buried in an unmarked grave in the East Richwoods (Kemp) cemetery on Luber along with many other slaves and former slaves who are buried there and throughout Stone County. Gravelly worked as a stone mason on a number of the buildings around Batesville and died there in September 1921 at the age of 86. The William Dillard home of 1837 at Round Bottom is on the National Registry of Historic places.

Riggsville was a frontier settlement and booming town at least 35 years before the Civil War broke out. Serving as the main center of commerce for the area, it had a brothel, tavern, livery, watermill, tan yard, black smith shop, mercantile stores and both Flatwoods and Methodist churches. The Rich Woods Riggsville settlement had postal service from 1838-1860. "Old Military Road" was likely installed along with the dam in the early 1830's, leading up and over the mountain it was a difficult road to both climb and descend. Because of the road, and having both a grist mill and a whiskey still, Civil War records document it being frequented by both Union and Confederate soldiers. Although the springs at Riggsville still produce enough water to supply the town of Mountain View, it is believed that the necessity of a new road was one of the primary reasons that former Union soldier, William Harrison Rosa, was able to secure the relocation of the center of commerce from Riggsville to what is now Mountain View.

Following the Civil War, the town of Riggsville began moving down the creek closer to a 'better' road. Only two structures still remain of the second settlement, a barn built in 1890 by John Cartwright and a store. The cleanup in the aftermath of the 2008 tornado on the farm of Mister Richard Decker, removed the last of the foundations of settlements leading to Riggsville including the Indian Trading Post and the Methodist Campground, the site of the first church of Stone County sanctioned by the Missouri Conference in 1826. The majority of the rock foundations of the homes and businesses have been removed from the surrounding fields by people and nature, including Indian grinding stones and artifacts, now gone entirely. The stone walls and spring jonquils stand as proud testaments to the home places that once thrived.

1848 Harris House built by slaves, used by Union & Confederates

The murder of Thomas Riggs son, John, likely contributed greatly to his efforts along with at least 50 other prominent men of the Ozark region to influence Governor Rector to call for Arkansas to conduct a second vote, to leave the Union, becoming part of the eleven Confederate states. The voices of prominent men such as Thomas Riggs who was succeeded by Jehoiada Jeffery served in the Arkansas House of Representatives in 1844, Jared C. Martin was State Treasurer from 1838-1843 were heard and the vote was re-cast, 69-1, reversing the previous decision to go with the north. Riggs losses, personally and financially resulted in most of the family selling out and moving to Texas in the midst of the Civil War in 1863 or 1864. These losses also contributed to the death of the town of Riggsville and paved the way for "Mountain View". In 1867, Thomas A. Riggs died at the age of 65 in Texas.

The 1862 marker on the dam denotes a place and time almost 150 years ago. Near the dam, the foundations of the first settlement, the still, mill, homes and businesses remain. Boulders in the creek, strategically placed supports for the flume that fed the mill, remain. The rock fences built by slaves, Indians and frontiersmen, settlers that likely did not include ladies and gentlemen lined the road into the valley; the knoll on which the homes stood and "Old Military Road" beautiful in the fall sunlight hold our heritage as a not only a town, but as a people. Although many of the Riggs family moved to Texas, it is clear our area is populated with descendants of the Riggs' and the first settlers including Hollandsworth, Younger, Stewart, Davis, Decker, Harris, Beckham, Storey, Walls, Creswell, Clark, Jones, Lancaster, Ausborn, Steven, Teague, Rushing, Ross, Long, Fulks, Whitfield and Martin. People who eked out a living in the rocky terrain giving all of us who call Mountain View home, its very beginning, 180 years ago. The remains of both the original 1819 settlement of Riggsville near the spring and the post Civil War settlement are located on land held entirely in the Kemp Trust, bordered by land owned by the Decker families, Danny Stewart, Joey Dobbins, Ken Jones and Dr. Ron Simpson. Located entirely on private property Riggsville is not currently accessible to the public without permission.

1890 John Cartwright Barn at Riggsville

Mountain View is isolated, defined by the river and the mountains that continue to make access difficult. Small towns across America, even along infamous Route 66, die everyday, just as Riggsville did over 100 years ago, when politics and new roads, by passes, supporting new businesses, new wealth, today a Wal-mart, pass the heart of the town by. It has been said that visiting Mountain View, is like stepping back in time, the richness of our past present in our daily lives. The ability to recognize who was from "off" and what your sentiments were an important part of individual survival and the very survival of our present day town may rest in our ability to hold onto our rich cultural past.

I have just returned from a trip to New England where dry stack conservancies protect the rock walls, foundations and buildings that denote the beginnings of our nation. I saw nothing more beautiful in the grand states of Vermont, New York, Maryland, Pennsylvania, Kentucky and Ohio than I have seen throughout Stone County and at Riggsville. Arkansas offers no protection and land owners are allowed to sell off pieces of history, stone walls that are easily accessible are most vulnerable. Homes, barns and cemeteries on the National Registry of Historic places fall to their demise or worse fall into the hands of people who have no respect for the people who came before them as they fall to ruin, burn, tear down or remodel these structures. I encourage people to hold onto the history in our land, our rocks, barns and old homes, just as we have learned to hold onto the washboards, the kettles and everyday household items we once threw into the trash or gave away, now antiques selling for high dollar. Your land is worth more, because of that rock wall, that Indian grindstone, old well, building or barn. Riggsville first heard the sounds of laughter, of sorrow cried and music played nearly 200 years ago and may hold the key to Stone County's place as a national treasure as we approach the bi-centennial of our place, this place, in our nation's history. Just as a road away from it, around it, may have led to the demise of Riggsville, it may now prove to be all that has saved it, much like Blanchard Springs. Isolated, resistant to change, Stone County is its perfect home. There is no amount of money, no legacy of your name on a building, a church or hospital, nothing greater that any one family could do for this county, for our people, for our nation than to endow the perpetuation and safeguarding of history, a perpetual legacy. Riggsville could be a county or state park; "Kemp State Park". Perhaps.

Alvin Pitts - Ruddells

Sitting at the Stone County Historical Society, I ask, Alvin Pitts and Edwin Luther, "Is it Ruddell or Ruddle"? Both agree, "It is Ruddells, with two "d's" and two "l's"," and a "s" named for a descendant of the Ruddell family who maybe was part owner in the lime quarry or maybe the train conductor, first known as "Ruddell's Station" the place where the train stopped to pick up the limestone." Our Ruddell likely became "Ruddles" after the train depot was gone, physically moved to Sylamore where it continues to sit and "Ruddell's Station" no longer existed.

Unidentified woman at Ruddells train depot circa 1920

The Ruddell family history has more bearing on the history of Stone Co. Abraham, 6 and Stephen Ruddell, 9 were captured in June 1780, adopted and raised by the tribe of Shawnee War Chief Pucksinwah, father of Tecumseh (1768-1813). Both Stephen and Abraham rose in the tribe and as brothers to both Tecumseh and The Prophet they were involved in numerous battles and tribal decisions. In 1797 when Stephen and Abraham returned to their families neither was able to speak English. Abraham maintained his Indian ways most of his life while Stephen received an education and became a missionary. Abraham served as a scout in the War of 1812 from the Missouri Territories and was instrumental in persuading many of the Shawnee to side with the U.S. instead of the British. In 1820 he settled near what is now Batesville. In 1824, he and another brother, John, established Ruddell's Mill (NRHP) situated about one mile inland from the White River, 3 miles west of Polk Bayou where the first ferry (1819) crossed the river. A close friend of the Jeffery family, they worked with Sam Houston and Chief John Jolly securing the safe re-settlement of many of the Shawnee and Cherokee people along the White river between Mt. Olive and Walls Ferry. Ruddell was principally responsible for the four major Shawnee settlements in Stone County; Optimus, Livingston Creek, Sylamore and Upper Walls Ferry. His 1841 obituary in the Batesville News citied Ruddell as "a real life inspiration for "The Last of the Mohicans"" (by James Fennimore Cooper 1826). The 1952 movie Brave Warrior is based on Stephen's life. A hundred years later, we have another, "Last of the Mohicans" Alvin Pitts, the son of Harvey and Dixie (Covey) Pitts, born, August 1, 1930, almost eighty years ago, he is the last known person born at Ruddell.

Until he was seven years old, Alvin lived near the base of the mountain where the limestone quarry was at; what is now Coolwater Retreat. He recalls "cables ran along the hill and loaded cars pulled the empty ones up to the pit for loading; the kilns were located at the base of the mountain near the rail road track, where our house sat."

Alvin on the porch of his grandpa's store at Ruddells

This area had one of the largest river port populations along the White River at the turn of the century. Prior to the time of the locks and dams the river ran shallow and often froze in the winter months allowing passage over the frozen river. Wooden ferries pulled by horses transported people, carriages, animals and later vehicles over the water while keelboats and canoes were the standard means of travel. The river was the road.

Steamboats traveled as far north as Springfield on the James including docking at Ruddell.

Then came the train and "Ruddell's Station". Whites and blacks alike came for the good wages and cheap housing offered by the Arkansas Lime Company, Superintendent George Wiegart (father of Dorothy Hinkle and Virginia Mabry of Mtn View). The company employed people from all walks of life, including transients, hobos and blacks, to work at the kilns and in the stave plant which made the barrels used for shipping the pressed lime. "Work paid generally about 17 cents per hour with housing furnished for employees at $2.50 a month. Employees were paid with paper money, called Cloney money that was only good at the company store, ringing true the song lyrics "I owe my soul to the company store"," Alvin says shaking his head. "1905 the first post office was put in at the store."

Parson Brown, a black preacher at Ruddell, had both white and black families who attended his church. He was known for seating blacks up front and whites in the back. The family of Will Harper was another prominent black family who lived at Ruddell along with Henry Harper and his family. They are buried at Ruddell cemetery; Alvin points out the grave markers in a once briar and thicket covered cemetery now being maintained. The Arkansas Lime Company was dismantled and moved to Limedale near Batesville, in 1930 around the time of Alvin Pitts' birth. The well house is the last remaining building in what was once the booming limestone company town of Ruddells.

Alvin at well house of former town of Ruddells

Alvin reports that the only electricity in Ruddell was an old Delco for the store and house where his grandpa lived. The Lancaster farm, present day Coolwater Retreat and across river at Round Bottom, was one of the largest in the area established in the 1800's and had one of the largest slave populations at the beginning of the Civil War. "My mother, Seddie Lancaster, taught school at Ruddell," Edwin adds. The Lancaster home and barn (NRHP) at Round Bottom is one of the oldest remaining homesteads in the county. The home has been extensively remodeled by its present day owners with disregard to preserving its historical integrity and has been removed from the national registry. The Lancaster cemetery has been surveyed for the sale of home lots, many of the over 100 graves have survey markers plunged into the heart of them.

After a short 25-year life, Ruddell no longer exists, but it flourished as a small company town from 1905 until 1930. With the closing of the plant, the train discontinued its use of the depot. The population devastated by both WWI and WWII, all that remains of this once thriving town is the old cemetery and well building. Alvin Pitts is a man to whom family and history is important, a man of whom Abraham Ruddell would have proudly called 'brother.' Alvin and I walk through the cemetery, a train whistle can be heard, the approaching click clack of the steel wheels. Alvin stands in the setting sun, his hand on his hip, watching as the train passes. He turns and smiles at me, I see that little boy that stood there in this spot a life time ago, waving again to the conductor.

Billy Wolfe - Wolf House 1819 to Court House 1924

Finishing up research on Stone county's courthouses, should have been simple enough, a 2 hour trip up and back to Wolf House (Norfork) with Mister Billy to get a picture and a little more information was all I needed. That was not to be, as we traipsed about the county on one of Miss Wilma's magical history tours that included the site of the second courthouse at Athens, the burial place for John P. Houston, first clerk of Izard County and brother to Gen. Sam Houston and the Katy Cemetery where Miss Bertha Williams "Lady of Color" is buried. Nine hours, long dusty roads and a flat tire later, we made it back, making this story not only richer but certainly more memorable.

Billy Wolfe, Wolf House c 1824 Norfork, Arkansas

Mostly the land of the Ozark region was left entirely to the Osage and Delaware Indians until the U.S. bought the territory in 1803 from France. Pictographs on the National Registry of Historic Places (NRHP) dating 500 A.D. are located in multiple locations throughout Stone, Izard and Baxter County. The west bank of the White River had been home to the Osage for over 1500 years when in 1817 the U.S. government relocated them to the western portion of the Arkansaw (all of the present state of Oklahoma was included in the Arkansas Territories of 1817). Designating the area west of the White River (Stone County to the present day Oklahoma border) as the Cherokee Indian Reservation from 1817-1828, the area of Oklahoma was the Osage Indian Reservation. During ownership under France, it was required that anyone traveling more than 20 miles from their home describe their route of travel in application for a passport from France which could take months.

Thus, leading to the usage of the term "can't get there without a passport" and those traveling more than 20 miles were from "off" – someplace else or more than 20 miles from where they had arrived at.

Jacob Wolf arrived in present day Norfork around 1820 immediately establishing a trading post and ferry operations along the converging rivers. When 'Old' Izard County was formed in 1825, it included all or parts of present day Van Buren, Carroll, Johnson, Marion, Baxter and Stone Counties. Wolf was appointed as Representative to the General Assemblies of Arkansas Territories representing in large part, both the Native Americans and the white settlers. A wooden two story structure was erected by Jacob Wolf at the mouth of the Big Fork River where it merges with the White. "Wolf House" served both as the county seat and court house. Built in 1829, 180 years ago, the Wolf House is on the National Register of Historic places and is considered the oldest remaining settlements in Arkansas. Stone County's Dillard settlement of 1837 at Round Bottom (NRHP) only 8 years younger, is considerably more remarkable than even present day Wolf House as it includes on site the home, barn, slave house and foundry; only the foundation stones remain of the Dillard Mill. Operating the ferries and the only mill provided Wolf with a unique trading opportunity among the settlers that began arriving both by land and water.

Jehoiada Jeffery Home built 1816 photo circa 1930

Before Wolf there was Jehoiada Jeffery who had been granted 160 acres following service in the War of 1812. He brought his young wife and children on mules from Southern Illinois homesteading land around Mt. Olive in 1816. Jeffery's double log home built with a broad axe and his bare hands served as both home and fort. It supported small window like openings on each side just large enough for observation and to fire a rifle through. Like Wolf, Jeffery had a number of slaves and a highly successful cattle and hog farm and in addition he grew corn and wheat. He shipped these to New Orleans and Memphis. In turn, this enterprise brought both supplies and settlers into the regions south of Mt. Olive, including Sylamore, Round Bottom, Rocky Bayou, Walls Ferry at Buckhorn (St. James) and O'Neal Ferry at Hess Town (Marcella).

In 1825 Jeffery was elected to the Fourth Territorial legislature, one of 18 members representing the entire Arkansas Territory. He introduced bills creating Izard and Fulton County. In 1830 the county seat was officially relocated from the Wolf settlement to the settlement of Athens which is about three miles down river from present day Calico Rock. Little Rock lawyer, John Paxton Houston, brother of legendary General Sam Houston, had been convinced to serve as the first county clerk of (old) Izard County by Wolf which included present day Stone County, serving from 1825-1830 and 1832-1838. He is buried at the site of the second courthouse at Athens, if you've got the time, "just ask Miss Wilma."

Athens – historical marker by Daughters of the American Colonists includes gravesite of John Paxton Houston, first clerk of Izard County, brother to
General Sam Houston

The 50 years before Stone County became a county in 1873 was a unique time in history for this area. A time when the Native Americans brought the first slaves here to the 'new reservation' in 1817, followed by a heavy influx of peoples of Scottish and Irish descent. A blending of those four cultures created a new Ozark culture that is distinctive in its music, its dance, its speech and attitudes resulted, a culture that is on the cusp of being lost.

In 1829 Sam Houston was elected Governor of Tennessee and got married. Both his marriage and governorship lasted only three short months. Upon resigning as Governor he came to the Arkansas Territories to live with John Jolly, Chief of the Western Cherokees who later adopted him. Jolly had voluntarily relocated a portion of the Cherokee tribe to Arkansas in 1818. Houston had spent much of his younger years living with the Shawnee as the son of Chief Tecumseh, brother of Jolly and nephew of Abraham Ruddell (one of the first settlers of Batesville). Ruddell captured by the Indians at the age of 6, was adopted and lived as an Indian until the age of 24. In April 1829 Houston appears to have traveled from Tennessee first to Batesville to see his uncle (Ruddell) and then to see his brother John P. Houston, before joining Chief Jolly at Spadra near present day Clarksville (Johnson County).

John Houston is reported to have been found dead at his desk in the wooden structure that served as the courthouse at Athens. The cemetery where he was buried is about 300 yards away under a falling down chicken house. Izard County and the Daughter's of the American Colonists commemorated his life and service with the plaque and headmarker at the Athen's site in 2005.

Between 1829 and 1832 Sam made a number of trips into the region of present day Stone, Independence and Izard County to visit family and friends Jehoida Jeffery and Thomas Riggs. These men may have been responsible for the route now known as the Trail of Tears leading through the

Ozarks, including crossing Izard and Independence Counties from which Stone and Baxter were formed. Many of the Native American families that settled along the White River were guided here by the efforts of Chief John Ross, Sam Houston and Abraham Ruddell including the Woods, Ausborns, Ross, Burns and Fulks who settled along the White river rather than continue to the reservation. During the last movement by water, in 1839, Elizabeth Ross, "Quatie-woman of the Wolf Clan" wife of Chief John Ross died. She is buried in Mt. Holly cemetery in Little Rock. Many of the Ross descendants live in Stone County.

The Fulks of Stone County are direct descendants of Cherokee Chief Fivekiller (Francis Ward). A member of the 1730 delegation to King George II, the portrait of the delegation including Chief Kollanah Fivekiller hangs in the British Royal Museum. The sons and daughters of the Indian Chiefs were encouraged to inter-marry in the century's old tradition set by the ruling families of the British Crown, thus cementing relationships between the Scots, Irish and English who made their way into the New World, and ultimately, the Ozarks.

1836 A.C. Jeffery Home, Mt. Olive, owners Carl and Carol Jeffery Cooper

The clannish nature of the people from the Ozarks is inherent and inherited, strong and often unyielding be it Scottish, Irish, Negro or Indian. The people who made it here 50, 75 years before Stone County was a county before Mountain View was a town, drove another people, the Osage off, to claim this land. Not unlike the wars between the peoples of Scotland, England, Ireland, France and Spain that lead to Columbus arriving here, the Creek, Delaware, Shawnee and Cherokee claimed this land warring with other tribes. The Indian people who stayed here in the Ozarks when the 1828 reservation ended and new boundaries were established in the western territories of Arkansaw (all of present day Oklahoma) and the frontiersmen who lived here alongside them, they were the settlers, the ones that made a frontier into a place others could call home. It is said a person from the Ozarks, a descendant of those original settlers, can recognize someone from "off" in their demeanor, their attitude, in the way they jig dance or play fiddlesticks, because those are unique to the Ozarks in the blending of the cultures that determined us as a people 200 years ago.

Prior to Sam Houston going to Texas and assuming the command of the Texas Army he enlisted Jehoida Jeffery to work on the military road project, known as the Southwest Trail which ran from St. Louis southwardly across the length of Arkansas to the Red River Valley of Texas, including supporting roads through Batesville and Riggsville, portions which were later used as "The Trail of Tears" (NRHP).

Jeffery then served as Judge of Izard County from 1833-1838 his duties being that of a primary peacemaker between the settlers and Indians including the famous attempt on later Arkansas Treasurer and House Representative, Jared C. Martin's life by Big Charley, a Shawnee from around Yellville (then known as Shawneetown) and accomplice, Chief Syllamo of the Creeks (from whom Sylamore takes it name). His decision setting off a war between the settlers, officials and Indians may have in part lead to the death of "Chief Syllamo", shot and killed, branded a horse thief. The Jeffery's home built around 1836 is a magnificent example of the time and is the presently owned by Carl and Carol Jeffery Cooper. The bricks for the first floor, foundation and chimneys were made on site by slaves, most who remained with the family during and after the Civil War. In 1836 due to the prominence of the Jeffery family and the influence of Thomas Riggs, both who served in the House of Representatives, the county seat had moved away from the Wolf House, to Athens and now to Mt. Olive thus centering commerce there and down river at Sylamore and Riggsville. In 1873, after Stone County was established from part of Izard County Mt. Olive was no longer the strategic center of the county. The Izard County courthouse moved in 1875 to Mill Creek (Melbourne) and Stone County built its first courthouse, a wooden structure located on Main Street near the Auto Parts store. The site is denoted by a historical marker.

White River was the border between civilized and uncivilized lands, our first 50 years determined who we are as a people, still found in the attitudes of generational descendants, strong, independent, highly intelligent, resourceful and resistant to change. Wolf House settled by Jacob Wolf, was the first seat of jurisdiction in 1820 of what was to become Izard County in 1825. Stone County "was" Izard County until it was sectioned out in 1873 with the White River and creeks, the roads. The first recorded settlement is the Lafferty family in 1797 followed by the Jeffery's in 1816. The first trading post was established in 1817 at present day Allison. All of present day Stone County was the designated Cherokee Indian Reservation 1817-1828. It was against the law for non Indians to travel into the reservation for any reason other than trade. Therefore the early settlements centered on trade with the Indians. "By 1818, a thin chain of log cabins extended up the White River some three hundred miles to points near the future site of Forsyth, Missouri" - (Elmo Ingenthron White River Valley Historian). Thomas Riggs first set foot in the Cherokee village located on the property of Mister Richard Decker, South Bayou Drive behind Wilson's Town and County and the area of what would become Riggsville around 1819. Buckhorn and Walls Ferry are found on territorial maps dating 1824 along with Riggsville, Round Bottom, Sylamore and Table Rock. The York and Hess families homesteaded what is now Marcella (Hesstown) in 1820. Dating around 1830, the oldest rock walls in Stone County with a distinctive Irish style found at St. James and Marcella were likely built by the hands of men black, white and Indian who found reprieve in the music and dance that became distinctive to the Ozarks in the blending of those cultures. A hoe down, particular to the Ozarks, is a reference to the end of the days work when the hoe can be laid down and presumably the fiddle picked up. Rich Woods maintained postal service for the Riggsville settlement and surrounding area from 1830-1860. Sylamore (Allison) and Riggsville were the largest settlements when the Civil War (1861-1865) broke out. Riggsville, about 2 miles from our present day courthouse, had a water and grist mill, a livery, tavern, store and two churches. Defeat of the South in the Civil War and death of Riggs' son John in an Indian massacre, lead Riggs to sell out and move to Texas in the midst of the Civil War. This served to fortify the influence of northern settlers who began moving into the area; their arrival and the land grants resulting from the Civil War also clearly contributed heavily to the relocation of Riggsville to Mountain View. Following the defeat of the Confederacy, homes and businesses along what is now highways 5, 9 and 14 began to appear. Several locations were considered for the courthouse including sites near the present day Levisy Flat church, Stevens Ready Mix and the hospital, each of them closer to the river landings. In 1873 just after Stone County was formed the name of the 'new' town, Mountain View, was drawn from a hat and the first courthouse, a 10x12 log structure erected.

The site of that structure is now denoted with a historical marker situated on East Main Street near the Auto Parts stores. The wide tree lined street it faces appearing as a private street for the homes', was in fact, the 'wagon parking and turn about' for the courthouse. The log structure that served as the original Stone County courthouse from 1873-1888 was later moved to the W.H. Miller property where the family used it as a barn for their milk cow. The property changed hands and currently belongs to the family of Van Rosa. The family reports that nothing remains of the first courthouse.

In 1874 the land where our present court house is located was deeded to the county by two families; the Brewer's for the sum of $1.00 and the Lancaster family who owned the north half of "the square," gave their half of the land taking money for it. Lancaster's Hardware is the oldest remaining business on the square from that time, owned and operated by the Lancaster family in its present location since around 1898. Many of the businesses on the south side of the court square on highway 66 were built by the Brewer family. In 1888 a two story wooden frame structure was built on "the square" and served as the seat of county jurisdiction until the completion of the construction of the present day courthouse.

1888 Wooden Courthouse now sits at corner of Evans & Oak

Finished in 1924 it is situated immediately in front of where the wood frame second courthouse sat. After the new sandstone court house was finished, Dwain Nesbitt was who was about 7 years old, tells, "Somebody bought the old courthouse, paid $200 for it. Then some fellas moved it down the hill on logs by a team of mules, when the team tried to make the down hill turn, right there where the telephone company's at, might near tore off most of the second floor." Our second courthouse which has been extensively remodeled sits at the corner of Oak (Telephone Hill) and Evans Streets and is a private residence in the Fiddler's Valley R.V. Park.

1888 Courthouse as it appears today
Fiddler's Valley R.V. Parks, Evans Street

Both Mister Decker and Mister Nesbitt agree; "The jail was moved by mules on logs about 10 years later around 1934. It (the jail) was across the street in what is now the parking area next to the old Lackey Building (Tres Amigos). (Great photo of old jail hangs inside the Stone County Tax Collector's office at the Stone County Courthouse.)

1924 Court House is on the National Registry of Historic Places

They doubled it in size and re-rocked it. You can see the work in the floor inside where they added on. The wall around the square was erected from stone and rocks from the four corners of the county. Every family in the county was invited to bring a rock; finished it in 1935... might near every farm and family in the county has a rock in that wall." The courthouse, including the wall, is on the National Register of Historic places along with over fifty businesses around the square, homes and barns and structures throughout Stone County.

Although court houses are the place to find records, I must say that nine hours of digging through archival records, rarely yields me as much information as one afternoon with Carol Cooper, Mister Richard, Mister Dwain or Miss Wilma, where dusty roads, ticks and chiggers, downed trees, the possibility of snakes, a flat tire and a little trespassing doesn't mean a thing when you're on a mission, yours or theirs. I smile as I pick up the phone and Miss Wilma says "Oh girl, have I got something to show you..."

Sam Younger - "The Buckhorn" (St. James)

Sam Younger is descended from Armistead Younger (1811) and wife Rebecca Crews (1814), whose brother James Crews (b 1816) of whom I am descended, arrived in the 1840's to Anderson, across the river from the Buckhorn. One of Stone County's Civil War battles was fought at Buckhorn, present day St. James, east of Mtn. View. Other than that, although I had grown up here, I didn't know a lot about its history prior to the Civil War. As Sam, Bob and I drove along Martin Access Road, Sam pointed out where the Civil War troops came across the river, commandeering both the Walls and O'Neal ferries for two weeks as they made their way across the river, up the banks and through the hills toward Riggsville.

Civil War Hospital – Battle of the Buckhorn
Steve Younger Farm, St. James

As we traveled the road to Younger Access Sam pointed out locations that were historical references in his child hood including the "Military Hospital" on the farm of Steve Younger (above), trading post, Indian burial grounds, old cabins, stills, mines, and Penter's Bluff. The oldest white family to settle Stone County was here, the Lafferty settlement of 1810 (old Izard County), on Sam's land across from Penter's Bluff. The bluff was named for the John R, George and William Penter who made it their 'fort' and lookout point in the late 1840's. The boys could see up and down the river and thus they could alert the men in the valley to the steamships, keelboats, travelers and trouble along the waterways. Locals still enjoy the hike out to the point for the view and can be heard talking in normal voices by persons standing on the opposite banks of the river's edge (Younger Access) 500 yards or more away.

Henry Rowe Schoolcraft descending the river from Calico Rock recorded on "Sunday, Jan. 17, 1819: ...we stopped for the night at widow Lafferty's, on the right bank of the river (Stone County). Some excitement prevails among the people occupying the right bank of White River, on account of the recent treaty concluded with the Cherokee Indians. By it those Indians relinquish certain tracts of land in the state of Tennessee, but are to receive in exchange the lands lying between the north bank of the Arkansaw and the south bank of the White River. Those people, therefore, who have located themselves on the right bank of the river, and improved farms, are now necessitated to relinquish them, which is considered a piece of injustice."

State, national and historical records of the Lafferty's support John Lafferty had a fur trading business with the Indians as early as 1801 in the area known as "The Buckhorn," a hunting ground of the Osage. Hunting and trapping allowed Lafferty a freedom of movement among the Indians as a trader, a requirement for white men to enter Indian territories. He would then take their furs to New Orleans for trade. Born in 1759 in Ireland, John Lafferty immigrated to America with his family as a small boy. He married Sarah Lindsey in 1786. They had 3 children born in GA and 4 in TN. He traveled the White River trading with the Osage as early as 1797. He decided to move his family to The Buckhorn around 1810. He was denied his original application for a land patent based on the fact that he had not continuously occupied the land for 10 years. His daughter Elizabeth married Charles Kelly in Sumner, TN just prior to their departure in 1810. She died while traveling near the mouth of the Arkansas River only two months after her marriage. Her husband, Charles Kelly became the first Sheriff of Independence County. Lafferty and his wife set up the trading post and river landing at The Buckhorn. During the 1811 New Madrid Earthquake Lafferty described being witness to a huge explosion that opened a pit over 200 feet deep near his river landing. The once visible pit located on Younger Bottoms was filled up around 2005 by Lyon College (formerly Arkansas College) who owns and maintains the Locks and Dams.

John Lafferty served in the Revolutionary War and when the War of 1812 broke out, he joined again. Wounded near New Orleans, he died in 1816 from complications from the injury. Although most of the family chose to move across the river to the mouth of the creek that now bears their name (Lafferty Creek) out of the newly established Cherokee Indian reservation, their mother, Sarah, "widow Lafferty" continued to live among the Indians in present day Stone County until her death in 1836. The Lafferty's were granted an Indian land patent for land in 14N 8W, Stone County in 1824 applied for by John Jr. and an additional 80 acres in 1836 applied for by son, Lorenzo. Margaret Lafferty married James L Criswell they acquired a large portion of Lafferty land just north of Younger Bottoms on Cagen Creek. Armistead Younger homesteaded nearby land in 1853.

Schoolcraft refers to both Hardin's Ferry on the south side of the river and Morrison's Ferry. One of the Lafferty sons married Hardin's daughter. Hardin sold the ferry to Abijah O'Neal, then it was ran by the family of Margaret Houston Grigsby until it was sold in 1902 to the Hess family. The Walls family operated the ferry while it was owned by the Grigsby's and the Hess', which gave rise to its current name of "Walls Ferry landing". O'Neal is situated across the river in Independence Co. Margaret Houston was a cousin to Gen. Sam Houston and his brother, John P. Houston, first clerk of Izard County. John Lafferty (Sr) operated a boat landing near present day Lock and Dam #3, which was later a ferry but never with the heavy use of the Walls Ferry.

Sam at Younger Access, Penter's Bluff seen in background

Sam remembers the ferries were in heavy use to Croaker Station across the river north of Penter's Bluff, so named for the bull frog's loud croaking. Its name was later shortened from Croaker to Croker. Then the locks and dams were put in, steam boat travel stopped, rail took over. In the 1950's the road to Batesville was paved and commerce moved away from the river. "The only activity on the bottoms these days besides a little fishing is Kent Brewer and the Foll boys farming," Sam says. Younger Bottoms and Younger Access were officially named for Sam in the 1960's when he gave the state the right of way across his land to the river over 100 years after his forefather homesteaded the land and 150 after the first boat landing was established there. In order to secure a land patent in Indian Territory a white man had to show he had established a trade with the Indians civilizing the frontier. For an Indian to secure a white man's land patent he had to have a white assurer or designee. Many land speculators came in and bought or traded for the Indian lands after the 1828 reservation ended, while others helped the Indians secure the land allowing them to remain here, blending with the settlers to create a unique Ozark culture on the edge of "civilization." And for Stone County, that began with The Buckhorn.

Lafferty Settlement 200 Years: 1810-2010

Sam pictured with Mary Cooper Miller and Mary Lafferty Wilson

This past week brought a burst of spring. Jonquils dotting the landscape are sweet reminders of home places that no longer stand. The Exploring Izard County (.com) crew joined Sam Younger and me for the first filmed trip of Exploring Stone County. We were joined by Mary Cooper Miller and Mary Lafferty Wilson, descendants of John and Sarah Lindsey Lafferty, who settled in present day Younger Bottoms in 1810, the first "white" settlement of Stone County. Until today, these distant cousins had not met each other or Sam. Arriving around 1840 the Younger family has called this home for 170 years.

We marvel at the rock wall that runs from Younger Access to Cook Holler stretching almost a mile. The wall was built pre-Civil War by slaves hired for 6 cents a day and turnips for lunch. Although it later served to hold in livestock, "it was built as a defense wall, to fend off the riff raff that came along the river wanting to steal and rob. It wasn't the Indians that folks worried about, it was other white folks," Sam offered. With talk of civil war in the air long before it was declared, including rifle ports, the rampart was first line of defense against Union soldiers. There are numerous accounts of both Union and Confederate soldiers crossing the river at Wall's Ferry (Lafferty Landing), including the Battle of the Buckhorn.

Mud holes along the road into Younger Bottoms were full and the possibility of getting stuck risky. Sam took us to the Indian burial grounds where in the 1920's floods and later archeologist's unearthed pottery, utensils, and at least one Indian whose remains were found buried sitting in an upright position. Although this was Osage land for 2,000 years, it is the Quapaw who buried their dead in the ground, in mounds or in the clay floors of their homes, frequently strapped to a stake in a sitting position then covered with earth. Now the burial grounds are gentle rolling slopes in a field populated by cattle. There are two other cemeteries nearby one whose rock markers have eroded and now rest at the river's edge; the other lost in the moss and undergrowth in the shadows of the trees. Sam recalls only one headstone as having a carved name, "Ennis". Sam stops at the edge of a field, near the convergence of Younger and Martin Access roads. "Your grandparents are likely buried here," he tells our two Mary's. There's nothing here now but a beautiful river bottom field. Sam remembers when the cemetery was there with 30 or so graves. "It grew up and when it was cleared for the field, the head rocks were leaned up against the trees over there. They were there for a very long time then one day, they were gone."

Pre-Civil War rampart wall almost perfectly intact, built by slaves

John Lafferty a fur trader first arrived here in 1801 running the waters of the White River in a keelboat. Likely around 1804, he brought his older sons and built a cabin. In 1808, he brought cattle and slaves. In 1810 he brought his wife Sarah and remaining children here. The oldest Lafferty daughter Elizabeth married Charles Kelly in Sumner TN June 11, 1810 just before beginning the journey with her parents. She died during the move at the mouth of the White River. Charles became the first Sheriff of Independence County. According to the New American State Papers, the Lafferty's applied for a land patent in 1810 but were denied for the primary reason they had not been here 'continuously' for 10 years. This documented denial is the first settler's claim to land in present day Stone County, 200 years ago.

Dec. 16, 1811 John and Sarah witnessed the New Madrid earthquake that caused the Mississippi to run backwards, creating Mud Island at Memphis. They saw huge clouds of dust, rocks, fire and water shoot into the sky, leaving behind a 200 foot deep pit that when the river rose water would run from into the fields. Around 2005 while completing work on Lock and Dam #3 under the direction of Lyon College, the sinkhole, one of the greatest geological remains of the 1811 earthquake was filled in. Nearby is an Indian thong tree, strategically cut to grow this way by the Indians and adopted by the settlers as early road signs, markers to indicate shelter, settlements, caves, springs and waterways. Denny catches sight of another one on the upper embankment and before we leave, a third on the edge of the marsh.

John and Sarah Lindsey Lafferty arrived here as a family in 1810. Mourning the death of their daughter they forged a life here on the right banks of the river among the Indians. John died at home in 1816 of complications from a wound he suffered in the War of 1812 near New Orleans. The Osage had agreed in 1808 to leave with the land being designated for the Cherokee setting out the reservation of 1817-1828 that included all of present day Stone County. In 1799, Tecumseh brought his mother Methoataske and his older sister, Tecumpease, to the Missouri territories. Tecumpease is buried near Gainesville, MO. In 1817, Stephen Ruddell brought his adopted Indian mother deeper into the Missouri Territories, to a place just up the river from his brother Abram. Documents suggest that place was Lafferty's settlement and that Methoataske, Tecumseh's mother and the adopted mother of Abe and Stephen Ruddell more than likely is buried here in Stone County or at the very least, the mouth of Lafferty Creek in Izard County. After the death of her husband in 1816, Sarah remained living in the reservation continuing the fur trading business thereby meeting the requirements to live within its boundaries. Sarah's older children had moved across the river out of the reservation establishing homes near present day Lafferty Creek. It is likely these two remarkable women were friends in the last days of their lives.

Schoolcraft traveling down river wrote on Jan 17, 1819 about "stopping at the widow Lafferty's on the right banks of the river." Although surrounded by Indians he made virtually no mention of them anywhere in his journals, his purpose ore and mineral explorations. Personal hand written letters and a biography of Lorenzo Dow Lafferty, the youngest son documents his life living among the Indians in Stone County. He married Elvira Creswell. In 1836 he homesteaded the land his parents called home. The knoll on which it is believed that the home of John and Sarah Lafferty sat, is just a few hundred yards from where Sam indicated the cemetery had been. Just to the east, Lafferty's Landing and the bottoms where they witnessed the earth erupt, leaving the sinkhole in its wake lays. Penter's Bluff is within sight to the west. It is believed that Sarah and John Lafferty, Stone County's first white settlers, are buried together here in this still beautiful place 200 years ago they called home, The Buckhorn. Today, Sam Younger, Mary Lafferty Wilson and Mary Cooper Wilson came home and remembered.

Chief Syllamo of the Creeks

Chief Syllamo by Native American Artist, Thurman Horse

The life of Chief Syllamo is documented in a number of places including the journals and writings of frontiersmen, J.J. Sams, Jehoiada Jeffery and Jacob Wolf. One of the earliest territorial maps lists Isllamo at the present day site of Allison, Arkansas, (Stone County) while only two list it as Syllamo. After the end of the Cherokee reservation of 1817-1828, it is consistently listed as Sylamore. The area does not become Allison until 1905.

The land east of the river was "civilization" with Batesville the center of commerce downriver. The western side of the river was Indian Territory with trading posts established at The Buckhorn, Sylamore and Table Rock. Entering from the White River, Sylamore became the point of entry into the Ozarks, into the reservation, the wild frontier, the point of departure where cultures did not assimilate one into the other, but blended, creating a vernacular of speech, in song, in music and dance, in the way we still live our lives, a bit guarded some might say, and resistant to change.

The Isllamo's were one of nine Creek Indian families moving to the new Cherokee Indian reservation here. Isllamo pronounced eye- Sĭl'-ă-mō

50

when spoken, sounded like "I – Syllamo" (two ll's spoken like an "i") more like an introduction rather than a whole name. It would have been easy for the settler's to mistake the spoken name as I - Syllamo. The name means "My Jesus Everywhere" in Algonquin. They established the first trading post around 1817 which sat in the same proximity of Angler's restaurant. The trading post provided guns, knives and staples to settlers and natives alike. The conditions were rough, rowdy and often resulted in conflicts leading to a few killings by stabbing, gunshot, arrows and tomahawks. There were at least two large Creek encampments in Stone County, the largest on what is present day North and South Sylamore which includes Gayler on the south, Blanchard on the north and Roasting Ear and Big Springs to the west. Relocated Muscogee Indians from Alabama and Georgia, the Creeks were given their name as "Creeks" from the English who noted that they lived in picturesque areas that were prone to flooding.

Indian burial site

Many of the Native American's were buried in above ground cairns that many people mistake for big piles of rocks such as this one in Stone County with an incredible view of the valley and creek below. Chief Syllamo was known to be antagonistic and belligerent, supporting raids and the stealing of horses, thus among the settlers he was known as a 'horse thief'. Stories go his horse thieving lead to his eventual death as he was tracked down and killed following the trial of Big Charley under Judge Jehoiada Jeffery for the attempted murder of Jared Martin. Big Charley, a Shawnee from Shawneetown (present day Yellville in Marion County then part of Izard County) had been hired, perhaps by some political rival of Martin's, to go to Little Rock to kill him. Martin served in both the House of Representatives and as Arkansas State Treasurer. Martin got word of the impending arrival of the Indians and their intent. Therein he shot instead, Big Charley wounding him. Chief Syllamo aided Big Charley in his return to the White River area of Sylamore. A pursuant trial over seen by Judge Jehoiada Jeffery found no one guilty. A kind of local war ensued between the settlers and Indians which resulted in Syllamo being shot and killed somewhere near the mouth of the creek around 1838, where the 1938 bridge leading to Calico Rock and Angler's boat dock now stand. Over time, just as many family names changed spellings and pronunciations Syllamo was anglicized like so many names, Indian, blacks and white settlers alike, to its current form – Sylamore (Sĭl'-ă-mōre). The Creek settlement now Sylamore township (Newnata area) and the creek which flows through the Indian encampment bear the name of Sylamore after the family Isllamo. But it is Chief Syllamo that has been recalled and recounted, given credit.

Numerous documents legal and personal from the era support additional encounters and dealings with an old Indian named Syllamo, whether he was actually a chief of his tribe or simply the last representative of a once proud family is not clear. It is clear that the Creek Isllamo family was here 20 years before Chief Syllamo died, and many of the Creek descendants live among us still. The oral and written history of the early Indian settlements is not well documented here in the Ozarks. Family stories, letters, journals and war records hold the most reliable information. In 1819 Henry Rowe Schoolcraft records stopping 5 miles downriver from the Jeffery's which more than likely was Sylamore. His next stop was at Widow Lafferty's at The Buckhorn, present day Younger Access. After the reservation ended in 1828, the land was opened up to settlers. Those settlers who had married into the tribes or established trade first patented claimed land under Indian Land patents later homesteaded the same land. They had to prove that they had both occupied and improved the land for 10 years to qualify for a homestead land patent therefore the majority of settlers did not record homesteaded land until the late 1830's early 1840's; homesteads prior to 1838 were in most cases established first as Indian land grants. Because there were defined areas of Indian encampments, the white settlers traded or bought those lands, leading to a number of the early settler's not homesteading their land until around the time of the Civil War even though they had resided in the area in some cases as much as 40 years. When word got out that the slaves if freed were going to be granted 80 acres and a mule, everyone who had not previously homesteaded or bought their land, made claims and when necessary, denied their Indian heritage as a new influx of settlers moved into the area.   Not because they were "dirty injuns" but because the U.S. government required that they assimilate or move to the reservation which is like the Vatican, a nation within a nation, and until only recently without representation as Native Americans on reservations were not granted the right to vote until 1956. The Indians often had to have a co-signer on land patents which led to a number of Indians taking on the family name of their friends, white wives or husbands in order to qualify for a homestead under white man's laws.

L.C. Sutterfield - Sylamore "East & West"

Ridley Polk – Polk Mtn is west above Sylamore in Izard County

It's a cold bleak day as L.C. and I venture out to the cemetery at Sylamore where our grandmother, Josephine Johnson Crews is buried. L.C.'s mother, Clementine was a sister to my grandfather, Sanford Crews, children of Granny Fine', L.C. and my dad, first cousins. Digging into the people and places of Stone county, of the White River Valley the line between civilization and the frontier, the relationships between people defining who was who, who is whom, has given me a greater understanding of not only my family but of the strength and inter-dependency of the people who arrived here in this valley 200 years ago.

L.C. was born on Polk Mountain in the hills above Sylamore in Izard County. Polk Mountain is named for Ridley Polk, a former slave who lived his life there. "One night Ridley came to our house looking for a doctor, his wife in labor. While he went to look for a doctor, mom and dad (Clem & Berry Sutterfield) went to their house. Mom delivered the babies, twins. Ridley came back without a doctor. Daddy showed him one baby then folded back the covers to show him the second one. There wasn't much he wouldn't have done for my folks after that. Grand daddy, William Crews was a doctor. He died while out making rounds on the White river around 1910. His horse fell on the ice, broke its leg. He froze to death on the banks of the river near Sylamore.

Circa 1930 White River with floating ice before Norfork Dam was built

A couple of times in the last 50 years people have wanted to change the name of the mountain to Sutterfield Mountain, and I think one suggestion was even Pleasant Hill or something. People who had been born and raised on this mountain, including our own, wrote, called, and protested from across the nation. The extended family of this mountain and there are a lot of us, the Sutterfields', Crews, Johnson, Sanders, are honored with the history in the name of this mountain, "Polk Mountain.""

We drive through the old town of Sylamore, at the foot of the mountains on the east banks of the river in Izard County. Buildings that were once bustling stores, the train depot and cattle yard now falling to ruin; a place that is said to have been the port of distribution for more raw timber following the Civil War continuing through the 1930's than any other port in the south. Muscles mined from the rich riverbed were made into pearl buttons and sold throughout the world. Everything that entered into present day Stone County arrived first at the port of Sylamore, present day Allison. Both the steamboat and ferry landing was at the base of the hill where Angler's Boat Dock now sits. The Mississippi River was the interstate of the era, with the Ohio and Tennessee both major connecting routes. The Ohio served as the boundary of the Northwest Territories, flowing into the Mississippi where the Convergence of the America's met at Paducah, Kentucky and Cairo, Illinois bordered by Arkansas, Missouri and Tennessee, about four hours from Sylamore by vehicle today. Traveling south to the mouth of the Arkansas and White Rivers, many settlers came up the White river first to Batesville, then

"The Buckhorn" and Sylamore. Making their way into the hills they built homes above the high water lines. They proved their resiliency and strength in the isolation as they forged out a living from the land. There were few overland roads well in the mid 1900's. Because "civilization" lay immediately across the White river to the east and the Indian territories to the west, Sylamore, in Stone County became the port of entry into the frontier.

The name Sylamore is an anglicized form of the Creek Indian family name Isllamo. Pronounced "Sil a Mo", the family established the first trading post at present day Allison around 1817. All of the land laying to the west of the White river, extending south near Batesville to the western borders of Oklahoma, was the Arkansaw Territories and Indian country. Stone County along with all of the Arkansas Ozarks and southern Missouri to the eastern boundary of present day Oklahoma was the new Cherokee reservation of 1817-1828. Mostly settlers held to the east side of the river as it was 'against the law' to cohort with the Indians, or enter the Indian reservation unless you were part Indian or doing business with them. A number of Osage had land grants from Spain and France and did not leave the area. Settlers often traded for the Indian land rights occupying and settling the land long before they were ever allowed to homestead. Land transactions such as these between the whites and Indians although not recognized by the U.S. government were nonetheless encouraged as a means to open up the frontier west of the White river. After the reservation ended in 1828, the land was officially opened up to settlers. They had to prove that they had both occupied and improved the land for 10 years to qualify for a homestead land patent therefore many settlers who had married into the tribes or established trade first obtained land under Indian Land patents. Therefore the majority of settlers did not record homesteaded land until the late 1830's early 1840's and some not until they were faced with the Civil War, many having lived on the land as much as 40 years.

Arkansas became a state in 1836. Henry Harris and his brothers purchased Indian land patents in excess of 640 acres along the river bottom between Sylamore and Optimus. Henry homesteaded the 40 acres between Sylamore Creek and the White River at the base of present day Government Mountain in 1849, building his home there prior to his death in 1852. It is the current home of Guy and Liz Harris. His brothers and extended family homesteaded the outlying areas hence our present day Harris Township. The Harris cemetery was washed clean of its markers in the flood of 1982. A number of the markers have been found in the river with many reported to still be in the wash near the cemetery. The Hayden's have allowed descendants to mark the location with a large boulder and plaque denoting the portion of the cemetery near their home. Historically the cemetery lay on both sides of present day highway 5, next to the Hayden's home on the east and south of the barn on the west along Green Mountain Road. Highway 5 is reported to have taken the path of the road that bisected the cemetery with the west side abandoned long before the flood of 1982. Many old timer's who worked on the road during the 1960's paving report when the road was improved and paved that markers and graves were destroyed on both sides, the present day right of way. While some suggest that graves lay beneath Highway 5, others maintain that the road took the existing path that ran through the middle of the cemetery, marking the distinction of who was buried where. Blacks and Indians buried on the west side of the road with the whites buried on the east side.

On February 5, 1851 Tobias S. Rudolph became the first postmaster in the newly established post office at Sylamore (present day Allison) on the west banks of the river. The Civil War (1861-1865) came to Sylamore with at least one battle and several skirmishes along Kickapoo Bottoms, North and South Sylamore to Cooper Mill (Big Springs) and Roeher (Rorie) Mill (Brewer Springs/Mill Creek), resulting in deaths ranging from one or two to over 50, for the North and South. Both before and following the war, Sylamore had taken on a true frontier town life with saloons, gambling and nightly dance halls at the edge of the Indian encampment (where Guy and Liz Harris' campground is on the west side of Hiway 5). Families who were living on either side simply forded the river in shallow places on foot, mule or horseback, while others crossed using a horse pulled wooden ferry to transport wagons and animals. The river is reported to have frozen over numerous times prior to the 1930's.

On December 18, 1905 a post office was established on the east bank of the river with William Brooks as the first postmaster of the new East Sylamore. The postal service was complicated and confusing as to which bank of the river to deliver mail. Therefore the U.S. Postal Service instructed the offices to change the names or one should close. East Sylamore had become a thriving community with churches, a school and they had the train station. They were historically the civilized side of the river. Now that they had the new rail road they predicted a booming future on the east side of the river and demise on the west due if for no other reason its wild frontier life style. Therefore in 1905 the east bank kept the name of Sylamore and Stone County's side on the west became known as Allison. Stories go it was named for a hobo, James "Dad" Allison who drifted in on a raft, looking for work at the limestone quarry (Ruddell). He had gained local popularity especially with the women because he had shown them an easier way to wash their clothes. He would fasten a can with holes punched in it to the end of a pole, thus they could stand and 'agitate' the clothes reducing the amount of time they had to bend over and scrub on a washboard. "Dad" Allison who died in 1948 is buried at Gayler Cemetery.

The rail road depot on the east bank of the river was named Ruddells Station. The post office of East Sylamore was actually housed in the general store of the limestone company store at Ruddell. When the limestone company relocated to Limedale, outside of Batesville, the post office closed August 15, 1930 having operated for only 25 years. This signaled not only the demise of Ruddell but of (East) Sylamore.

Steamboats were chugging their way up the White River with the last known docking in 1938, just prior to the completion of the bridge at the mouth of Sylamore Creek in 1939. They ported at the same landing used by the wooden ferry and later the motor powered ferry, situated between Angler's boat dock and the foundation of the Sylamore Creek Bridge precisely where Chief Syllamo is reported to have been shot. Train travel dominated over the steamboats and now automobiles were becoming the main means of transportation.

One of the last remaining dance halls of that frontier period was located near "Swinging Bridge;" a juke joint run by "Ma Cook" who provided services in the early half of the 19th century for the CCC boys and the workers on the railroad, bridges and roads of the 1930's. One story goes that some of the boys got pretty intoxicated and drove some pigs off the bluffs into the creek below. Then, they rounded up the hurt and dead animals for a pig roast. Other stories include Ma Cook herself acting as bouncer tossing drunken men off the porch to the ground. As Miss Neva (Foll) told me in the spring of 2009 just before her death at age 93, "no ladies ever admitted back then to having gone there. But the music was grand and lots of fun was had by all. There was always a ruckus of some kind, of that you could be certain. We supplied a little sugar to the moonshiners back then, had a store out in Happy Hollow."

For us Stone County natives descendants of the first settlers, the Irish and Scots, blacks and Native Americans, who trapped animals for meat and furs, who built the roads and mills, who sang the songs, Sylamore is not one place. It is not Ruddell or East or West Sylamore nor Allison. It is not Harris Township nor is it Sylamore Township. It is not Blanchard Springs or Roasting Ear. It is a time when places were known by the people who lived and died there. For us, it will always be Syllamo, the place of the "Creeks"; the path, the road, from the inland area along the creeks, from the Indian encampments, toward the river and the place where the streams meets the river, where "Chief Syllamo" of the Creeks lived and died.

L.C. shows my grandson Denali Gayler the medicine satchel that belonged to William Crews, my great grandfather, who died on the banks of the frozen White River around 1910 while out making rounds. "His horse fell breaking its leg and Grandpa Crews (husband to Josephine) froze to death." Denali listens wide eyed, "Now, my great grand father William Johnson was a prize fighter and a U.S. Marshall," L.C. continues. "His son, Sam Johnson, Granny Fine's brother was a doctor. They lived at Marcella. He had a son and a son in law who were doctors. Doc Johnson's grandson, Sam, a first cousin to my Momma and your grand dad Crews," L.C. says eyeing me, "was Sheriff of Stone County in the 1920's during the famous Connie Franklin murder case. But now that's another story."

Dr. Bill Crews was my daddy's and L.C.'s grandpa, my great grandfather and my grandson Denali's great great great grandfather. L.C. is sharing first hand stories about our family history that were told to him growing up. These stories some that go back to the Civil War are a priceless gift when shared in this manner. Just as Ches Beckham heard the stories from his grandfather who had fought in the Civil War and I heard them from him, although it is a 150 years ago, only a single lifetime separates us from these events when shared by our elders.

L.C. showing Denali the medicine bag of grandpa, Dr. Bill Crews

The bridge over Sylamore Creek completed in 1938 is under construction in the background as the mule drawn wooden ferry glides across the water. L.C. operated both the ferry at Sylamore and Ruddell using "horses at one time or another."

After WWII, L.C. Sutterfield ran the ferry from Sylamore to Allison, "when the river was low, it would take a horse or mule to pull it across and when it was high, you just tied it up, hoping it didn't break loose and get off down river."

L.C., his wife and children would cross the river and walk up the hill to Levisy Flat to church. Sometimes, there would be a ride, most times, not, "a life time ago, but yesterday in our memories, our life experiences." The bridge over the creek was built in 1938 but it would be almost another 40 years, 1974, before there was a bridge across the river. L.C. and his family lived at what was East Sylamore on the Izard County side of the river, where civilization met the frontier well into the 20th century.

Naomi Hedges Gayler -
Camp Hedges & Fifty-Six, Arkansas

In 1903 Fred Hedges made his way from Illinois to Arkansas by ox wagon. Fred homesteaded 80 acres in what was to become the Ozark National Forest, Sylamore District.

Naomi at Camp Hedges - Gunner Pool Recreation area
Pictured with her grand daughter Mariah & great grandson Denali Gayler

Fred ran the first post office in the area. The mail route was operated by mule and ran on Monday, Wednesday and Friday from Sylamore to Hedges post office then on to Big Flat. He maintained a small shed and stall to keep the mule in at night. Fred was not paid a wage as post master instead he received a compensation for the cancellation of stamps which may have amounted to as much as $4.00 in a good month. The area was generally known as Hedges until the 1920's when the U.S. Postal Service determined that the mail service was sufficient enough to be included in their official routing. However, the settlement would need a name. Fred served as a minister at the Spoon Flat community church and shied from the vanity of having the town named for him as first suggested by the United States Postal Service. The entire community was invited to attend a meeting at the Newcomb Country Store to decide upon a name. It seems it was a good thing that only six people showed up to make the decision as there was considerable dispute and discussion. A list of all the people who had been getting mail which was a total of 60 people had been prepared which lead to the suggestion of "Three Score, Arkansas". Then it was learned that Mr. and Mrs. Hay had moved. Lotty Low had died while having her baby a month ago and old George Shaw had also just died, therefore "Three Score will not do," a Mr. Turnaway announced as another suggestion of "Three Score minus Four" was made. Finally a Mr. Revy who was moderating the meeting suggested everyone write down their favored name and he would submit them to the U.S. Postal Service and let them decide. Everyone agreed, leaving the meeting feeling they had all had their say. About 10 days later news arrived from the U.S.P.S. that the name of the town would be Fifty-Six. It is unknown if the list of suggestions was submitted or if the postal service just shortened the "Three Score minus Four" suggested by Mr. Revy to "Fifty-Six."

Newcomb Store & Post Office, Fifty Six, Ark

The land Fred Hedges had homesteaded thirty years before on North Sylamore Creek became Camp Hedges in 1933, home to Civilian Conservation Corp (CCC) Company 743 serving until 1942, and home to the first forest rangers, game warden and firemen were the father's of Alvie Green (Green Tower) and Jack Thomas and Carl Ward. The CCC began in 1933 under President Franklin Delano Roosevelt as a means to provide outdoor employment to young men to both improve the economy of the Great Depression and to protect, improve and develop our country's natural resources. Camps were set up in every state with 106 located in Arkansas. The CCC workers planted trees, built parks including cabins, lodges, campgrounds, bath houses, picnic pavilions and beaches, dams, bridges, roads and hiking trails, along with saving over 40 million acres from erosion through soil conservation. Working eight hours a day, five days a week, they were paid $30 a month for their services, with most of the young men sending home the maximum amount of $25.00 living on only $5.00 a month. The majority of young men enrolled in the CCC served in World War II, which ultimately led to the closure of the camp.

Arkansas' first state park, Petit Jean, near Morrilton was built by the CCC, along with Mt. Nebo, Crowley's Ridge, Devil's Den, Lake Catherine and Lake Leatherwood. Locally much of the improvement of Blanchard Springs including log cabins, campsites, recreation hall, and pavilions was completed by the CCC. Blanchard remains remarkable and more beautiful because of the now historic rockwork of the CCC including the beautiful stone walk ways, bridges and dams still in use today, Gunner Pool Recreation Area, Hedges Dam, Mirror Lake and Mitchell Mill.

Naomi Hedges Gayler is the great niece of Fred Hedges. She is the daughter of Abram Hedges and Vera DeCamp Hedges. She is married to Carl Gayler, whose sister Opal Gayler Thomas' husband Dexter (Jack's dad) was the first "Refuge Keeper" in the Ozark National Forest. The Gayler's, Thomas' and Hedges, descendants, friends and family of the native people and the first frontiersmen who settled the White River Valley: John & Sarah Lafferty (Younger access 1801), Abraham & Mary Culp Ruddell (Ruddell's Mill across the river in Independence Co, from Marcella 1816), Isllamo family of the Creek Indians (first trading post at Sylamore 1816), Thomas Riggs (1820 Riggsville/Mountain View), Thomas & Lavina Jeffery Culp (Culp 1822; Lavina is the daughter of Jane Mason Jeffery, who settled south of Mt. Olive. Jane is remembered today as Dr Quinn Medicine Woman. Jane Mason and the Hedges family came from Martinville, Hedgesville, VA, to Kentucky, Illinois and the Missouri/Arkansas Territories) and Isaac Teague (who first arrived at Blanchard Springs in 1834); each contributing greatly to the history of the Sylamore District of the Ozark National Forest, the White River Valley and the culture that defines the Ozark region.

Hedges Dam, Gunner Pool erected by the CCC

Virgil "Jack" Thomas - Gunner Pool & Hedges Dam

It was a beautiful day in early August when Jack and I headed out through the hills of the Ozark National Forest. Down the road to Gunner Pool Recreation area, a favorite spot when we grew up, a favorite still to locals and visitors alike. The creek remains clear and brisk, the towering bluffs stunning in their beauty, children who don't know each other play as if BFF's (best friend's forever) if only for today. Parents nearby with watchful eyes enjoy the warm sun, the tranquility brought on by the chirping birds in the trees, gurgle of the creek and the sounds of children laughing. Jack points to a place on the bluffs above the creek now filled with cedar and pine where the CCC (Civilian Conservation Corp) boys put boulders forming 743 designating the CCC Company that was "Camp Hedges" from 1933–1942. "The boulders are still there," he says, "you just can't see them for the trees." Camp Hedges was named for Fred Hedges who homesteaded nearby land in 1903. In 1931 the Arkansas State Highway Commission built a bridge across North Sylamore Creek a connecting road to "old Highway 5" whose primary path was through the forest, rather than along the river as it is today. That bridge remains in use, 80 years old in 2011 it is in much better shape than a majority of our more modern structures. It has recently been placed on the NRHP.

Gunner Pool swimming hole just below Hedges Dam

WWII arrived and most of the young men who had comprised Company 743 left to defend our country and "Camp Hedges" fell to the administration of the Ozark National Forest. Jack and his family moved to the vacated buildings of the camp making the hospital their home. His father, Dexter Thomas, was the first "Refuge Keeper" for the state, a precursor to the game wardens, for the Sylamore District which included the Livingston Creek Refuge, approximately 8,500 acres and the Barkshed Refuge, approximately 5,300.

Several local men were part of Company 743, at one time or another including Tollie Leonard, Firse Brannon and Alvy Mitchell. I am told that the men became friends, survivors of a different kind; they wanted the camp to be remembered. They wanted to be remembered. While many people want to remember the men of CCC in the name of Gunner Pool, for those that went on to fight, there's another story about a dog that liked to swim in the water and his name was Gunner. People would drive by and say, "There's old Gunner in the pool." The dog got in a fight with a bear and was killed and Gunner's Pool stuck.

Civil War smeltor kettle used to make ammunition

However, there are others who tell a story that is much older and makes more historical sense. "During the Civil War, Union commander Baumer sent men repeatedly up the Sylamore Creek in search of the gun munitions. The Confederate milita under J.J. Kemp had been put in charge of making ammunition for all of Arkansas' troops, right here on the Sylamore. It was being made out of the nitrates that were coming out of the caves. When you work with nitrates, puttin' on your garden, they burn your hands. They had to make the gun munition right there on the banks of the creek. That place was there at what's known as Gunner Pool." In researching the Civil War records and bills of laden for steamboats on the river, it was clear that not just one or two but huge numbers of steamboats landed at Sylamore bringing with them the smeltors kettles (photo above) and other items needed for the powderworks. Several of the steamboats carried mail into the region and were not immediately suspect, however, with the river being the great divide once again, travel on the river became hugely risky. Smeltors were found throughout what is now the Ozark National Forest Sylamore District well into the 1900's with many used as rending kettles and damaged ones as flower pots or feeding kettles for animals.

Jack and Bob are like two young boys slipping and sliding in the moss on top of the dam, trying not to fall in… they didn't.

I ran across another interesting piece of information in researching the people who died during the Civil War that were not soldiers but were nonetheless casualties of war. I found names, repeatedly, of people who had died in Bermuda, from the Ozarks. Just as with Vietnam many of our young men were used as snipers due to their expert skills at hunting. But in the Civil War marksmanship combined with expertise in maneuvering the rivers and coastal waters they were sent to Bermuda, which was a neutral port, to secure guns and smuggle them back into the South. On July 13, 1864 the Mary Celestia hit a coral reef and sank off the coast of Bermuda. It's well documented that the ship was part of a gun running effort for the South. Lincoln had authorized Union men to stop the ships and shoot or hang all the men without question if any contraband Confederate arms were aboard. That fateful day, the Mary Celestia was attempting to get out of the coastal waters and out of sight and was unable to avoid the coral reef at the speed they were traveling. This information along with the steamships that were coming in and out of Sylamore assures me, Gunner Pool is a hold over from the Civil War.

One of the duties that fell to a young Jack Thomas (born in 1933), son of Dexter and Opal Gayler Thomas, and his friends Carrol and Von Ward whose father Carl Ward was the first "Forest Ranger" of the U.S.F.S for the area, was opening Hedges Dam to free the waters of Gunner Pool cleaning the leaves and debris preventing it from filling up. Jack told me the story of their work as young boys with great pride. Shaking his head anger and sorrow evident in his words and on his face, he spoke of how some of U.S. Forestry Service had considered tearing it down in their frustration of not knowing how to clean it. He volunteered to show them how to remove the leaves and debris using a garden hose and piping to remove enough leaves and debris to expose the levers of the release door that had become hidden. He had expected a couple men to show up to help and learn but instead dozens showed up, stunned that it was something a couple of people could do, three young boys had. Afterwards, he went back with a boat and motor to stir up the leaves from the bottom so that they could flow through and instead of being allowed to finish the job, was ordered out of the water by the ranger who was incapable of understanding without a proper cleaning it would fill up, "rules you know about boats and motors."

Today it is clear, spring floods and rains have brought in new debris and gravel seriously encroaching into the pool again putting it at risk. Ultimately without the proper maintenance, that even three young boys did for years, Gunner Pool will fill in like Riggsville Dam. Both of these are remarkable examples of rock work and ingenuity, but even more, they are examples of the spirit that makes our county, our state, our country special, our spirit of independence, of doing what's right when it's the hardest of choices. Riggsville Dam honors the Native Americans, slaves and frontiersmen who forged a path for others to follow, settling this part of old Izard County when it was the Cherokee Indian Reservation and may represent one of the oldest remaining pre-Civil War structures in the White River Valley. Hedges Dam and Gunner Pool, they honor the boys who worked for their families during the Great Depression and who defended our country regardless of how it got its name. These places, like the people who lived their lives here and remember the stories of their fathers and grand fathers, should be honored and respected. Only Mirror Lake is on the NRHP; Mitchell Mill, Gunner Pool, Hedges Dam, the walk ways and bridges that make Blanchard all the more special, nor Riggsville Dam - are not. Thankfully the process has been started to place the bridge over the North Sylamore creek at Gunner Pool on the NRHP.

I am certain there are at least three old historic fellas, Jack Thomas, Carrol and Von Ward who would gladly instruct a couple of young fellas on how to properly maintain Gunner Pool should the U.S. Forestry Department be interested setting up a volunteer maintenance program.

Peggy Lester - Culp

When I lived in California, I loved getting the newspaper from home with the news of Guion Road, Herpel and other small communities. It was important when someone visited and shared a piece of Momma's fried peach pies along with news of weddings, illnesses and birthings. Visiting with Peggy Lester took us both back to a place and a time when neighbors were friends, if not family. Miss Peggy moved here from Pennsylvania in the 1940's when she was 10 years old. Her parents bought and ran the store at Optimus until the 1960's (a later story, when she and I can get with Von Ward). Miss Peggy's home is the last remaining house in what was the once thriving community of Culp, with a doctor (Dr. Joe Gower), a post office, church, school, lumber yard and sawmill (Thomas Marchant, Joe's son in law), general store (Joe Emmett) and grist mill (Sam Hall & Joe Emmett). Miss Peggy visited with a Mister Sexton in the 1980's at the rest home at Calico Rock. He was born in the early 1890's and lived his life at Culp. He identified all of the buildings that in 1980 were falling to ruin, now gone, and the families who lived there in 1900 including the bootlegger. Thomas Marchant married Effie Emmett. Their daughter Claudine married Harold Culp. Dr. Joseph Gower and his wife Rebecca moved from Timbo and built the biggest house. They had 6 sons. Without his story and Miss Peggy's curiosity, this history would be gone.

Painting of Culp from a photo circa 1900 of Mister Sexton's

Thomas Culp, a brother of Mary Culp Ruddell, wife of Abraham Ruddell who had been captured and lived 15 years with the Shawnee as a brother to principal chief Tecumseh, arrived in the Ozarks around 1815 to find his sister Mary. His family was tanner's by trade. He and John Milligan established and ran a successful tannery at the southern edge of present day Sharp County prior to entering the military in 1821. After mustering out, he and his wife Lavina Jeffery, (daughter of James "Ol Jim" and Jane Mason Jeffery and a sister to John Milligan's wife, Eda Jeffery), moved to the west side of the White River on land presently owned by Hayden Wyatt. Lavina had been married to Wiley Sams and had one son, Jehoiada J. Sams, whose writings although highly embellished and often simply fictional reveal a rich history and insight into the families of the White River Valley. The trail into the 'reservation' on the west side of the White River began at the Culp property near Optimus. The largest Shawnee settlement was located near City Rock Bluff overlooking the river leading to Table Rock; the present day route of "Culp Road." The new U.S. government in the early 1800's encouraged settlers to move into Indian territories however they had to be part Indian, marry an Indian or establish trade with them in order to do so. As a tanner Thomas was able to meet the requirements and established a trading post and staples store with some ease. His brother in law Jehoiada Jeffery had perhaps the largest established trade route in the region taking furs, crops and timber all the way to New Orleans from Mt. Olive, Sylamore and the Lafferty settlement at Buckhorn. Jane Mason Jeffery, Thomas' mother in law was the doctor for the settlers in the region. The Culp Post, point of trade with the Indians at what was then the 'end' of Culp Road where Peggys' house now sits, in the Indian settlement was the beginning of the Town of Culp, and the bustling community that existed there after the Civil War until the mid 1940's when small communities everywhere began to die as automobiles and better roads transformed our nation.

It was a cold and snowy day when I visited Miss Peggy. She graciously showed me the remains of the old post office near the creek and where the old road crossed the mountain.

Thomas Culp served as Ark State Representative 1836-1838. Decisions made by the friends, family and elected officials set in motion historical events and forged relationships that shaped our nation; among them Thomas Riggs (settled Riggsville, first settlement of Mtn. View, served Ark House of Rep 1840-42), Jehoiada Jeffery (settled Mt. Olive, Ark House of Rep 1842-44), Sam Houston (aided in settling Cherokee into the White River Valley, Father of the Republic of Texas and brother to John Houston, Izard County's first clerk), the Hardin's (daughter married into the Lafferty family, ran the first ferry at present day Marcella that Riggs crossed in 1819; both Joseph and Jacob Hardin served AR House of Rep) and Abe Ruddell (brother in law to Thomas and one of the founders of Batesville).

Although Thomas had no formal training, he may have learned some "doctoring" from his mother in law Jane or from Abe who was known to have practiced a little herbal healing, "Indian doctoring", or from the Indians themselves. Thomas and Lavina had eight children - Jane, Josiah, Daniel, Abraham, James Jeffrey, Thomas, Jr., Ambrose and Letty. Thomas and Lavina's nephew Daniel Culp became a doctor and served as personal secretary to Sam Houston. When Daniel died in New Orleans, Sam had his body returned to Texas for burial declaring him a "Son of Texas."

Culp Road is situated off Hiway 5 in Stone County 1 mile south of Calico Rock. The former Town of Culp is six miles down Culp Road, about one mile over the Stone County line in present day Baxter County. Thomas Culp died June 27, 1846. It is believed that Thomas and Lavina Culp may be buried in unmarked graves at Table Rock, Culp or Optimus.

City Rock Bluff (Stone County) looking toward Calico Rock

It is clear that the pioneering families here made lasting relationships amongst themselves and with the Indians contributing to the birth of the Ozark culture in the White River Valley that remains unique in its attitudes, politics, speech, song and dance, even its horse's, the Missouri Territories "foxtrotter". Many people move here, perhaps with former roots here, perhaps no association at all, and purport that the music they play and the jig they dance is "traditional Ozark" or that there is no right or wrong way as anything goes. Although we may love the sound of your voice, applaud your skill on the instrument and share a dance with you, we recognize that the traditions of the Ozarks are being lost as what is taught and understood as Ozark often bears no more resemblance to our culture than naugahyde is to the leather produced by the hands of Thomas Culp. And if you run for office, you might consider the value in asking for a person's vote, looking them in the eyes and shaking their hand as more than water runs deep in the White River Valley.

Merlin "Skinny" Blair – "The Lower End"

"My brother could pick me up by the straps of my overalls setting me up on the old mule with just one hand," Skinny explains, "that's how I got my name. But you know, everyone had a nickname, rarely did we go by our given names," as he runs through a list of family and friends asking if I know them, "Cooter, Boog, Shorty". I do, or at least I remember them, most of them now gone. Skinny is the son of Clyde Blair and Mabel Goodwin, his grand father James Avery Blair owned the mill at Pleasant Grove. Avery's parents Samuel and Elizabeth Porter Blair moved into the White River Valley in the 1840's from Tennessee. They had thirteen children.

In 1913 Clyde, Earl, Albert and Hershel cut wood out at Novell Mullin's house for $2.50 a cord. The steamboats picked it up at Smith Landing. With part of the money they ordered their first instruments from Sears and Roebuck, a fiddle, two banjos and a guitar, delivered to O'Neal.

Around 1914 they started playing with some of the black river boat men; "Whistling Rufus", Roy Reel from Vincennes, Indiana. They would stay on a day or two while the steamboat was being loaded and unloaded. Around the time of WWI they learned the "Spanish Two Step" from Roy. The Blair brothers helped Leslie "Boog" Walls (1915-1980) and his brother Raymond learn to play. Skinny recalls his dad telling how this fella played the guitar using a figure eight pattern they taught to Boog later made famous by Johnny Cash (fellow Arkansan) who learned it from his dad, who also attributed it to black men who worked the river boats in south east Arkansas along the Delta. Skinny recalled some of the songs they sang that have since been attributed to more learned white people, folks who took credit. "Will the Circle Be Unbroken" although known as a traditional Ozark hymn with the chorus

71

recalled by people prior to the Civil War sang by slaves in the fields is now attributed to Ada Haberson as having written the lyrics around 1907. It is more than likely that Ms Haberson who lived in England received the words in a letter from friends or family who had emigrated to the U.S. and the White River Valley and heard the song sang in worship or in the fields. Southern spirituals are a result of the interaction of music and religion from Africa with music and religion of European origin. This interaction and creation of music occurred only in the United States. It is no less important that the people of the Ozarks claim and celebrate what is ours, what makes us who we are, than it is any other ethnicity or region of the world that is facing extinction. Holding onto traditions isn't easy any where in the world, for any one.

Avery Blair Mill – Red Stripe (Pleasant Grove)

The Blair family brought with them not only a love of music and dance but a work ethic that made Avery Blair one of the richest men in the area. When he died, each of his children received 40 acres. Avery Blair and his sons ran the grist mill, cotton gin and saw mill at Pleasant Grove employing not only their family but members of the community. The mill sat in the location of Dwain Logan's house across from the Pleasant Grove store. Before it was Pleasant Grove, it was Red Stripe, so named during the 1817-1828 Indian reservation by the Shawnee who called it the Land of the Red Stripes, a red striped water snake that is found in the cool rocks, hollers, marshes and sloughs. The first mail route was established by John Hatfield who rode a mule from O'Neal crossing the river at Hesstown (later named Marcella) then onto Red Stripe. Mail was delivered to a single metal box for everyone in the community. In 1911, 100 years ago, the first post office was officially set up by Mabel Blair Davis. The first mail carrier, Claire Hess, used a wooden wagon to deliver mail. The name Red Stripe was changed following the 1929 Connie Franklin murder trial in which Franklin returned. The publicity and curiosity seekers were so great, the community elected to change the name submitting three suggestions to Washington. The name Pleasant Grove was chosen.

The 'lower end' of Stone County has a rich history important to the culture of both Ozarks and the White River Valley. Skinny tells how the holler there above twin bridges east of Marcella is known as Hub Chute Holler. The loggers set up a trough in the trees in which cut timber could be placed then chute down the holler to the creek and from there to the river. The main road ran from the steamboat landing and ferry on the river to the community topping the hill near where the twin bridges now stands. When the river traffic ended and rail slowed in the 1930's, the improved road to Batesville was not unlike some of our remaining gravel roads in the county today. Hiway 14 became Stone County's first paved road in the late 1950's.

The huge sweeping curve as you approach the twin bridges east of Marcella remains known as "Fruit Jar Bend" where the men would leave their mason canning jars with money in them for the bootleggers. They would take the money and leave the jar in its place filled with moonshine. Stills were legal in Arkansas until 1868. Then the government bonded the stills in order not to ensure safety of product but rather to collect taxes. It is the failure to pay taxes that was illegal, not the actual production until Prohibition in the 1920's. It became known as moonshine due to the distilling process taking place at night under the light of the moon in order to avoid detection by the revenuers. The Hess family of Marcella ran one of the largest and most profitable stills in the region contributing greatly to their overall wealth.

As people sell their land, new homes are built and a new kind of settler moves in, one who believes anything goes, jigging for instance characterized as like "stepping on fire ants", perhaps if you've had a little too much shine. Preserving your heritage preserves more than your family history, it preserves the history of our culture. It should be remembered – the history of your land, the buildings, the barns and rock walls, they are the antiques of the land and irreplaceable. They make our land significantly more valuable when preserved. Beautiful as our hills are we are the reason people move here, how we have chosen to live our lives, what we have held onto and no matter what the hymn book says, "Will the Circle Be Unbroken" was sang in the White River Valley of the Ozarks pre Civil War. It is no more written by a white woman from England than a black man from the Ozarks wrote God Save the Queen.

"Rock Throwing Rebel" – Bob Porter

My mother, Ima Fulks Cruse is remembered for many wonderful and funny things, including her incredible ability to hit a moving target with a rock. Edwin Luther, a child hood friend, who witnessed her killing a rabbit as they walked to high school tells me how even 70 years later, he's still never seen anything like it. As a kid, I had been threatened and subjected to her rock throwing, felling me like a tree when I would run from her rather than take a whipping. She would call out, "Stop or I'm gonna knock you down," precisely indicating where she was going to hit me, on the ankle or lower leg. This just made me run harder but she never failed to down me and the whipping was then worse for having run from her.

Skinny Blair comes from another historic rock thrower. The son of Clyde and Mabel Blair, grandson of Avery and Alberta Blair and great grandson of Samuel and Susan Elizabeth Porter Blair;   Susan's brother, Bob Porter, is the legendary "Rebel Rock Thrower" of the Civil War. The official Civil War reports of Martin Beem, Arkansas Mounted Infantry (considered deserters by the Confederacy), "Early this morning, unfortunately Bob Porter succeeded in eluding the vigilance of the guard and made good his escape, much to our regret... He is a sharp, desperate fellow... Porter stated that they were all to concentrate at Clinton, 60 miles from the post. Killingsworth, Second Lt. Captain West's company is reported near Buck Horn with about 20 men."

Porter had been captured by Yankee's a few days earlier on Jan 16, 1864. He was reported to be a big burly man with an arm that was strong and accurate. On more than one occasion he had warded off the Federalists' with nothing more than rocks. The most famous is the story of his dismounting Yankee horsemen. Attacked by Porter he hit one of their horses in the chest causing the horse to rear up. The soldier fell to the ground as Porter then pelted the others with rocks until they all fled. When later captured he was determined to escape. He feigned illness however they didn't believe him and marched on in the bitter cold. Undiscovered, he swallowed a plug of tobacco and soon was violently throwing up, then the 'back door trots' hit. The group decided to take refuge in an abandoned cabin for the night to shield them from the freezing rain that was falling on top of the already deep snow. As each new attack of vomiting and dysentery would strike, the guard would have to follow Porter out into the cold. After several trips he took to simply running out in his stocking feet and under garments. Finally the guards stopped following him and told the now seemingly very weak and sick man that he need not try to escape because they were ordered to shoot to kill. No one thought that any sane man would try to escape into the bitter cold of the night with freezing rain falling in only his underclothes and socks. But escape Porter did. The sentry soon realizing he had not returned alerted the others and they took out after him on horseback, however, Bob had numerous 'stockpiles' of ammunition along the familiar ridges and managed to again knock soldiers from horseback into the cold snow. They abandoned the chase for the crazy man in his underclothes. He ran about 4 miles through the woods to his sister Susan's. Banging on the door in the middle of the night her husband Sam Blair answered the door to find a frozen, spiked hair, icicled man standing before him. Family stories describe him as having ice frozen in his eyebrows, hair and chest. Fearing the safety of his sister and her family, he stayed only long enough to warm up, gather clothes and move on. Then knowing the soldiers would be searching for him come day break, Sam and Susan hid his tracks, leading to and from the cabin by brushing over them with limbs.

Skinny's grand father Avery Blair, the son of Samuel and Susan Blair, ran the Mill at Red Stripe, named by the Osage due to the numerous water snakes with a red stripe that inhabited the sloughs. Avery secured the parts from the original Ruddell Mill, built by Abraham, John and George Ruddell, original settlers of Batesville. The site of Ruddell mill is now on the NRHP. The Blair's were prosperous providing a number of jobs at the mill for the thriving community of Red Stripe. Avery's wife, Mabel Goodwin Blair served as the first post mistress of Red Stripe and was responsible for getting the name changed to Pleasant Grove, following the sensational 1929 Connie Franklin murder trial. The Blair family made frequent trips across the White River at O'Neal Landing (Grigsby Ferry) to Batesville carrying both mail and supplies. Although Skinny is a barber by trade, I think it probably best not to challenge his accuracy.

Brook and Josephine Linker Hart - The Lost Indians

As early as 1820 the Hart family homesteaded land in Izard and Independence County. Brook Hart's grand father chose Stone County and patented land on the ridge above Meadowcreek home to Indians for over 2,000 years. Brook married Josephine Linker of Cherokee descent 37 years ago. Jo's family who settled on the Arkansas River lost the majority of their land in the development of the Arkansas River project. In 1972 Jo began practicing law in Mountain View. In 1998 she made Arkansas history when she was elected to the Arkansas Court of Appeals from District 2 which among its 16 counties includes Stone, Izard, Independence and her native Pope County, as the first woman elected to this position from Stone County since its formation in 1873, a 125 years, and since territorial days 1820. After serving for 12 years she was re-elected in 2010 for a final term.

Brook and Josephine Linker Hart

The Ozarks, Arkansas and Stone County are rich in Native American heritage. But the questions remain; "What happened to the Indians?" "Didn't they all leave here when the reservation ended?" Unless you were a slave, the people, Indians and whites alike, that came here to the Ozarks, to the White River Valley were invited here by other friends and family. After the Louisiana Purchase, the Osage agreed to a treaty moving them further west, out of the Ozarks and White River Valley. In 1812, the Missouri Territories were created from which the Arkansas Territories were formed in 1819 including all of present day Oklahoma. The new U.S. government was actively encouraging people to move west, to forge the path into the new frontier. The Indian census between 1780 and 1820 were estimates based on the Indian agents reports some of whom never set foot in the territories. In order to reduce the anxiety and fear of potential settlers the agents greatly under estimated the numbers of Indians. Schoolcraft who made a journey along the White River in 1818-1819 made a concentrated effort not to discuss the Indians he encountered along the way. His official purpose and funding was based on mineral and ore explorations. His depictions of the rugged frontiersman and the primitive manner of life was one of the first efforts to portray the area of the Ozarks as a land ripe for settlement with only a handful of settlers and Indians alike, all primitive and in need of "civilization". It is clear he encountered at least a dozen or more significant settlements during his explorations. Shawneetown, present day Yellville had one of the largest settlements under Chief Lewis.

Near Wolf house, Table Rock, Optimus, Livingston Creek, Sylamore and The Buckhorn, each had 100-300 tribesmen. Although Schoolcraft stopped at the widow Lafferty's on the south banks of the river in the reservation, he noted only that there was concern about settlers having to

Indian's buried their dead often in rock shelters and caves, marking them, such as this one near Dry Creek, circle on left rock

move back across the river out of the reservation. Visitors were always a curiosity and although there is no doubt he was surrounded by Indians at

Widow Lafferty's there was no mention of them. The eastern boundary of the reservation lay near present day Stone and Independence County lines south of The Buckhorn at Harden's Bluff. Stone County was the wild frontier, injun' country, while Batesville, down river represented civilization. Batesville is the second oldest city in Arkansas and the oldest surviving city. So, what happened to the Indians? Didn't they all leave?

Sage Holland with 2,500 year old pictograph

The Ozarks has the highest known concentration of pictographs, paintings on rocks, in the nation, with a large concentration of petroglyphs, pecked images also found here. There are at least 5 on the National Registry of Historic Places in Stone County. On private land, they are not accessible to the public. This particular one is a favorite among anthropologists and archeologists worldwide with its smiley face. Authenticated to 2,500 years old, it is red and approximately 4 feet tall (NRHP) and has been nominated as a World Heritage site.

The frontiersmen that were part Indian could establish homes in the reservation. While whites had to establish trade with the Indians or marry an Indian to live in the reservation. There were a number of outpost, stations and landings, along the White River where trade was established, such as Lafferty's Landing. A larger number of early frontiersmen moved into present day Stone County by marrying into the tribes. Not many white women made the initial journey here in those early days so nature took over if greed for land didn't. The men found Indian women in a matriarchal system that afforded them access, land and protection. Indians were unable to patent land after the 1828 reservation without a bond signature by a white person, therefore the Indian women had the land and their white or half breed husbands became their bondsmen, such as with the Harris family at Sylamore.

It was traditional that men took the names of their wives therefore as the Indian men married white women they took their family names while many Indian women adapted to the tradition of taking the white man's name. For example, Chief Peter Cornstalk (1755-1838), married Mary Frances Avey and became Peter Cornstalk Avey. Peter Cornstalk Jr (1785-1841) married Mary Adams in 1826 at Wolf House and became Peter Cornstalk Adams. He and Mary lived at Bear Creek in present day Searcy County. The Cornstalks were relatives of Tame Doe (Catherine Carpenter) Moytoy who married Francis "Chief Fivekiller" Ward. The Ward descendants settled at Optimus. Nancy "Beloved Woman of the Cherokee" daughter of Chief Fivekiller and Tame Doe, married Kingfisher, Nancy's daughter Catherine Kingfisher married John Walker, their grand daughter, Caty Walker married David Fulks. The Fulks settled land east of Rocky Bayou on Dry Creek near the Buckhorn. Perhaps the southern naming traditions of giving your child your momma's last name as a first name finds its roots with the Native Americans. So, what happened to the Indians?

In the flood of 1927, people tell me how the Indian graves washed open, revealing bones, skulls, arrowheads and pottery. Elders have told me as children, they kicked the skulls like they were footballs or tossed them about in the air. Mommas wore out their behinds and under Daddy's watchful eye, they reburied them. Archeologists from a number of places including St. Louis came, surveyed, excavated and retrieved numerous items now housed in museums throughout the region. For decades people found arrowheads in the river bottoms. Most, not unlike historic white and slave cemeteries, are abandoned and forgotten with only a few known Indian burial grounds remaining. Although there are a few people with Osage ancestry in this region, most left, either by agreement of treaty or due to the conflicts between the resisting Osage and the first arrivals to the new reservation. These new arrivals that populated the White River Valley reservation of 1817-1828 were predominately Shawnee, Creek, Cherokee, Chickasaw and Choctaw and within those each family knew their blood lines - Algonquian, Delaware, Pekowi, and others. Many Indians did leave. But most, chose to stay. The people that came here were invited here, they knew someone. They were friends and family. And most, had a reason to hide their heritage; British who stayed after the Revolutionary War, Scots, Irish, indentured servants, former prisoners, Native Americans, slaves, no one was immune and no one was without reason to be a little wary of people that came here. They all wanted an opportunity for a better and freer life. It was important to know your neighbor and of new people to determine, "Who's your people?" Alliances and family relations determined survival and may still. The inherent clannish survival in keeping outsiders at arms length has been misunderstood and portrayed negatively for over 200 years. So, what happened to the Indians? We live everywhere, in the Ozarks, in Arkansas, in Stone County. We the descendants of the native people write for the paper, teach your children, doctor you when sick and walk the halls of justice.

Ken Coon Jr – "The Old Perrin Place" - Daniel Jeffery Farm

The best stories always start out with, "it was a dark and stormy night or a cold blustery winter day," descriptions as foreboding and difficult as the choices the pioneers who settled this valley were faced with. It was a cold winter day as Ken and I drove over melting snow, icy and muddy roads to "The Old Perrin Place", historically first homesteaded in the 1840's by Daniel Jeffery, son of James "ol Jim" Jeffery and Jane Mason Jeffery, old Izard County's Dr. Quinn Medicine Woman.

Identified on territorial maps, Ken points out the path of the Old Military Road and mail route that crossed the Daniel Jeffery farm, Jehoaida Jeffery surveyor.

Jane Mason was born in 1769 in Virginia. She married "old Jim" in Alexandria VA in 1789 at the age of 20. He couldn't read or write, which was not untypical of the day but stories go that Jane's father vehemently opposed the marriage. Besides being illiterate James was an Englishman of British loyalty. Most British families returned to England after the Revolutionary War, the Jeffery's chose to stay. While many family members believe Jane is not found in the Mason family records in VA, likely because her family disowned her for marrying beneath her status, there are others who have researched Jane Mason from another perspective, that she was the daughter or grand daughter of a slave, raised in the Mason household. One theory has that she was the grand daughter of Gunston Nell, a slave in the home of George Mason who "did a little doctoring, attending to birthings and war wounds" during the American Revolution and thereby taught Jane these skills. It is also suggested that she was perhaps indeed the daughter of George Mason, making her mulatto. It is more likely that her mother was of Indian and black ethnicity a blending that creates often incredibly beautiful people in skin tone and features, which would have made Jane Indian and Metis, a more plausible reason along with her possible parentage as to why she would have been able at such a young age to marry an older illiterate white man.

Jane became the doctor of the day and legend has her as our own "Dr. Quinn, Medicine Woman". While some family stories state she had medical training, there is no record to support that claim as the first woman admitted to a medical school was not until 1838, 50 years after Jane left Virginia. It seems more reasonable that she learned her skills from her mother or grandmother regardless of race, as anything related to women's reproductive health, birthing babies and all, was entirely womenfolk's job, indecent for men, even those trained as physicians.

Incredibly beautiful reflected in the pristine waters of the pond
Daniel Jeffery Slave Barn

Whatever their positions there, Jane and old Jim left the Southern Virginia Plantation society behind making their way to Rutherford Co, NC to Tenn in 1798, then to the Missouri Territories settling first around the Strawberry River of old Lawrence County, present day Sharp County before making their way into the White River Valley. Jane was an early human rights advocate in her willingness to provide care regardless of race, color or creed; Indian, white, black, she would often travel 50 or 60 miles by foot or horseback to aid a woman in need. This eventually led to a falling out with her husband who had demanded that she stop providing care for individuals who were unable to pay. Against the wishes of her husband, she responded to a Indian woman in need, crossing the swollen White River in a canoe during a heavy rain storm into the Indian Territory's of present day Stone County. She knew that Jim was angry but she defied him which lead to him throwing her out of the house and the Jeffery family. This resulted in her living for periods of time between her daughter, Lavina and son in law Thomas Culp, and her son Daniel Mason Jeffery and his wife Mary Bowcock who was part Indian. Having been orphaned she was raised in the Bland home taking their name. Even though Jane was the matriarch of the Jeffery family (wife of Old Jim, mother of Jehoiada, 1790, Daniel, 1797, Lavina, 1798, Nancy 1799, Eda 1800, James 1802 and Jesse 1804) and outlived old Jim (d. 1843) by 10 years (Jane d. 1853), she was not buried with other family members at the Jeffery Family Cemetery north of Mt. Olive. Instead she was buried on a lone knoll in a private spot on the farm owned by her son Daniel. A prominent man, Daniel Jeffery served as Sheriff, County Judge and Ar. State Rep 1846 for Izard Co. The farm was a fertile 320 acres. Daniel exported corn and cotton to Memphis and New Orleans. His wife Mary died in 1862 followed by Daniel a year later in 1863. The farm was sold and is known today as "The Old Perrin Place".

Born in 1840 in Ohio, Franklin Perrin moved to Batesville with his parents prior to the 1850 census. He made friends with the Jeffery's. In 1870 he was living at Sylamore with Jehoiada Jeffery in the home of Ceila Harris, 50, a mulatto. This Jehoiada was the grandson of Jehoiada, who first settled in the White River Valley in 1814 and the son of Miles whose 1858 home place, barn and slave barn are on the George Hinkle property at Livingston Creek and on the National Registry of Historic Places. In Feb 1888 Miss Celia Harris deeded Frank the 80 acres on which they lived on Green Mountain Road overlooking Sylamore, a portion of which is presently owned by Stan Townsend. Frank also bought the Daniel Jeffery's farm on the Izard County banks of the river. Frank had one older brother David and two younger brothers, Samuel and James and a sister, Sarah all of whom lived their lives in Independence and Izard County. The clapboard dog trot house now falling to ruin was likely built by the Perrin family as the timbers are milled rather than hand hewn. It would have been relatively easy to get such timbers from the Emmett & Marchant saw mill at Culp in the 1890's. The cistern includes broken mussel shells in the mixture called tabby and likely dates around the same time as the clap board home circa 1890. The pre Civil war (Daniel Jeffery) slave cabin remains in solid condition, with distinguishable hand forged square nails and a dozen or more slave pegs.

Franklin Perrin died in 1917 at the age of 77 in Batesville, Arkansas. The parents of Ken Coon, Jr are the current owners of "The Old Perrin Place", the homesteaded land of Daniel Jeffery, son of Dr. Jane Mason Jeffery and "ol" Jim. The farm is traversed by the "old military road" and mail route which ran from St. Louis through the Missouri and Arkansas Territories to the Red River Valley. This was implemented by Sam Houston and other leaders of the Texas Revolution, and of which Jehoiada Jeffery, brother to Daniel served as a surveyor. It is where Jane Mason Jeffery, Medicine Woman and matriarch of the Jeffery's one of the oldest pioneer families of the White River Valley lived out the last years of her life and the site of her final resting place. The farm is not simply rich in White River soil, but rich in White River Valley history.

The Exploring Izard County (EIC.com) crew and members of the Izard County Historical Society returned when the weather warmed to assist Ken Coon, Jr, his children, Heston and Katie Rose and parents, Ken and Sue Coon, in the cleanup of the historic resting place of Jane Mason Jeffery. Note the location of where Missy is standing as compared to later photograph of Dale Hanks, in Mothers of the White River Valley, before and after cleanup. Missy Irvin pictured above assisted in the cleanup of the historic cemetery and in November 2010 was elected as Arkansas State Senator for this district which includes Stone, Izard and Independence Counties. Since Jacob Wolf was first elected in 1820 to represent the Arkansas Territories, Missy is the first woman elected to hold this position from our district. Jane Mason Jeffery is smiling.

Dale Hanks - Mothers of the White River Valley

I was flattered when historian Dale Hanks called me. I had read a great deal of his work about the early days of the White River Valley, including "The Falling Out", which relates the story of why Jane Mason Jeffery was buried separately from her family. Dale had heard about the recent cleanup of Jane's gravesite. He drove from his home in Richmond, VA for a visit to her grave, honoring this incredible woman who was his grandmother. Born and raised in Batesville, Arkansas, Dale graduated Batesville High School in 1946. He has lived in Richmond, VA since 1965. We drove over to the "old Perrin place" now owned by the Ken Coon family, mid afternoon Thursday in what turned out to be a hot spring day. Our visit included a drive up to the slave barn followed by sweet tea on the deck at JoJo's Catfish Wharf.

Dale Hanks with the restored headstone of Jane Mason Jeffery.

In order to understand who we are as people of the Ozarks, we must first understand from whom we are descended. Some remarkable women lived here in this valley between 1810 and 1850. These women walked here, rode a mule, carried a pack or if they were lucky toiled with a push cart. These unyielding first women personified the embracing nurturing spirit that is the foundation of our present day women.

The first known white woman to settle in Stone County was Sarah Lindsey Lafferty, arriving in 1810, 200 years ago. Her oldest daughter Elizabeth, a new bride, died during the journey at the mouth of the White River. Mourning her daughter, Sarah settled into Indian Territory where undoubtedly she was consoled by and made friends with the native women. Elizabeth's husband, Charles Kelly completed the trip with the Lafferty's and later became the first Sheriff of Independence Co. Sarah's husband John had established trade with the Indians in 1801. Now alongside him Sarah operated Lafferty's Landing, near present day Younger Access. After the death of her husband in 1816 she continued to live in the reservation maintaining the outpost. In 1819 Henry Rowe Schoolcraft wrote of stopping at "the Widow Lafferty's in the Indian reservation".

In 1774 Chief Pucksinwah, father of Tecumseh was killed. His death lead to his wife Methotaske, Tecumseh's mother, a Creek losing her standing in the Shawnee tribe. By 1779 she was forced out and moved with her Creek family from the Ohio River valley to the Missouri Territories. Methotaske brought her two youngest children with her leaving her oldest daughter to raise the children she had to leave behind, including Tecumseh and the Prophet. In 1780 after the attack on Ruddell's Mill, KY captives included George Lail, Stephen and Abe Ruddell. White Wing, the daughter of Young Cornstalk/44 and Eliaabeth See (Seay)/54, became the fifth wife of Tecumseh. After Tecumseh's death in 1813, the last of the Northern Shawnee moved from the Ohio River valley to present day Cape Girardeau, Missouri. Although white traders preceded him, George Lail arriving with the Shawnee became the first white settler. Many of the Franks and Burns of Stone County are descendants of his sister Elizabeth Lail. Also taken captive at Ruddell's Mill she was sold to the British for a key of whiskey. She married British solider John Franks.

White Wing's first cousin, Chief Peter Cornstalk/85 along with Abe Ruddell brought a large contingent of the Shawnee further south and west into the White River Valley. In 1817 Stephen Ruddell brought an aging Methotaske from near Gainesville, MO, to live closer to Abe who had settled west of Batesville. In 1826 Chief Peter Cornstalk/85 married Mary Adams at Wolf House. Mary was a sister to the first white settler of Searcy County, Robert Adams.

Abe Ruddell married Mary Culp, sister of Thomas Culp, whose wife Lavina was the daughter of Jane Mason Jeffery. Thomas and Mary Culp's nephew, Daniel D. Culp, by their brother Josiah Culp, became the private secretary to Gen. Sam Houston. When Sam Houston heard of Daniel's death, he had Daniel's remains moved back to Texas and proclaimed him a "Son of Texas". He is buried in Galveston.

Sam's older brother John Paxton Houston was the first clerk of Izard County. Their cousin Margaret Houston married James Grigsby. The Grigsby's ran the ferry between Marcella and O'Neal. Their daughter Martha Houston Grigsby married Elias Elijah Fulks. Another relative Ann Houston married John Walker III. Her son John became "Chief" Walker of the Cherokee when he married Catherine Kingfisher, daughter of Nancy Ward Kingfisher, grand daughter of Tame Doe (Catherine Carpenter) Moytoy and Francis "Chief Fivekiller" Ward. Sam, Abe and Chief Walker were actively involved in the treaty and voluntary settlement of the 1817 Indian reservation. Catherine arrived here with her grand daughter Caty Walker and husband David Fulks.

Jane Mason Jeffery was known as "the old medicine woman". Subsequently Jane had a "falling out" with the Jeffery family over her willingness to treat white, blacks and Indians alike. As a result she lived the last years of her life with her son Daniel and his Indian wife, Mary Bowcock Jeffery. Upon her death in 1853, Jane was buried on their farm, separate from the Jeffery family at Mt. Olive.

Jeffery family historian, Dale Hanks with the Hanks children grave markers. He is standing in approximately the same location as Missy Irvin during the cleanup of the historic and beautiful resting place of Jane Mason Jeffery.

There are now a total of 9 nine graves there; 6 unidentified, possibly four adult slaves and two native or black children. Two Hanks children are also buried near her; William died in 1886 at the age of 9 years, Willie Hanks only a few days old died in 1902. These were the grand children of Jane Mason Jeffery and descendants of the Nancy Hanks family, mother of President Abraham Lincoln.

Jane is buried on a grassy knoll, with the sound of a gurgling creek, rolling hills and the White River in the distance. Around 1970 the rock walls that surrounded the farm along with the foundation and chimney rocks of the family home were sold and hauled away. The mock orange, lavender and prim rose bushes are tell tale signs of where the house once stood, where lives were lived, and where friends and family, mothers, Mary Bowcock Jeffery, Mary Adams Cornstalk, Lavina Jeffery Culp, Martha Houston Grigsby, Caty Walker Fulks, Mary Culp Ruddell, Methotaske, Sarah Lindsey Lafferty and Jane Mason Jeffery may have dressed a deer or doctored a child. It's a beautiful spot and a beautiful resting place in the shadow of ancient trees.

Chester Beckham - Rocky Bayou

Ches Beckham was born in 1919 to Dow Malone Beckham and Retha Poff. He is the grandson of Elihu Beckham, whose parents Joshua and Catherine (Hinkle) Beckham settled Rocky Bayou long before the Civil War. Ches married Omalee Decker in 1941. These families are some of the earliest pioneering families of Stone County.

Mister Ches and Miss Omalee, April 2010

It was a beautiful warm winter day as Mister Ches, Mister Billy and Miss Wilma Wolfe and I started out with the Jan. 1864 Civil War record of Union Lt. Col. W.M. Baumer in hand. Mister Ches was both proud and disappointed that one of the local newspapers had run his grandpa's civil war journals and hadn't bothered to pick up the phone or come over and talk to him. He didn't know what download meant, but he didn't think it was a good thing. He explained that his grandpa Elihu did not write the journal during the Civil War, but compiled it afterwards and that he and his father heard stories from his grandpa, both of them keeping stories alive that were not among those that made it to paper. He was proud to spend this day not only telling the stories but visiting the places.

Baumer cites locations chasing Freeman's Confederate troops up the Middle Fork of Sylamore Creek where they had burned and destroyed Rorie's Mill (present day Mill & Roasting Ear Creek), captured seven prisoners and then killed three men at Cooper's Mill (Big Springs). They were searching for a gun powder mill on North Sylamore Creek which they believed to be in Rorie Cave but was actually hidden deep inside Salt Peter Cave. A second unsuccessful detachment searching for Freeman at Sylamore joined Baumer at Andrew Hinkle's Farm (South Bayou Drive near Mill Pond) where they confiscated his livestock and slaves. From there the Union troops proceeded down Batesville Road to South Rocky Bayou creek, across the Beckham farm where bandits were seen in the hills, two were shot and killed by the Union, several wounded and a number of horses captured.

Area of unmarked Civil War graves

Mister Ches pointed out areas where the snipers attacked Baumer's troopers and were killed. Buried among the rocks in the style of Native Americans, "it was not something people talked about. But occasionally over the years, people have come and asked me to show them where it was at, putting flowers there. I reckon they was family. I never said no," Mister Ches told us. "The fear of being found out to be one side or the other could bring troops down on you, or even worse, jayhawkers. People buried the dead where they found them." These men were not soldiers like so many other casualties and nothing denotes their having given their lives other than

Baumer noting that two men were killed. Baumer's troops then marched to the White River fording at the mouth of Rocky Bayou, camping on the plantation of rebel Col. Thomas Black (Cajen Creek/Dugan area of Stone County and directly across the river in Izard) confiscating additional livestock and slaves. The following morning they continued their march to Wall's Ferry (Marcella) then taking the main route to Batesville.

Mister Ches knew each of the areas where the troops had converged and traveled including Sylamore and the Burning of Rorie's Mill. The recent rains had caused the creek to swell, but the water was clear and falling, not alarming to Mister Ches or me as we barreled through them none the less thankful for 4 wheel drive. I could see the quiet smile on Mister Ches' face as Mister Billy would tense up every muscle gasping in a deep breath, water splashing the windows as we dropped off steep embankments into the moving water. Both Mister Ches and I knew the creeks well, the routes in and how to cross. Our cows would routinely cross the ridge ending up on the Nesbitt, Beckham or Wade land on Rocky Bayou. Momma (Ima Fulks Cruse) and I would ride horses with the cattle dogs to herd them back. Without the gravel haulers the creeks are filling up, becoming hazardous not only to cattle and wildlife but blocking water and causing bank erosion. The waters ran clear before the land eroded from reckless and unplanned timbering, mostly by the Missouri Land and Title Co who shipped more timber down the White River, loading steam ships at Sylamore, than any other port in the South. Now its new housing going in, land stripped clean for a view.

Elihu Beckham

89

The Beckham family farm consists of hundreds of areas along Rocky Bayou Creek, with Herpel on the other side at the far end, where Howard Wade and Monroe Burns lived and Round Bottom further north to the river. I grew up on the other side of the ridge on Dry Creek, where our family still has hundreds of acres, some homesteaded as early as the 1817 Indian reservation. The home where Mister Ches was raised still stands, his daddy died when a tractor turned over on him and so he never got to live in the stone house, what was clearly a mansion on the hill overlooking Rocky Bayou.

Mister Ches recalled his grandpa Elihu dying when he was young boy having spent the last 29 years of his life in a wheel chair paralyzed. He was living with his daughter Alpha Beckham Hinkle, (rock house currently belonging to Jo Hinkle Mitchell and husband Mike across from the new forestry services office and Harps Grocery on East Main) when he died. Elihu is buried along side his father Joshua at Flatwoods Cemetery.

Mister Ches was only 4 when he started school at Burr College in the Rocky Bayou valley. His older brother Blake refused to go to school unless Ches had to go to. "So, off I went with him," he says laughing. "John Hinkle was the teacher. He would stop at the house and let me ride with him on the back of the horse to school. One of the McCasland boys snuck out of school and went up to the Davis place and stole a jar of moonshine. He came running down off the hill and didn't see the barbed wire fence ahead of him. He plunged into that fence, broke the jar, he was all cut up. It was a bloody mess. He wore them scars the rest of his life." Mister Ches attended school at Flatwoods and graduated Mountain View High School in 1937, but he loves to tell how he attended college, Burr College, first.

We approached the creek just above the deep hole where the spring flows where students carried water from for the school. Anxious, Mister Billy had to get out and look at this one before we crossed. I waded into the cold water up over my knees. Standing there, in the rushing water, although deep I could feel the rocks were solid. Shaking his head "No" Mister Billy climbed back into the vehicle. Mister Ches smiling motioned with his hand for me to ford the creek. Although nothing like the pioneers or the Civil War soldiers, it was clear, Mister Billy's heart was beating faster as the water topped the wheel wells splashing the glass but Mister Ches with the window down and the breeze in his face, just smiled.

Mister Ches died a few months later. I talked to him just weeks before he died about the Beckham Cemetery at Round Bottom. The deaths of men like Ches Beckham are stunning losses not only within their family but within our community and our state. One of the last things he said to me was that I'd given him "the gift of going home." It is I who was given a gift, of understanding "home". I am deeply honored to have spent time with both him and Miss Omalee.

LC and Francis Gammill - Dark Holler

LC and Francis Gammill live on the western end of Dark Holler, just off the hard road (Hiway 263) near Timbo. LC is the son of Earl and Ola Martin Gammill. The Gammill's settled the area pre-Civil War, in what was then Searcy Co. Francis is the daughter of Tom and Retha Cross Burns, born and raised on the ridge above Rocky Bayou. The Burns are descendants of Elizabeth Lail who was taken hostage by the Shawnee in the 1780 raid on Ruddell's Station, Ky and then sold along with her two sisters to the British for a keg of whiskey. Elizabeth's brother George Lail spent 15 years living with the Shawnee along with Abraham and Stephen Ruddell, adopted brothers of renowned Shawnee Chief Tecumseh. Abraham Ruddell was one of the first settlers of Batesville, the oldest surviving city in Arkansas. The Shawnee made their way here into the Timbo Valley sometime around 1816. Although once full of mountain lions, Panther Mountain and Panther Creek that traverses Dark Holler to flow into South Sylamore Creek are more than likely named for the Shawnee family M'-se'-pa-se or Panther.

LC, Bob Fleming, Francis and Martin Darrell trekking into Dark Holler. Home of Civil War soldier John William "Bill" Dark.

Bill Dark, represented by future Arkansas Governor Henrie Massey Rector, was convicted of the murder of Hardy Foster in 1858 and sentenced to five years in the Ark state pen. When Civil War broke out, Rector who was now Governor of Arkansas and serving as a Capt in the Confederacy released Dark in June 1861 with the commission of rooting out northern sympathizers in the area of Searcy, Van Buren and Izard County, which included present day Fulton, Stone and Marion Counties. Initially he served with a regiment engaging in a number of battles, however as outcroppings of dissent arose he was given greater authority to "act on matters of importance" to seek out and rid the area of northern sympathizers.   With little oversight by his commanders he was able to act at will, accusations were the same as guilt and the assaults that followed acts of war.   Dark was never a deserter as some reports suggest. His last paid commission was in Nov 1862, just before his death, thus confirming his status with the Confederacy. Dark married Rachel Adeline "Addie" George of Timbo in 1862.   Addie's parent's had homesteaded land on the hill above Panther Creek currently owned by Jackie Trammell (son in law of LC and Francis Gammill) and J. Adams, east of Dark Holler and south of Rorie Cave which became two of Dark's hideouts. Laudis Brewer was raised in the home that Addie and Bill had near her parents, known as "The Jimmy George House."

One of the two locations Bill and Addie had houses in Dark Holler

To a number of prestigious members of the Confederacy Dark's actions were considered necessary in pursuing and expunging the enemy. The Izard County Investigative Committee reported anti war activities to Governor Rector of individuals at Sylamore, Mt. Olive and Calico. In Nov 1861, a group of over 100 young men known as the Peace Society were rounded up at Sylamore, while 47 elected to join the Confederacy "wiping out the foul stain of their foolish youth," the rest who refused were shot or hanged. Those remaining 47 young men were marched to Little Rock, not everyone made it there alive.

While the Confederacy may have seen Dark's actions as over zealous, for the local people Dark was to be feared. Confederate Civil War records contain letters of people from the area asking for compensation from the Confederacy for stolen property, cattle, horses, wagons and reports of cruelty which give credibility to the abundant folk history of Dark's actions. L.C.'s great grandmother, Martha Gammill requested compensation for her cow that Dark "killed, gutted, butchered and bagged to feed his troops." Jane Stevenson's "cow was "freshening", ready to deliver" therefore her request was for both the cow and calf." There are numerous accounts of cruelty and death including the killing of women and children. He "taunted Mrs. Farris with the ribbons and lock of hair from her deceased child, all that she had left." An old farmer by the name of Lee near Big Springs reported having "buried 5 or 6 children beneath the rock wall" he was constructing as "Dark and his men have robbed and desecrated graves, looking for hidden guns and supplies buried there. They killed the children of the daughter of William Moore, a solider in service. The children's aunt Cathy Cole and grandmother buried the children in the field" wherein Mr. Lee continued the rock wall to secure their graves from future atrocities. The stone wall where they are believed to be buried still stands along the gravel road behind Pleasant Hill Church north of Dark Holler.

Stone Wall behind the Pleasant Hill church that remains undisturbed for 150 years may be the resting place of several children in order to keep Bill Dark from robbing their graves looking for hidden food, valuables and guns.

The Home Guard was different than the Peace Society. The Home Guard was made up of both northern and southern individuals to protect against the jayhawkers, bushwhackers and specifically Bill Dark and his troops. According to the Civil War record and report of the incident leading to the death of Bill Dark, two Confederate soldiers, "Pvts. Robinson and Hoffman," were home visiting their wives during the killing of a hog, above Arlberg near Sally Flats in present day Stone County. One of the women saw Bill Dark and his men riding up on horses. The soldiers and their accompaniment ran through the cornfield into the timbers to hide. One of them left his gun behind and according to the Civil War report filed "a young Jim Berry, about 10 or 11, positioned himself on a log in the front of the house aiming the gun toward the men. Bill Dark dismounted his horse and taunted the young man, calling him 'a young puppy'. The young man waited until Dark was only a few feet away, firing he hit him square between the eyes, the ball exiting the back of his cranium. Dark fell forward face down dead." The women exited the home kicking Dark's body. His men loaded him onto a horse and rode away. Presumably fearing for their own lives they allowed the body to fall to the ground where it came to rest under a large oak near the slough of the Little Red River and Little Tick Creek. Fearing reprisal the first official report by Dark's men states that "Dark was gravely wounded and could not likely make it back to the post," three days later they confirmed that he met his death at the hand of a young Jim Berry, and lay beneath a tree not far from where he was felled.

Pvt. Johnson was a relative of Addie George's. He went to her home "The Jimmy George House" alerting her of Bill's death (Jan 1863). Addie George was pregnant with her son Willie. According to family stories he helped her get to her sister's house at Sylamore where she crossed the White River headed to family in Izard County. In 1880 Addie and her son are found on the Izard County census in the home of William Aiken's family. She remained there until she married a much younger D.H. "Hugh" Martin in 1881. Although there is little documentation as to what happened to her son, Willie Dark, it has been reported that he drown in the river near Sylamore around 1900. Their children left a number of descendants including families of the Gammill, Gower, Long, Avey and George. Addie and Hugh are buried at Big Springs Cemetery.

There are no Civil War markers denoting the men, women and children who died, at the hands of Dark (CSA) or Col. Baumer (Union) at Sylamore. No markers for Rorie's Mill the Union soldiers burned in 1864 or the men they killed there, or the others they took as prisoners, or Cooper's Mill at Big Springs, where they rested, but killed two more people or Beckham's farm where two men were killed, but there should be. Arkansas is a Southern state, a Confederate state, and this is our history. Whatever it may be, it is more about the remarkable people who lived and died here. Because just like in the "Dark" days, people here in the Ozarks will band together regardless of their differences, to defend each other, to fight for our families and our way of life.

Don Long - Dark Holler, "Legends & Lies"

Don Long at his boyhood home built by his parents in 1932

It was one of those really beautiful cool days when Don Long, his wife Shanelle and I rode out to the old Long house behind the Varela farm at Newnata. Don grew up in a one room house that is not only still standing but is one of the most perfect examples of 1930's depression era housing I've seen. His folks built the house in 1932 within a few hundred yards of his grand parent's house. Don was born there in 1934. "This was a great place for a young boy to grow up," Don says with a look of warmth in his eyes. He proudly shows me the spring where they got water and remembers the trips he would make back and forth along the wooded trail.

As a kid in high school he worked for Jack and Lenelle Jones at the cleaners (now owned by Charlie King), took tickets at the theatre staying afterwards to cleanup and racked balls at Buster's Pool Hall. Don Long is the son of James and Myrtle Gower Long. He is the grandson of Mollie Mae Martin and Francis Luther Long. Grandma Mollie is the daughter of Rachel Adeline "Addie" George and second husband Ben Martin.

Addie was born at Green Bush, in Sylamore Township. In 1862 she married her first husband, notorious Confederate solider and marauder Bill Dark. They had one son Willie born in 1863 just after his father's death. Addie was the daughter of Margaret Stewart and James George whose homesteaded land later became the home of Mollie and Luther Long, currently owned by Charlie Varela, Jimmy Long and Kenneth Crymes. At the time of Bill Dark's death January 28, 1863, at the hands of a young Jim Berry, Addie and Bill had a place near Turkey Creek.

Headstone of Addie George (Dark) and D.H. "Ben" Martin
Parents of Don Long's Grandma Mollie Mae Martin

According to Civil War records and a number of reports of the events of the actual shooting. After Dark was shot by a young Jim Berry, his men loaded him onto a horse and rode away. A piece down the road, his body fell from the horse to the ground where it came to rest under a large oak near the slough of the Little Red River and Little Tick Creek. Presumably fearing for their own lives his men left his body behind. Joe Moody found it and is reported to have tied him to a horse. Then Joe proceeded to pull him about the area showing people that he was dead and gone. This may have contributed to the stories, including Joe's own story, that it was Moody who killed Bill Dark. He may not of been dead when Joe found him, but died in the process of being dragged behind Joe's horse.

Represented in 1858 by future Governor Henrie M. Rector in the murder of Hardy Foster, Dark was convicted and sentenced to serve 5 years. Rector had Dark released in June 1861 and consigned to the service of the Confederate Army with the charge of routing out the northern sympathizers in Izard, Searcy and Van Buren County (including present day Stone County) creating a wide berth for an already convicted murderer. Supported by a number of prestigious members of the Confederacy his actions were considered necessary acts of war in pursuing and expunging the enemy. He was in effect an early CIA operative. There are a number of stories about the atrocities of Bill Dark and his men. Legends and lies, embellishments to the truth, or facts too horrible to repeat, his actions as a Confederate solider seeking out Union sympathizers make water boarding seem child's play. It is no wonder that historians from any angle prefer to consider him a deserter and rouge. However, both Civil War records and personal family stories demonstrate he was acting however loosely interpreted, within the guidelines set by the Confederacy and Gov. Rector. The Izard County Investigative Committee reported activities of individuals at Sylamore and Mt. Olive. This lead to the arrest of 103 men and boys, known as the Sylamore Creek Massacre at least 56 were hanged or shot until dead as spies, with another 47 mostly young boys taken to Searcy County and from there, along with other captives from the area, marched in chains to Little Rock. Families from across the region have shared letters and stories of their fore fathers, older men mostly unable to serve having died in the massacre, killed indiscriminately on the word of a single person, suspicion all that was needed. Descendants believe that Dark was among those responsible for the execution of the men.

The Home Guard made up of men throughout the Ozarks, for Stone County included Timbo, Newnata, Onia, Mozart, Sally Flats and Meadowcreek areas was different than the Peace Society which was made up of individuals who were northern sympathizers and or anti war. The Home Guard was made up of individuals both northern and southern throughout North Arkansas and Southern Missouri to protect against the jayhawkers, bushwhackers and specifically the gangs of Samuel Hildebrand, Frank James and Bill Dark. The Battle of the Buckhorn (St. James/Younger Access) was a result of "Federal" bushwhacker Bill Williams being defeated by Gen. Shelby in 1864. Had Bill Dark survived the Civil War it's more than likely he would have joined the ranks of the James and Younger gangs. Given the authority during the Civil War to act in accordance with what was necessary to seek out and destroy enemies, these men acted exceedingly outside the confines of that order.

Addie George (Dark) Martin is buried at Big Springs Cemetery. Although there is little documentation as to what happened to her son, Willie Dark, family stories say that around 1900 Dr. Bill Hayden found him floating dead in the river near Sylamore. It is believed while attending a wedding, he passed out in the water and drown while having had a little too much to drink. These same families report that Addie's husband Hugh arrived by mule to claim the body for burial. It is believed that he is buried in an unmarked grave at Big Springs Cemetery near his mother.

Don Long was born in what remains as an almost perfect 1930's Depression era home that sits on land that is rich not only in his history, but the history of our county and state. The homes, barns and rock walls are the antiques of our land, irreplaceable and significantly more valuable than any present day construction will ever be. The Noah McCarn home on Hiway 5 South on the NRHP was allowed like so many others, to fall to ruin and has now been bulldozed. The value of the land lost in the demise of the home, irreplaceable, it is now just a place on the side of the road like so many others. The CCC buildings which were torn down at Blanchard would now be a draw. State and national parks now realize they attract more people because of the old buildings. From Rorie's Mill to Cooper Hill and Big Springs, our history is felt in every step you take; National Registry of Historic Places include the 1925 Clarence Anderson Barn, 1918 Roasting Ear Church and

School (which needs a new door), 1906 John Avey Barn, 1890 George Anderson House, 1858 Wesley Copeland House and 1922 Orvill Gammill Barn. The Long house which sits on Crymes land should be on the NRHP, as not only is the house an incredible testament to 1930's Depression Era construction and how Ozark families lived, but the history of Dark Holler is here, in this valley, on this land. There are no Civil War markers denoting the men, women and children who died but there should be. Perhaps, the Crymes family will donate a piece of history to our county to protect and maintain, allowing future generations to understand the roots of who we are as a people. Don Long's great grandmother, Addie George Dark Martin, lived out the remaining years of her life tending to the care of her family, friends and neighbors, trying like so many others to put the Civil War behind her. Arkansas is a Southern state, a Confederate state, but mostly, just like present days, people here in the Ozarks will band together regardless of our differences, to defend what is right.

Frank Foll – Happy Holler aka Happy Hollow

I had the good fortune to interview Neva Petty Foll born 1916 prior to her death in 2009. She was featured in my book Voices of Our People, published in Oct 09. Miss Neva and her husband Ralph Foll were two of the most respected people in Stone County, with roots going back almost 200 years. Miss Neva was full of stories telling how "Frankie was born in 1937 in a one room log home and store we operated right near your house." I didn't know where she was talking about. But a few nights later at a church dinner, Ora Mast pointed it out, sitting between my house near the convergence of the springs and the Happy Hollow Mennonite Church, directly behind Mister Ora's barn.

"Frankie" is Mr. Frank Foll. He and Miss Julia Holt Foll taught almost everybody in this county my age, older and younger as teachers at Mountain View. They have two sons, Stanton and Barton.

Frank Foll with his son Stanton and grandson Jonathan

Happy Hollow located about 4 miles west of the court square on Hiway 66, traverses the valley ending back at Hiway 66 at Timbo. The name comes from a church that was situated in the valley during the late 1800's when the religious fervor of the day included the shakes, talking in tongues and hollering. Preacher Jess Goodman continued the tradition well into the 1900's. He would ride up to the church just off Cane Spur on his spotted pony. Making sure not to get caught, he would finish off the last of his moonshine and toss the bottle into the brush pile before entering the church. His voice would echo up the hollow towards Cane Spur and White Sands Spring. "People would sit on their porch and could hear Jess' Happy Holler."

It's not Happy Hollow, someone just corrected the spelling thinking they were fixin' someone's mis-spelling. Preacher Jasper Cooper would ride his mule from Sylamore to do some preaching too. He had a hair lip contributing to his inability to talk plainly. "Uncle Sol Everidge couldn't read or write, so he'd hold the Bible up like he was reading and quote from memory," Frank adds to the story his Mama told me. "His eyebrows were thick and furrowed, earning him the title Beetle Brow. Slamming his fist, shaking his head and furrowing his brow were especially effective in getting both the men and women to holler more than "Amen.""

Mister Frank's mom and dad like many folks went to the bottoms (any where on the Delta where they grew crops) to work the cotton fields during the depression. In 1934 they came home with only $10 in their pocket because the rain had rotted the cotton bolls. They gathered up their livestock out of Bull Pen Hollow and drove them across the ridge down Licking Creek to South Sylamore to the Dobbins place at Allison where the U.S. Government killed and burned them. "I don't know why they did that exactly cause people was starving. They put in some dippin' vats for the ticks and fleas but oncest they got out in the fields, it didn't make no nothing. They paid Ralph $92 which was enough to stock the store. We lived in the front part and Ralph he built on a little room in the back with a window that we traded through. People would come any time of the night or day." Mister Frank adds, "The neighbors gathered in and built the cabin in one day."

"After them men built the store we had a big dance all night; squaring and jigging, Book Miller Shannon on the banjo, Espier Shannon had his fiddle, Than Martin's played the guitar and Collie Dodson the banjo," Miss Neva told me with a soft smile on her face, remembering that day, I'm certain. "Hayden Shannon would always jig dance on one side while a square dance was going on. One night he got so drunk that he jig danced all-night on his knees and had to be helped to the wagon. It was several days before he could walk again."

The Foll's had a wagon road from the back of the store direct to Finis Shannon's still which was ¾ mile away. Sometimes Hayden Shannon would run all the way to the store where Ralph, would throw a sack of sugar on his shoulder for the distilling process. "We sold Hale Hayden two model T loads of whiskey with Stone Mountain watermelons on top for a political gathering at Timbo. Hale won, then built old No 5 hiway to his farm by blasting off the bluff where the road runs today," Miss Neva said. "I'd like to think we all had our part in getting that road put in."

"The young boys were all into gaming, betting who could shoot off this rock, or can, or something. Bob Whitfield had a Stephen Cracks shot that Leslie Shannon had been trying to trade for. One day they both got drunk, and Leslie gave Bob 23 gallons of moonshine for that rifle. Most expensive rifle in these hills," she continued laughing.

Frank shaking his head remembering, "When we sold the store to Ross Webb, eggs were a medium of exchange. We didn't have any money, but my older sister, Faye, found where a hen had hid her nest. She traded the eggs to Ross for a piece of bubble gum that we'd heard of but never experienced. Several of us would take turns chewing it. We kept the contraband concealed on a fence post at night. In the morning, the whole bunch would head for the gum hollering "It's my turn." I don't believe we had any sense."

Before Miss Neva died, she told me what my momma also told me, "Some things don't need said until all them people's dead." She was mostly talking about Ma Cook's place and the bootlegging and moon shining. Miss Neva, my momma, nor I mean anyone alive or dead any harm or humiliation. The early days of Stone County were filled with people who were trying to survive. People bartered, traded goods and services and whiskey was the currency of the day. It wasn't called Liquid Gold for nothing. It made the Hess family rich and kept many others from starving. Preacher Jess Goodman should be remembered, not for his taste of moonshine, but for the souls he saved, the joy he brought and the holler that still reverberates with the sounds of children laughing, preachers preaching, pickin's on the porch and some Happy Hollering.

The Prices of Bull Pen Holler

The expansive shelter is flanked by a beautiful waterfall on the right.
Stanton, his mother Julia Foll, son Jonathan and daughter Megan
are dwarfed by the massive shelter.

"It's hot and snakes are out," I thought as Stanton Foll sprayed me down for ticks just before we headed off down the hillside into the deep gorge and box canyon known as "Bull Pen Holler." Miss Julia, Stanton's Mom, Jonathan and Megan trekked along with us. Of course heading down into the holler we had gravity on our side and the journey was complete with Miss

Julia taking a slight tumble, catching her leg on green briars. The devastation from the 5 natural disasters our county has endured over the last two years was evident. Landslides from torrential rains, washing mud, rocks and trees down the hillside. Trees broken like matchsticks in the ice storm and debris from the tornadoes, natural and manmade littered the landscape. It looked like a war zone.

Brothers, Samuel and John Price arrived in the Missouri territories of "old Lawrence County" present day Batesville, around 1820, according to tax records, census and land patents. The Cherokee Indian reservation has just been established across the White River in present day Stone County. In order to enter the reservation you had to be part Indian, married to an Indian or establish essential trade. The Lafferty's, the first white settlers and fur traders, ran the first outpost here in 1810 at what is now Younger Access. The Creek Indian family Isllamo (pronounced Sil A Mo) operated the first trading post where Angler's restaurant now sits. A band of Tsalgi Indians had a post behind Wilson's Town and Country on land presently owned by Richard Decker, near the original settlement of Mtn View, Riggsville, after settler Thomas Riggs. Although much of the natural wildlife had been hunted out in the droughts of proceeding years when the Osage had to rely primarily on game for food, this county still had razorback hogs, deer, panther, coyote, mink, bear and buffalo. We had enough bear that Arkansas was originally called "The Bear State." John Price could have been a trader, a hunter or married an Indian but he hunted with the Indians in an area that maintains two names today – Bull Pen Holler or Price Holler. The holler is a huge, monsterous box canyon with two creeks running through and out of it, feeding Lick Fork Creek. The Indians would run the buffalo into the canyon from which there was no escape. They would move trees into the narrowing creating a barrier so they couldn't escape making the slaughter easier.

Lick Fork Creek at Happy Hollow Road & Hiway 66 West

From a top the ridge above Bull Pen Holler you can see west and north to Cow Mountain near Newnata. The mountain is named for the buffalo cow that John Price killed there. Directly west towards Happy Hollow Road, between the artesian spring that feeds my house and White Sands Spring, Stanton points out the flats which became known as the Killing Fields. The buffalo would come through in the spring and fall, coming up Lick Fork Creek, crossing present day Hiway 66 on present day Gammill and Richardson land adjacent to Happy Hollow Road. They would cross then up the left fork of the creek where Murphy Hollow runs into Bull Pen Hollow, next to the Mark Miller farm.

Megan and Jonathan make their way to the pool of water
at the base of the larger waterfall in Bull Pen Holler

He would build a fire then take a shiny piece of metal and use its reflection to shine eyes. It is reasonable assumption the he was Stone County's first spotlighter. The Indians also showed Price how they trapped the buffalo using the cedar logs from which Bull Pen got it's name.

In the fall of the year the Prices would go on camp hunts that lasted several weeks. Some of their camps were Sugar camp, Brown's camp, Bee Bluff, Wild Goose, Chinquapin Ridge, Painter (Panther) Hollow, and Yellow Bluff. After the Civil War, Sam Hess told of the Prices going to the Grand Prairie and killing wagonloads of prairie chickens while on camp hunts.

By the time of the Civil War, Grandpa's Widow, Elizabeth, my mother's great grandmother (Elizabeth Church of Sugar Hill was named for her) lived two miles west of the top of Dodd Mtn in a cabin in Squirrel Hollow. The family hid from southern sympathizers led by Bill Dark, Bob Lancaster, but the renegades found them and poured their cornmeal on the ground to feed their horses. They also bent their rifle barrels around trees. The family scooped the corn meal up. Then they would pour some into a pan with water and drain it. They did this repeatedly to remove most of the dirt. Aunt Jane Williams was Elizabeth's daughter and living with her at the time. Aunt Jane only weighed 90 lbs but she once picked up her grandson Ed Williams who weighed about 60 lbs and carried him four miles across two creeks and up Sugar Hill with his feet never touching the ground.

The Prices were great bear hunters. They hunted barefoot in the snow and stood in the creek to warm their feet. Aunt Jane was no exception to this bear hunting tradition. She had a hidden gun that she used to kill a fat fear while their men were gone to war. The bear was on the hillside and rolled down the hill into the yard. They rendered 25 lbs of lard from it as well as all the meat that could be piled on a table. They scooped dirt from the floor of the smokehouse, soaked it in water, then boiled it down for the salt to cure the bear meat. They would boil a kettle of bear meat that still had a lot of fat on it. When it was almost done they added a lot of turnips or turnip greens, and seasoning. Salting the meat before it was tender would make it tough. Then, using bear grease to make cornbread, they ate fat, lean meat, greens and cornbread. Sometimes they hulled white oak acorns then place them in water to leach them. After doing this the acorns were dried in the sun, parched in front of the fireplace and ground with smooth stone. The acorn meal was used to thicken meat broth. Ground hickory nuts and ground dried sassafras leaves were also used to thicken meat broth.

Aunt Jane's husband and brother, Jack and Sam, were sharpshooters in the 7th Arkansas CSA. They were on a skirmish line in the Battle of Shiloh when Uncle Jack was shot "through the hollow." The shooter was so close his wadding entered Uncle Jack along with the bullet. A ramrod with a silk bandana was shoed through him from his back, then the bandana was pulled through to get the wadding out. In the same battled, 15 year old Sam killed his first man, a Union sharpshooter in a duel when the sunlight reflected off his opponents' belt buckle. A remorseful Sam said, "He didn't aim for me to go home, so I guess I aimed for him to go home." They hadn't written home in three years because they couldn't read or write, and they were presumed to be dead. But in the early spring of 1865, when Lee surrendered, Aunt Jane, who could read a cup (of tea leaves), predicted that they would be back. Right on schedule they came walking in barefooted after wading water from Memphis to Oil Trough, and they made a crop in the ridge field with their muzzleloaders tied to their Georgia Stock plows.

When I was just a boy, Uncle Zed Price lived at the crossroads where Wilson's store is now. He would go barefooted up Stair Gap – the old timers pronounced it Star Gap – to the Mabry Farm where he'd get his team by the crack of dawn. He'd plow until dark then walk home. His wages were 50 cents a day for twelve hours of work.

The Prices were always real superstitious. No axe or other tool could be brought into the house. They were always hunting for gold, but they wouldn't stick a shovel into the ground until the stroke of midnight. Once, when Epps Price was hunting for gold, they were scared off by a strange light. When they got home, Aunt Jane told them exactly where they had been digging. She said they should have dug one foot deeper. The approximate location of two saddlebags of gold double eagles was handed down to me. They were hidden by a Union officer in a black gum tree where someone had chopped a rabbit out. The officer's two boys came back after the Civil War to hunt for it.

Thong trees were early road signs used by Native Americans adopted by the early settlers. Near Murphy Hollow this one points the way to the shelter and box canyon of Bull Pen Hollow. Most roads today lay in direct line with the early animal trails and buffalo paths. It's entirely possible many of these trees were the work of John Price.

Cecila Wood - The Death of Chief Peter Cornstalk (III)
Born 1785 Murdered 1841

Ticks, chiggers and the possibility of snakes didn't deter Cecila Wood and me but the dead fall from last year's ice storm did as we headed off to the base of the mountain at the back of her farm in Searcy County (Arkansas). B.T. "Satch" Smith joined us but decided to sit and wait, watching as "us girls" climbed the mountain. The "round mountain" that can be seen in the background is noted in numerous places as references to both the Sequatchie Village of Chief Peter Cornstalk and his final resting place. We edged our way over rocks along the ledge searching for the rock box (cairn) the reported final resting place of Chief Peter Cornstalk.

Satch finding a place in the shade as Cel and I get ready to climb.

Young Hokolesqua Cornstalk/b1710 of Chalakatha/Mekoche (Shawnee) lineage became Chief of the 20 tribe Northern Confederacy in the Ohio Valley in 1755 serving until his death in 1777, Point Pleasant, Virginia. Hokolesqua was given the name Cornstalk by whites due to his height of over 6 ft 6 and his flowing white hair. His first son, Peter/b1744 was the first "Peter Cornstalk". It's difficult to sort out who is who in the Cornstalk family lineage because the Shawnee like most early Native Americans were a polygamous due to the high mortality rate. Young Hokolesqua (1710-1777) had at least 8 wives and possibly as many as 30 children. The lineage may be tedious to follow but four of his son's are important to our local history; 1) Young Cornstalk born 1744 by his 1st wife Helizikinopo, 2) Peter Jr (I) b. 1755, 3) John Wolf b. 1750 and 4) Black Wolf/41 by his 2nd wife, Ouanacona Moytoy. Since first writing the piece for the Stone County Citizen newspaper, I have spent hundreds of hours pouring over historical documents, bibles and records and listening to the stories handed down within families in order to be as accurate as possible in the ancestry of our people.

Hokolesqua's son Young (I)/44 married Elizabeth See, his adopted white sister, the daughter of Hokolesqua's 5th wife Catherine Vanderpool Sharp and Frederick See (Seay). Young (I)/44 and Elizabeth had White Wing, b. 1770 and Son of Young b 1772. White Wing aka Nancy Adkins had two husbands, Elijah Adkins and the legendary Tecumseh. Young Peter I/44 was Tecumseh's father in law. Black Wolf/44, Peter Jr. II/55 and John Wolf/50 were White Wings uncles. Their children were cousins, a relationship that can be seen in the settling of the White River Valley. In 1774 Tecumseh's father, Chief Pucksinwah was killed, his mother Methotaske, Creek was not well treated within the Shawnee tribe following her husband's death and eventually was driven off. In 1780, the Shawnee raided Martin and Ruddell Station's capturing over 200 prisoners. Among those were siblings George and Elizabeth Lail and brothers Abraham, 6 and Stephen Ruddell, 12. George, Abe and Stephen would continue to live with the Shawnee for almost 20 years, as brothers to Tecumseh. It is more than probable that Tecumseh after locating his mother brought her here to the White River Valley where she is reported to have lived and died in the vicinity of present day O'Neal across the river from the Lafferty Settlement.

Chief Young Hokolesqua's second wife was Ounaconoa Moytoy (1718-1758), mother of Black Beard born 1735, Black Wolf/41 John Wolf/50, Peter Jr (II)/55 and Susannah/57. The lineage of Ounaconoa is impressive. She is the daughter of Swan Wapehti Hop and Oshasqua (I) Muskrat Moytoy (V). It her family along with the Wards, that aligned the British with the Shawnee in 1730. Their portrait known as the Trustees of Georgia painting hangs in the British Royal Museum in London.

Black Wolf/41 fathered a child with Jenny Sellard Wiley, captive white woman. She reportedly gave their son to Black Wolf in order to be allowed to return to the whites. Upon returning to the whites, she told her captives had tomahawked the child. That child is Chief John Black Wiley. His settlement in Searcy County, Arkansas, known as Wiley's Cove was renamed Leslie, Arkansas after the Civil War. Peter Jr (II)/55 married his adopted sister captive Mary Francis Avery (Avey)/b. 1764, ½ white and half Shawnee who had been raised by Chief Peter's 5th wife Catherine See (Seay). They had a number of children between 1785 and 1805 including their oldest Peter/85 (aka Peter Avey) and their youngest Nancy Jane Avey b 1805 who are important to the White River Valley.

John Wolf/50 married a Shawnee woman with whom he had a daughter, Black Poddee/85 and sons, Henry Clay/90, John Wolf Cornstalk (II) Jr/92 and Peter Wolf (III)/94. John Wolf Cornstalk (II) Jr took his first wife at Shawneetown (Yellville, then the Louisiana Territories) with whom he had Andrew 1819, John (III) Jr 1822 and Daniel 1824 all born in Missouri or Kentucky, near Paducah, Kentucky across the river from Cape Girardeau, MO where many of the Shawnee settled including George Lail. In 1826 at Norfork, Arkansas, Wolf House, John Wolf/92 took a second wife, his first cousin, Nancy Jane Avey b/1805, the youngest daughter of his uncle Peter II/55 and Mary Francis Avey. It is at this time that he and all of his children became "Avey's"; with Nancy Jane/b1805 he had Peter "Pest" Avey b 1829, Jacob "Jake" Avery b 1835, Elizabeth b 1843 and Mary b 1845. Chief Peter/85, now 40, married his 3rd wife, a young Mary Adams, in 1826 at Wolf House at the same time his sister Nancy and John Wolf (II) Jr/1794 were married there. Mary Adams was the daughter of Robert Adams & Elizabeth Ferguson. White Wing, Peter III/85, Nancy/1805, John/92, Peter (III) 92 and John Black Wiley/87, were the grand children of Chief Hokolesqua Cornstalk b 1710. Peter II/85 had taken the name of his mother, Mary Frances Avey but after marrying Mary Adams, it is reported he used both the name Peter Avey and Peter Adams. The Adams family resides primarily in Searcy and Marion County. It is the descendants of Peace Chief John Wolf Cornstalk (II) Jr (Avey)/92 whose descendants we find in Stone County. He settled west of Mountain View, near Big Springs at Newnata which means "My big spring there" in Algonquin.

Of greater importance is the relationship created between the Moytoy's and the Cornstalks with the marriage of Young Hokolesqua Cornstalk to his second wife, Ounaconoa Muskrat Moytoy. Ounaconoa's brothers and uncles were of the Principal Chiefs, members of the 1730 Delegation to King George II. Their portraits hang in the British Royal Museum in London. Francis "Chief Fivekiller" Ward married Tame Doe (Catherine Carpenter) Moytoy, their daughter, Nancy Ward, Beloved Woman of the Cherokee, married Kingfisher, their daughter Catherine Kingfisher married John Walker. Their grand daughter Caty Walker married David Fulks, the first of the Fulks to arrive in Arkansas along with Peter (Avey)/85, John (Avey)/92, Peter/94, John Black Wiley/87 and the Wards around 1820. Elias Fulks, son of David and Caty, married Martha Houston Grigsby, a cousin to brothers, General Sam Houston and John Paxton Houston, first clerk of Izard Co, buried at Athens, 3 miles south of Calico Rock. Although many Cherokee came through Arkansas on the Trail of Tears (1831-1838) these Shawnee and Cherokee came here voluntarily, were not assigned roll numbers and contrary to belief most did not leave when the 1817-1828 reservation ended. The Native Americans who moved here voluntarily were among the first to circumvent the U.S. patent laws by adopting the white man's names and thus patenting land as such. It is the fear of the loss of their land that for years forced silence and denial of their Indian heritage.

Chief Peter's settlement known as Sequatchee was located on Bear Creek in Searcy County. Some say the creek is named due to the abundance of bear in the area, while others say it is due to the fact it was the location of the Bear Clan of the Shawnee of whom Peter/85 was Chief. Cecilia Wood who lives in Mountain View, was born and raised north of Marshall where she retains ownership of a portion of the former Shawnee land not far from Bear Creek. She is a descendant of Peter Adams Tyler, son of Baker Tyler and Agnes Adams. According to the Adams family bible, Agnes is the daughter of Matthew Adams and Catherine Ferguson; brother's Matthew and Robert Adams, sons of James Adams, married sisters Catherine and Elizabeth Ferguson. Peter Tyler married Eveline Manerva Price daughter of Elizabeth

Brewer and Buck Price, believed to be relatives to John Price who settled Bull Pen Holler in Stone County around 1820 and the Brewers of west Stone County.

According to a number of sources including family members, family bibles and Shawnee Heritage by Don Greene, "In 1841 Chief Peter Cornstalk (Peter III/85) was killed in Kansas by Peter A. Tyler, a former family friend." Both family and local stories report that while at a tribal gathering near where the Buffalo and White River's converge, Chief Peter (III)/85 became enraged when a child stepped on a stick at the fire circle flipping fire sparks onto him. Chief Peter (III)/85 struck the child in anger killing him. Realizing what he had done he fled. On the decision of the convening chiefs, members of Chief Wiley's clan along with Peter Adams Tyler pursued Chief Peter (III)/85 into Kansas. Therefore Mary's first cousin Agnes' son Peter Adams Tyler killed Mary's husband Chief Peter Cornstalk (III/1785).

Little is known as to what transpired that they did not bring him back alive other than Chief Peter (III)/85 was killed by 18 year old Peter Adams Tyler and his body was brought back to the Bear Creek settlement for burial. He is reportedly buried in an above ground three sided rock box, cairn, at the face of the mountain overlooking Bear Creek Valley. Tyler's Bend located on the Buffalo River, north of Marshall is named for the Tyler family. Peter Adams Tyler was one of the men marched to Little Rock in chains as a member of the Searcy County Peace Society which then included most of west Stone County. He died during the Civil War at Bowling Green, Ky. Mary's father, Robert Adams and her brother, Robert Adams Jr. are reported to be the first white settlers of Searcy County.

Due to the marriage of John/92 and Nancy, children of brothers John/50 and Peter/55, their descendants Peter "Pest" Avey b 1829, Jacob "Jake" Avey b 1835, Elizabeth b 1843 and Mary b 1845 (m Peter Mann) are the "double" grand children of Young Holokesqua Cornstalk 1710-1777 and Ounaconaoa Muskrat Moytoy 1718-1758. The Cornstalks and Moytoys are the Royal family of the Native Americans, members of the 1730 delegation to King George II. Attributed to the Cherokee, it is the Moytoy's and Cornstalk's (Sequoyah) who developed the first written language of the Native American people. It is important to document the lineage to prove the Northern Confederacy which included the Shawnee and Cherokee remain here in the White River Valley. Some of the known families of the "Royal Family" here include my line (Fulks/Chitwood family) – Martha Roper Blackwell, Stone County Judge, Stacey Avey, Laudis Brewer, Bill Wallace, Von and Fred Ward and many others. At the time of her death in December 4th, 2010 Faye Willie Ward-Wallace was the oldest living descendant of Chief Hokolesqua Cornstalk and Ounaconoa Muskrat Moytoy. The Native Americans who moved here voluntarily were among the first to circumvent the U.S. patent laws by adopting the white man's names and thus patenting land as such. It is the fear of the loss of their land that for years forced silence and denial of their ancestry upon the people who moved here.

I have included some lineages of those above within the book in individual stories – however, I have chosen to specifically include the ancestry on the AVEY line at this juncture due to considerable confusion within the family due to naming patterns, coupled with the errors of census takers. Lineage is back to Chief Hokolesqua Cornstalk 1710-1777 Principal Chief of the Cherokee and 2nd wife Ounacona Muskrat Moytoy – Children – full blood – Chalakatha/Pekowi/Mekoche/Metis (1/2 Shawnee and ½ Cherokee) – Shawnee were polygamist and had multiple wives through the early 1800's. John Wolf Cornstalk Avey b 1794 who settled in the Missouri Territories, became the Arkansas Territories, then Lawrence County, and finally Stone County was a Peace Chief over a much greater parcel of land than his 1st cousin and "father in law" Chief Peter Cornstalk b 1785, of Searcy County fame. More is written about Chief Peter Cornstalk because of his association with the Adams family, recorded marriage to Mary Adams in 1826 at Wolf House (Arkansas Territorial Documents) which allowed her father and brother to become the first white settlers of present day Searcy County. He was an old man who married him a young woman in a land deal. Peter/85 was killed by Mary's cousin, Peter A. Tyler. John on the other hand negotiated treaties and worked with Sam Houston, John Houston, Thomas Riggs, Stephen Austin, Chief Robert Benge, Jacob Watts, Chief John Jolly, Chief Ross and others to quietly move the Shawnee people into the White River Valley, making a conscious decision to create a place for these people the result – the Ozark culture as we know it today.

CHILDREN OF CHIEF JOHN WOLF CORNSTALK AVEY

B 1794 son of John Wolf Cornstalk/b1755 and Chalakatha Woman, Grandson of Chief Holokesqua and Ounacona Muskrat Moytoy –

1st wife Shawnee woman – children – full blood Shawnee & Cherokee: Daniel (1824-1880), Andrew (1830) John Jr (1835)

2nd wife, 1st cousin Nancy Jane Avey b 1805 daughter of Peter Cornstalk/1785 and Mary Avery, grand daughter of Chief Holokesqua and Ounacona Muskrat Moytoy – children – full blood – Shawnee & Cherokee "double" lineage to the Royal Family of Native Americans (1730 alliance with King George II): Peter "Pest" Avey (1829), Jacob "Jake" Avey b (1835), Elizabeth (1843) and Mary (1845).

Due to the need of white society to place children in chronological order and assign a single mother, often polygamous wives were not listed and the newest or one with the white name was selected as the mother of all the children. This is seen repeatedly in the census of Illinois and Missouri, and later in Utah and Arizona, when recording Mormon households.

It has taken considerable research including digging into the National Archives and reviewing countless family bibles, notations on photographs and documented Shawnee history to determine the correct lineage and authentication of the age of the original photo to determine this is Daniel Peter Avey (1858-1899), son of Jacob Avey (1835-1880), grandson of Chief John Wolf Cornstalk Avey b 1792 and Nancy Avey born 1805, sister of

Peter/85, children of brothers, Peter/50 and John/55, double great great grand son of Chief Young Hokolesqua and Ounaconoa Muskrat Moytoy of the Royal Family of the Native American's (1730).

DANIEL 1824-1880 m Tenessee Nancy Jane b 1833-1892 (Cherokee unknown lineage believed to be full blood)
Their SON–John Lee Avey b 1864 (full blood Shawnee/Cherokee) married sisters – Martha Jane Rorie and Ovie Rorie
Children with Martha ½ Shawnee/Cherokee – Nancy Della, James Marvin, George, Lillie and Sherman
Johns' SON – James Marvin Avey ½ b 1889 m Lavonia Cooper
James SON – Erstle Elmo Avey b 1924 ¼
Erstle's SON – Stacey Avey 1/8th Shawnee/Cherokee

DANIEL PETER AVEY (1855-1910)
Son of Jacob "Jake" Avey b 1835

Daniels' 1855-1910 DAUGHTER/w 2nd wife Fanny Bradsahw –
Martha Jane Avey b 1884 1/4th Shawnee married John Thomas Roper
Martha's SON 1/8th James Coleman Roper
James DAUGHTER Martha Roper married Rex Blackwell
Martha CHILDREN" Jessica and Roper Blackwell are 1/32nd Shawnee/Cherokee(Chalakatha/Kishpolo/Shawnee, Cherokee & Metis)

Roper killed this huge bear in Stone County with a crossbow 2010

Jessica with her dad Rex after bagging this beautiful turkey.

JACOB "Jake" AVEY 1835-1800 married Martha Jane (?) also believed to be part Indian but unverified so following lineage is Jake's only: Children ½ Shawnee/Cherokee
Jake's SON Daniel Peter Avey (PHOTO) buried at Alco married 1st Fanny Bradshaw and 2nd Sarah Ann Cynthia Jane Paxton
Daniel's SON w/Cynthia 1/4th Charlie LeRoy Avey b 1899-d1947
Charlies Children 1/8th Grand children 1/16th
Dulcie 1924 married Hugh Kirby, children Gloria and Daniel
Dorothy 1936 m Carson Finch, children Linda and Lisa
Bernice 1935 m Charles Allen, girls Susie, Barbara, Marilyn, Paula
Charles 1922 m Alta Ivy son Joel Lee

Dulcie Avey Kirbby holding the original photo of her grand father Daniel Peter Avey. Her father was his only son Charlie LeRoy "Lee" Avey

PETER "Pest" 1829-1860 full blood Shawnee/Cherokee m Martha Jane George 1830-1860 sister of Rachel George, wife of Bill Dark
DAUGHTER – Nancy Jane Avey ½ b 1855-1938 m Henry Harris (believed to be Metis – white, black and Indian undefined)
Nancy's DAUGHTER – Anna Lou Harris 1/4th 1872-1949 m Joseph S Ward (1/8th Shawnee/Cherokee See Ward Family) 1862-1942   Anna Lou's DAUGHTER – Faye Willie Ward b 1915-2010 1/8th Maternal and 1/16th Paternal or 3/16th or 1/4th Cherokee/Shawnee married Phillip Ray Wallace 1910-1970
Faye's SON – Billy Joe Wallace b 1949 1/8th
Bill's SON Jeff Wallace b 1974 1/16th

Lakesha 2010 Stone Co Rodeo Queen
takes the barrel with force, ease and grace.

Jake ropes his calf with a single throw of the rope. Traditions and ways of life continue in the Ozarks in the way we hunt, fish, trap, walk, ride, dance, sing, play music and revere God is in the way we live our lives as people of the Ozarks.

Truman Bullard - Mt. Joy Church

"In the chapel they were singing." I can still hear Jim Ed Brown's deep inviting voice, his firm handshake and warm bear hug. But tonight it was Truman Bullard doing the inviting and the singing was rousing, soulful and uplifting being sung at Mt. Joy. Truman is the son of Clyde and Zelda Gammill Bullard. He has been preaching at Mt. Joy for just over a year. On the second Tuesday of each month they have a gospel singing and tonight, a beautiful warm spring night, the church was full, inside and out.

Truman Bullard at Mt. Joy Church

The original Mount Joy church was built long before the Civil War, at the back of the Chitwood farm on Cajen Creek. It served the community for over 100 years until 1953 when the new Mt. Joy church was constructed. Joe Buck and Ima Canard donated the land next to the newly hardtop road (Hiway 14) at Roaring River (a creek) east of Mtn. View. An ever frugal community, they brought the church bell from the old church and salvaged useable lumber from it for the new one. Herman Chitwood and Arnold Brightwell hauled logs to the saw mill across from Tater Shaw's house at the start of Guion Road for Elmer Fulks and my daddy, Ed Cruse to saw. Wayne Turner remembers working at the mill along with many other friends, family, neighbors. Alvin McCarn. Tillar Ruminer Britton. Ima Fulks Cruse. Burns. Brightwell. Brown. Pitts. West. Hess. Chitwood. Fulks. Lambert. Shaw. Webb. Morris. Sutterfield. Price. Canard. Aiken. Creswell. Carter. Pilcher. Davis. Thompson. Foster. Killion. Rorie. Turner. These were just some of the people who worked on the church and have called it their own, names in the church book when it was dedicated April 1953 as recorded by Glenn Woody, sermon delivered by Orf Sutterfield.

Growing up on Guion Road, "the lower end", this was the church where we held my grandma's service and Uncle M's; where my children and I had dinner on the grounds and hunted eggs on Easter Sunday with my momma. "Yes, this is my church." It was old home place as I entered, familiar faces from the pews greeting me. These folks were at my daddy's funeral, my momma's and my daughter's. They were there when my house burned and when the tornado hit, when the ice storm and floods ravaged our county. Perhaps some of the older women here took a switch to my bare legs as a child, or doctored me when I was sick. Tonight they hugged my neck and shook hands with the politicians. They like us candidates standing in front of them singing, sitting in the pews or visiting outside, are Republicans and Democrats, Baptists, Methodists, Pentecostal. The fence between us has never been very high in this county whatever the name we wear. We are a devout people, moral, conservative and rich in our history and traditions.

The 71 mile stretch of the White River Valley we settled, from Buffalo City where the White and Buffalo Rivers converge flowing south to Batesville gave birth to the Ozark culture. Over 85% of the land in Stone County is still held by the families who homesteaded after 1810. The deep respect we have for our families, our friends and neighbors, is ingrained in our character. People came here seeking freedom, the American Revolution (1775-1783) fresh in their lives. 1 in 10 died on the Patriot POW ships in New York, over 12,000, more than died fighting. A majority of the British soldiers did not return to England after the war, just as all of the Indians did not leave here when in 1828 the reservation ended. The Scots, Irish, British, Native Americans and Blacks blended, creating this place. It can still be seen, felt and heard in the way we live our lives, dance a jig or play a tune. Traditions run deep in all of us, how we mourn the dead, help our neighbor and celebrate new life. People desire to be part of it. Many who move here say it is like coming home. They love the people and our way of life. They become one of ours, devout and respectful of our elders and our heritage. But our history, culture, traditions, our morals and values, our way of life is threatened by some who would have us be divided, not remembering who we are. By some who believe we need big city law enforcement in our little county of 12,000. Who believe we are "weird", "stupid," and "in need of 'civilization'". And that we "would all be living in shacks at the end of gravel roads" if it were not for folks like them; folks who consider that a bad thing, believing somehow we are less than they are. A person who believes like this is a poor man. One who will never know what "neighbor" means, a person like this needs our prayer and pity but never our vote.

We grade our neighbor's road just because it needs it, or repair the gap in their fence so the animals don't get out. This is a place where the mail man still carries a shovel to fix the potholes and the ladies leave sweet tea in the mail box. We may fight with each other like cats and dogs, brothers and sisters, each wanting to "win", but we will also fight to defend each other. The road we may take will vary but it is headed to the same place, a place that takes care of each other. I fondly remember the trees that lined Guion Road before it was widened and paved. I would gladly travel that road still for the smell of the fresh rain that settles dust and for a taste of my momma's biscuits waiting. There's no where I need to get so fast that it makes much of a difference if the road is gravel or paved.

We are a people whose greatest treasures hang in the frames on our walls, sit with us when we sing God's praises, mourn the death of a loved one, or celebrate the birth of a child. Yes, Mt. Joy is my church, Guion Road home and my neighbors are not just my family and friends, they are yours. We have come a long way since the first families constructed the original Mt. Joy church but in the ways that count, we're still who we've always been. Whether united in song or by casting your vote, your voice and our way of life here in Stone County matters to all of us. Here, 911 is a response of the community, of your neighbors and not about an ambulance. And like Democrats and Republicans before us and now, we sing together, we worship together and live together as friends and neighbors, as family and that's always the right choice.

Bud Cooper - Round Bottom

Knowing we would likely end up with a load of ticks, not to mention the possibility of encountering snakes, Bud and I headed to the Beckham Cemetery, also known as Round Bottom or Lancaster Cemetery. Mister Ches was not up to coming with us but confirmed the location and history of the cemetery. Bud, who last visited the cemetery over 50 years ago, grew up across the river in Izard County at Twin Creek, once a flag station on the rail road. For 31 years his dad, Jeff Cooper was the postmaster there and operated a store. Many people, including Bill and Nettie Lancaster got mail at Twin Creek. As kids Bud and his sisters, Linda and Mary, could see the Lancaster's working Round Bottom, plowing their fields, cattle grazing. Jeff and Roland Gillihan taught singing school; Laudis Brewer, Howard Wade, Martha Mealer and Roland had a singing group, called the Happy Four Quartet. When Jeff died in 1963, they sang at his funeral in Melbourne.

We're searching for the graves of two children, George and William, sons of William "Monroe" Cooper and his second wife, Nancy Byler (daughter of James Taylor Byler and Mary Riggs). Monroe and Nancy were sharecroppers on the river fields of "Round Bottom". Born in 1863 during the Civil War little George died only three months later. In 1876 Nancy lost a second child William when he became ill and died at 12. These boys are the half brothers of Bud's great grand father, Thomas Jefferson Cooper. Bud recalls almost 200 graves at Beckham Cemetery, with markers running to the rock ledge where an old fence now stands, and north where bull dozing has scarred the land. The boy's graves were marked in the 1950's with new etched marble markers placed there by the Hinkle family but clearly have fallen over, buried or bulldozed and gone. After the death of her first husband

(Johnson), Nancy married Monroe Cooper. The Coopers are descendants of John and Sarah Lindsey Lafferty, the first white settlers of Stone County at the Buckhorn in 1810. When Monroe died, the "Widow Cooper" married William Riley Hinkle. Buried at Flatwoods cemetery, Nancy and William share a headstone.

Bud and Elinor with the still standing sandstone chimney
Wade House

Bud and I made our way down to the Wade place where we find Elinor enjoying the beautiful spring morning on her deck overlooking the river valley. Stone County has silica sand of the same type as mined at Guion. The lone sandstone chimney is the last remains of the home that Stanley Wade built where each of his children were born. While men used the stone as foundations and chimney's the women used the sand to clean the floors of their homes. Mister Ches was not up to going with us today. The Wade land was settled by his grandfather Elihu Beckham then sold to Wade McCasland, a half brother to William Wade. It has remained in the Wade family for almost 150 years. The Wade home faces the area of the White River known as Greasy Bottom, south is Dillard Shoals. Before the dam was completed, when riverboats plyed the waters, there was an area known as "Nigger Jailhouse" on Bird Rock Bluff. Discontents and miscreants, black, white and Indians, aboard the steamboats would be let off there as punishment. The bluff was too steep to climb and the water teamed with flat head bull catfish, some weighing in the hundreds of pounds, as big as a man could hold head high, and equally big alligator gar. The men would not dare step into the water, waiting hungry and cold until the steamboat returned for them.

There's Rock Island, Engles Eddy (an Engles man from Guion drown there), Fleming Bluff, Handford Bluff and Handford Spring where stories abound of bums and rail road workers staying in the early 1900's. Baby Face Nelson and Jesse James are said to have hid out there. Stories also report silver coins from the Spanish American War hid in the bluff hole, a spot in the mountain that even goats could not traverse. It would require a skilled rock climber descending the face to enter it then or today.

Bud in the field where Civil War troops camped, Twin Creeks in background

Next directly across from Round Bottom is Twin Creek, named for the two creeks which spill into the river about 300 feet apart. In the winter of 1864, the northern end of Round Bottom was the Civil War camp of 200 men of the 1st Nebraska Cavalry and a small detachment of 100 men from the 11th Missouri Cavalry, Union troops all stationed at Batesville. Food was scarce, unable to feed all the troops at Batesville soldiers were repeatedly sent out into the surrounding areas to fend for themselves. CSA Col. Thomas Black of Cagen Creek was married to Mary Byler, sister of James, aunt to Nancy. The Union troops took the slaves of Andrew Hinkle (Riggsville) and Col. Black, burned Rorie's Mill and killed dozens of people, including two men on the Beckham farm. Civil War records cite Round Bottom on a number of occasions, from troops crossing the river there, foraging for food and encampments using the Fred Lancaster barn on the National Registry of Historic Places.

Photo Civil War Re-enactment 2010 Battle of Lunenburg

Presently owned by Frank Foll, the barn was added on to in the early 1900's thus displacing its age for NRHP purposes. The barn has slave pegs and slave holes which clearly dates it prior to the Civil War. Round Bottom was a major route along the White River with two steam boat river landings. The path of the old military road led up and over the ridge through Herpel to Riggsville then south across Richwoods.

Slave peg holes are found throughout the White River Valley

One of the oldest remaining settlements in Arkansas, the 1837 Dillard settlement at Round Bottom is on the National Registry of Historic places. It consists of two barns, a triple pen log home, slave house and foundry. Just down river from the AG&F Round Bottom Access, on private land, badly in need of cleanup and repair it could be one of the most significant tourist attractions in the region. The restoration and preservation of the Dillard Settlement and Riggsville would be of equal historical significance to Stone County, the Ozarks and Arkansas as Jamestown is to Virginia and the nation. Development and preservation of our history, our cultural heritage, rock walls, settlements, music and dance, is our future growth with a goal of being more like Jamestown than Branson or even Gatlinburg (TN). People want to live next to historical sites, no one wants to live next to neon signs and amusement rides.

1837 Dillard Settlement Round Bottom NRHP
Stone County is the Jamestown, VA of the Ozarks

The Cooper, Brewer, Lancaster, Hinkle, Nesbitt, Decker, Dearien, Harris, Beckham, Wade and Burns families, along with many others settled and worked the area known as Round Bottom. The Buckhorn, Sylamore and Round Bottom are historic locations of the first settlers and natives of Stone County, rich not only in their soil but the deep roots of who we are as a people.

Donna Wilson - Rorie's Mill's

Short of emergency deliveries, home births and the short lived practice of a few doctors and skilled midwives, Donna Wilson is one of the last people actually born in Stone County. Delivered at Dr. Burton's Clinic on Main Street, she is the daughter of Charlie and Joyce Gullett and the GGGG grand daughter of Absalom Rorie who in 1845 brought his family here from Hardin Co, TN, 165 years ago. She serves as Stone County Clerk.

Donna at Rorie's Mill, the foundation rocks can be seen on the right of photo

After arriving here, Absalom and his wife Sarah (Meador) set about building a huge two story saw mill followed by one of the first and most prosperous grist mills in Stone County. These gave upper Middle Sylamore Creek its present day name of Mill Creek. Timber, logs and lumber were floated down the creek to White River where they were loaded onto steamships headed to Memphis and New Orleans. A small community was starting to grow including Aaron Stevens and his family, Jonas Brewer and his wife Margaret. Roasting Ear Creek did not exist until several years after the Civil War, when following a huge storm a new creek was pushed forth out of the mountain flowing through the Steven's and Brewer's cornfields taking the "Roastin' Ears" with it. After the flood, Roasting Ear Creek remained.

Absalom's business and family were thriving as talk of Civil War became a reality. In 1860 Arkansas required each county to maintain a militia; J.J. Kemp of Riggsville (Mtn. View) was appointed Colonel of the Izard Co Militia, a title he earned in the Civil War and maintained the rest of his life. A huge expanse of land with just over 6,000 residents it included present day Stone County and Mt. Olive was the county seat. May 6, 1861 Arkansas seceded. The Confederate Congress urged Ark to make provisions for the manufacture of arms and munitions, including saltpeter for the cause of the South. In June 1861 the Military Board of Ark ordered the county judge, sheriff, and clerk of each county to serve as a commission to procure supplies for Arkansas soldiers; H.H. Harris, age 34 (Melbourne) Judge, W.J. Cagle, age 31 from Riggsville (Mtn. View), Sheriff, W.C. Dixon age 29 (Mt. Olive), Clerk served for Izard Co.

In July 1861 Absalom and Sarah's 21 year old son, Absalom Josiah "Jody" Rorie joined the Confederacy as a Private in the Ark Infantry. On Aug 21 the steamboat New Moon arrived at Sylamore with cargo of 30 huge kettles, a steam engine and a hammer mill to produce gunpowder for the Confederacy. They were brought up the North Fork of Sylamore Creek to what became known as Gunner Pool. White oak baskets carried on the backs of oxen led into Saltpeter Cave were loaded with bat guano. The guano was placed in the huge kettles by the creek and boiled, leaving the saltpeter at the bottom. Charcoal made mostly from cottonwood was ground in the hammer mill powered by the steam engine. Sulphur was added to produce a more accurate shot. The Confederate Gov sent infantries to work and guard these powder works. As steamships loaded and unloaded cargo and supplies for all of North Arkansas to aid the munitions effort the river port town of Sylamore (Stone Co) became a critical location in the Civil War. The road from Sylamore, which parts of can still be seen today in the Ozark National Forest, led through the mountains crossing the Buffalo at Spencer Point then north on to Yellville and from there to Missouri. In the spring of 1862, Union Gen Curtis invasion of Izard Co began with skirmishes at Calico Rock and Mt Olive, with 20,000 plus soldiers spread out from Pocahontas to Yellville searching for the Confederate powder mills located throughout our hills in the many caves. He issued an order "If you can't bring it with us, burn it."

On May 29, 1862, Gen. Curtis sent 300 men under Major Drake and Major Bowen of the 3rd Iowa Calvary with two mountain howitzers to Sylamore. They were after Rebel's camped in Kickapoo Bottoms, (between Livingston Creek and Jack's Boat Dock). The Union, firing the mountain howitzers at them from the east side of the river, ran about 45 men out of a cane break, killing one and wounding two others. A mountain howitzer is a mini-cannon easily packed by one mule with cannon balls about three inches in diameter. For years well into the 20th century the three inch "mini" cannon balls were plowed up in the river bottom fields of Stone County. Curtis' invasion was a war against the population as a whole. In order to save official records, county clerk, W. C. Dixon, hid them in a cave.

The burning and pillaging of homes and churches was intended to produce beggary of the local population. Grist mills and agricultural equipment, private salt works, and other manufacturing were destroyed. The cartel of prisoner exchange suspended. No preaching allowed unless the preacher had taken the Oath to the Union. No traveling permitted without a pass. No marrying allowed and parents forbidden to name their children after Southern Generals. Military governors appointed. The atrocities of Yankee

Rule enacted in Izard County surpassed what was known in other parts of the Confederacy largely due to the well hidden munitions efforts.

Bud holds a mini howitzer cannon ball found in the fields at Sylamore

In Nov 1863, the drought was having harsh effects. With no fall rains, the river was low, just barely running, crops and gardens failed. In Jan 1864, Maj Gen Sterling S. Price commissioned Col. Thomas R. Freeman to raise and maintain a regiment for the Confederates in North Arkansas. The weather fell to 10 below zero and stayed there. The river froze over so thick loaded wagons could cross over it. Orders received "Sat, Jan 23, 1864, Batesville, Ark Hdq 1st Nebraska Cavalry to Lt. Col William Baumer. You will proceed immediately and attack every Rebel encampment you find. Move via Hookrum, Lunenburg, Sylamore. Shoot every Rebel soldier you find in Federal uniform and destroy all armed Bushwhackers. On North Fork of Sylamore you will find and destroy a powder mill operating there. Should the town of Sylamore be occupied and fire upon you, burn them out. The object of this expedition is to destroy Freeman."

The Burning of Rorie's Mills

"At 9:00 a.m. Jan 23, 1864, 1st Nebraska Cavalry and 6th Missouri State Cavalry 297 men strong and 5 guides moved north." The first night, they camped at Evening Shade, next day traveled through Franklin making camp at Lunenburg (Jan 24). The third morning two companies split off. One came down to Mt. Olive, there killing at least 3, including Isaac Jeffery, captured 10 prisoners and burned the town before crossing the river at Hell Creek Landing. From there they moved on the old road under the bluff to Sylamore

(Stone Co) where they burned most the town killing 4 and wounding one. The two story home of Lucy Dillard Harris built in 1848 which sits at the junction of 5/9/14 at present day Allison was commandeered as a base, saving it from being burnt. (Photo Riggsville story)

Re-enactment 2010 Battle of Lunenburg

Scouts were sent to find Freeman with the remaining Union troops moving to Riggsville (Jan 25) to join the 11th Missouri Cavalry that had gone south out of Batesville. The scouts reported back that Freeman was camped on Middle Sylamore at Rorie's Mill (Jan 26). Union soldiers were dispatched. Next morning, Jan 27th, 1864 Monks and the 11th Missouri Cavalry went in first, but Freeman had left before dawn going back northeast toward Livingston Creek. Official records report they burned both the saw mill and grist mill and killed three men. Freeman had left a rear guard as distraction which the Union chased a number of miles through Big Flat before capturing. After the eight men surrendered they were shot and killed. Capt Franks, a brother in law to one of the Rorie daughters, was among the casualties. Col. Livingston's monthly report states, "Of this scout to Sylamore 1 Union wounded." Although the river was reported as being frozen sufficiently solid for loaded wagons to cross, Col. Livingston says the "1 wounded man was put in a dugout boat with 3 men to bring him to Batesville." Confederate soldiers reported another story. The east side of the river is said to have at least 20 graves of Union dead.

In 1863 having served almost two years in the Confederacy, Jody Rorie deserted. Captured on July 9, 1863, at Port Hudson, LA., he was paroled four days later. A skilled wagon maker, he was allowed to return home to build wagons for the Confederacy. He had been back on the Middle

Sylamore with his wife and four children a few months when on the morning of Jan 27th, 1864, Monk and his men stormed the area looking for the powder works, Freeman and his Rebels.

Photos July 2010 Civil War re-enactment Battle of Lunenburg

Angry that Freeman had gotten away, they burned the now prosperous mills to the ground, but not before torturing and killing three of the Rorie men in an effort to determine the location of Freeman and of Rorie's Cave believed to be producing powder works. Absalom and his sons, Andrew and Hezikiah had their arms tied to separate horses. The horses pulled against each other exacting pressure pulling the men's arms from their sockets, dismembering them as they were ripped from their bodies. Each man was then shot. Whatever Young Jody said or did is lost to that day. It is a reasonable assumption he used his Confederate desertion and his ability as a skilled wagon maker as a maneuver to barter with the Union for his own life and the lives of the rest of his family. Presumably under the watchful eyes of Union guard, Jody moved the remaining family to Big Flat, buried his brothers and father and then, on Feb 1, 1864 only three days after the burning of Rorie's Mills, he joined the Union Army. Hezekaih Columbus Rorie (1822-1864), of whom Donna Wilson is descended, was tortured and killed along with his 18 year old brother Andrew and his 66 year old father Absalom.

Hezekiah left his widow, Louisa Ticer behind with seven small children. People tell stories of men who fought for one side and then the other, of brothers fighting brothers, without telling the whole story. The people here fought to protect their homes and families making untold sacrifices. Most people did not own slaves and were not fighting for or

128

against slavery. Of the 1047 heads of household, 78 were slaveholders. After the Civil War ended, Jody came home again. He and his wife Mary Snelgrove had 8 more children (a total of 12). He worked at the saw mill of Thomas Marchant and Joe Emmett at Culp until he could build a new sawmill near MacPherson just a few miles away up the old Civil War road to Yellville. Jody was a major supplier of the Missouri Lumber and Mining Company. He made a good living for his family. His friends the Marchant family put in the first lumber yard and supply store in Mountain Home. Taking in city blocks, it would have dwarfed a Home Depot. Jody continued making wagons with a great many of the wagons that can now be found throughout the Ozarks, treasured antiques, produced at his mill. He didn't like to talk about the war or the day they burned the mills. He died in 1916. Both he and his wife Mary are buried at Table Rock Cemetery at Culp. Donna Wilson is a proud member of the Rorie family.

The Ghost of Gettysburg - By Buddy Case

I'm the ghost of Gettysburg, I'm Picket, Mead, and Lee
I proclaimed my presence July eighteen sixty-three
Cannonballs, black powder and the sounds of endless woe
Were the reapings of the harvest that a wounded nation sowed
I'm brother fighting brother...

I'm the ghost of Gettysburg, I'm widowed and I'm maimed
While history keeps a movin in this graveyard I remain
But I am all the brave men still livin though they're dead
I am the ground they walked upon I am their guns and lead
And a child cries for its father...

I'm the ghost of Gettysburg I am some mother's son
I turned fifteen on the battlefield and now my life is done
I'm the ghost of Gettysburg, the mother of a son
And deep inside I'm dyin, right along with everyone
Will he be returning?...

The prophet speaks, the page is turned, the past you teach, but never learn.

Kenneth Rorie - Mountain Meadows Massacre
By Bob Fleming

Kenneth Rorie with treasured family heirlooms

In 1845, Absalom Rorie and his family arrived in present day Stone County. Followed by friends and more family the community around "Mill Creek" (Middle Sylamore at Newnata) became a thriving community long before the Civil War. The Rorie's built and operated a grist mill and a two story saw mill that in addition to producing the regions best wagons, provided white oak for barrels, bins and barns throughout the area. Kenneth Wayne Rorie, ggg-grandson of Absalom Rorie & Sarah Jane Elizabeth Meador, gg-grandson of Hezekiah Columbus Rorie & Louisa A. Ticer, g-grandson of Newton Monroe "Newt" Rorie and Sarah Beaver is the son of Eulis and Cleo Graddy Rorie. Eulis learned to make wagons from his father Newt. Kenneth learned as a young child how to guide a team, including the meaning and use of the words, Gee and Haw.

When the Baker family started making plans to go west to join the California Gold Rush, John Twiddy Baker from Searcy County purchased wagons built by the Rorie's knowing they would be the strongest and surest, able to make the torturous trek west from Arkansas. Outfitting a wagon suitable for a cross country trek was a special order, costing around $5,000, the "Aire Steams" of the 1850's. In March 1857, the Baker wagon train met up with other families from the area at Caravan Springs on Hiway 7 near Harrison to begin the journey. A monument stands at the site from which they departed. Squire Beaver, after whom Beaver Lake was named, operated a trading post in Carroll County where the wagon train made its last stop purchasing final supplies for the arduous trip.

In this photo of Kenneth and his cousin,
one of the Rorie wagons can be seen in the background

On May 13, 1857, in Alma, Ark, Parley P. Pratt, one of the 12 Mormon apostles, was killed by Hector McLean. Pratt had usurped the marriage of McLean and his wife Eleanor, taking her as his 12th plural wife leading to an outraged McLean stabbing then shooting him. Pratt died 2 ½ hours later from loss of blood. Word arrived to Utah of the murder making Pratt yet another martyr to the Mormons, who had been chased out of both Missouri and Illinois. In 1838, the state of Missouri had issued Executive

Order #44 also known as the extermination order which Gov. Boggs stated was a result of "open and avowed defiance of the laws, and of having made war upon the people of this State ... the Mormons must be treated as enemies, and must be exterminated or driven from the State if necessary for the public peace—their outrages are beyond all description." This order was not formally lifted until 1976. The fiery rants of Brigham Young citing the on going persecution led him to declare martial law in Utah issuing a command that they would not provide any supplies to passers through, directing followers instead to cache supplies of food, grain and munitions in the hills and caves in order to fend off aggressors. It was in accordance with Mormon policy to hold every Arkansan accountable for Pratt's death, just as every Missourian was hated because of the expulsion from there.

The following is excerpted from depositions in the National Archives given by survivors, Martha Elizabeth Baker and her brother, William Twiddy Baker during the post Civil War investigation into the massacre; "My father (George), mother (Minerva Beller Baker), grandfather (John Twiddy Baker), several uncles and aunts were among those killed." "My brother, sister and I were kept in the family of John D. Lee," leader of the Mormon sect who attacked the wagon train, "until the soldiers came a year later upon the insistence of families here, to retrieve the survivors." "Only 17 children under the age of 8, who were deemed "too young to tell" were spared. The wagon train was under attack for 5 days." "We ran out of water with people dying in the hot sun from thirst as much as from wounds. There really was no choice but to surrender to John Lee who said he had worked out with the attacking Indians to allow safe passage," "but the men had to give up their guns. They loaded us children into a wagon." Elizabeth recalled the last time she saw her mother alive was as she was being placed into a wagon. Seeing the men wash the Indian paint from their faces, they realized these were white men, dressed as Indians. But it was too late. Given a signal by Lee, the Mormon's turned and shot each unarmed person with whom they were walking. More than 120 innocent men, women and children over 8 years old were killed. The survivors recalled seeing their mother's dresses worn by the Mormon women, their daddy's guns used by the men and Brigham Young himself riding around in one of the fine carriages" made by Absalom Rorie. When the soldiers came to retrieve the children over a year later, they found the remains of the slaughtered and stopped to bury the bodies that had been left exposed, ravaged by animals. Elizabeth, Sally Ann and William's grandma Mary came from Arkansas to claim them.

In 1864, brothers, Andrew and Hezekiah Rorie were tortured and killed along with their father Absalom by Union soldiers who were looking for Confederate troops and the powder work munitions being made in the caves of Stone County. Hezekiah's widow Lousia Ticer was left alone to raise their young children, Martha 4, Sarah 7 and Alan 11. Their four oldest children, sons, became men and heads of the house overnight, responsible for not only themselves but their siblings and mother. Their 18 year old son Newton "Newt" Monroe Rorie had become a skilled wagon maker. In 1869 he married Sarah Beaver, niece of Squire Beaver, who had supplied the Baker wagon train. Sarah Beaver Rorie lived to be over 100. She was the oldest person attending the 1941 Folk Festival at Blanchard where she sang and played, and won the hog calling contest. The desecration and irreverence of our nation's history continues, from the horrendous unconscionable acts of bulldozing cemeteries to renaming roads, mountains and lakes. Squire Beaver's trading post lay's beneath Beaver Lake. Succumbing to political pandering Beaver Lake is now part of Hobbs Conversation District and is referred to as "Hobbs Lake".

1875 John D Lee Center, Prior to Execution
Courtesy National Archives

In 2006 the movie September Dawn was released. It tells the story of this shocking piece of our nation's history and the lengths to which people will go when they are fighting for religious freedom. A full investigation into the massacre did not occur until after the Civil War. In 1879 John D Lee was tried, convicted and returned to the site of the massacre for hanging. It was no small footnote that the Pratt murder occurred on May 13, 1857 and the Mountain Meadows Massacre, the slaughter of Arkansas' people in the Baker wagon train occurred just four months later on September 11.

In Memoriam
Robert "Bob" Jarvis Fleming   1946-2010

      Bob Fleming completed Mountain Meadows Massacre Saturday night May 22nd. He died the following morning. Born in 1946 to Beulah Bryce Fleming, he is the great great grandson of early Mormon settler Ebenezer Bryce (1830-1913), of whom Utah's Bryce Canyon is named. Raised as a Mormon he served as a missionary in Brazil. It was his belief based on a lifetime in the Mormon Church that his story is an accurate understanding of what happened. He also believed that his gg grandfather Ebenezer Bryce was involved in the planning and execution at Mountain Meadows, Utah. Bob was a devoted member of the community of Mountain View, assisting in researching, editing and photographing people and places to preserve our history. Although I couldn't seem to get him to understand the need to "stay on the trail" which inevitably he ended up with bagger lice and worse, ticks and chiggers, he was always willing to trek down paths to caves and old house remains, or visit for endless hours with whoever was willing to talk to me. The above photo was taken in January 2010 following one of worst ice and snow storms in recent history. Bob agreed to drive me down to Blanchard Springs for winter pictures. He took photographs for nearly 40 years of the Mills of Southern Missouri and for the Missouri Fox Trotters Horse Breed Association in Ava, Missouri setting the standard for horse show photography in the breed and he started the Ava Journal.

      He was an incredible story teller, writer, photographer and explorer. I will be forever indebted to him. We packed a lot of living into the five years we shared. He was always willing to "carry my bags" and open any door that was closed. I miss my friend. I love you Bob. – Freda

Caleb Branscum - Kahoka & Three Sisters

Caleb and his friend Eli atop one of the rocks in the Three Sisters formation

     Small communities exist all over our nation, often simply known by a family who lived there or a landmark. They are disappearing as the local church, grocery and post offices give way to improved roads and better communication. In 1900, Stone County had over 100 schools, now we have three. Stone County is full of once thriving community's including Luber, Hanover, Fairview and Kahoka. After Bob and I attended the Red Paint Pow Wow in Silver Springs, New Mexico in the winter of 2009, he became even more interested in our Indian heritage, wondering aloud to anyone who would listen, "Why isn't it better documented here in the Ozarks?" Chief Wilma Mankiller laughed with him at his favorite tee shirt, "I'm part White but I can't prove it," as an ironic explanation to the lack of documentation, then she began educating us both. Bob had discovered how close the Cahokia Mounds were to us and was anxious for our upcoming trip there. Wilma told us about Stone County's very own mounds and a site of tribal gatherings here over 300 years ago. But more importantly she told us about the dance of the "Three Sisters" and the rock formation that bears that name at the site of the gatherings.

     Kahoka or Cahokia (pronounced /kə ho ki.ə/) is the ancient indigenous city (ca 600–1400 CE) near Collinsville, Illinois, across the Mississippi River from St. Louis, Missouri, approximately 6 hours from Mtn. View. Although only 80 survive, the 2,200-acre site included 120 man-made earthen mounds over an area of six square miles. Cahokia Mounds is the largest archaeological site related to the Mississippian culture, which developed advanced societies in eastern North America centuries before the arrival of Europeans. It is a designated site for state protection and a National Historic Landmark. In addition, it is one of only twenty World Heritage Sites designated in the territory of the United States. It is the largest prehistoric earthen construction in the Americas north of Mexico.

"The Mounds were named after a clan of historic Illiniwek people living in the area when the first French explorers arrived in the 1600's centuries after Cahokia was abandoned by its original inhabitants. The Cahokia were not necessarily descendants of the original Mississippian-era people. Researchers do not know which Native American groups are the living descendants of the people who originally built and lived at the Mound site, although many are plausible."

Caleb points to a perfect bird point he found near his school at Concord

"The Illini lived in a seasonal cycle related to cultivation of domestic plants and hunting, with movement from semi-permanent villages to hunting camps. They planted crops of maize (corn), beans, and squash, known as the "Three Sisters". In the seventeenth century, the Illinois suffered both from diseases brought by the whites to which they had no natural immunity and warfare by the expansion of the Iroquois into the eastern Great Lakes region. The Iroquois had hunted out their traditional lands and sought more productive hunting and trapping areas. Then in 1769 when a Peoria warrior murdered the Ottawa war chief Pontiac, the northern tribes retaliated against the Illiniwek. They suffered greatly. Many of the Illinois migrated to our present-day Ozarks settling in areas from Eastern Kansas to Stone County to escape."

There are a number of towns and communities that bear some variation in spelling of Cahokia throughout Missouri and Arkansas. Our Kahoka is about 15 miles east of Mountain View, on hiway 5 south. The rock formation of "The Three Sisters" is on land belonging to Wheeler Watters it over looks Marcella and lays just north and east of Chalybeate Springs near Bob Davis Mtn.

Wilma told us that the Kahoka Indians settled the area of Stone County between Chalybeate Springs and Three Sisters sometime around 1775. The area of the Three Sisters distinctive rock formation served as a meeting ground for various tribes. Located about 5 miles from the White River, with an abundance of caves, overhangs, shelters, food and water nearby, it was the perfect place for spring and fall gatherings. The rock formation was something like "Pride Rock" in Lion King, serving as a stage and vantage point. A dance was held atop the rocks to celebrate the success of the crops during both planting in the spring and harvest in the fall, thus the rock formation took on the name "Three Sisters" which is corn, beans, and squash. Although celebrations and tribal gathering of many kinds were held here, it was the Kahoka's reverence to the land and its bounty that gave the formation its name.

Caleb Branscum is the 12 year old son of Lisa Watters Branscum and grandson of Wheeler Watters of the community of Kahoka. There were six members of the Waters/Watters family on the 1817 Indian Census. Sequoyah took Sallie Watters as his 8th wife. The 1,000 people who became known as the Old Settlers, they were never on a U.S. roll and received no allocations from the new government. The Watters family has a public fishing pond, pay by the pound. As I headed out along the edge of the field, the rock formation of "Three Sisters" was there along the road to the pond, jutting out in an otherwise beautiful rolling field, it remains striking. Caleb was Johnny on the spot to assist me, asking if I was looking for the pond. I didn't spend a long time with Caleb and his friend Eli, but these two young boys were gentlemen and excited travelers in life. Caleb recently found a bird point arrowhead in a cave behind his school at Concord. And near the "Three Sisters", he had located some shards and other arrowheads. Although open to the public for fishing, this is private land. The "Three Sisters" can be seen from Haywood Lane, the county road that passes in front of it and is one of the most prominent landmarks of the once proud Indian community of Kahoka.

Todd Hudspeth & Lance Bonds – History in the Making

History happens every day but more often than not we realize the significance of an event long after it's occurred. That's not the case with the primary election run off race for Stone County Sheriff, between incumbent Todd Hudspeth and challenger Lance Bonds. Mark your calendars. Keep those photos, these newspapers. June 8th, 2010, made not only county history but Arkansas and possibly national history in the run off tie between these two remarkable young men who want to serve us as Sheriff.

Lance Bonds and Todd Hudspeth Candidates for Stone County Sheriff

This began when each Democratic candidate received an equal number of votes, 1,383, in the June 8th primary run off here last week. Stone County has never had a tie in any primary election run off. In fact it appears no primary election anywhere in Arkansas or perhaps even the U.S. has ever seen this happen. Nationally we have experienced only three tied elections in the November general elections. Therefore the election laws regarding ties are designed for and applicable to the November general election leaving the interpretation of primary elections often unclear, vague or grey. This has set the stage for history making politics emanating out of what actions are decided in Stone County. State legislatures nationwide including our own will be addressing the issue of tied primary elections following this landmark case which has drawn national media attention.

Politics here and in small rural areas across our nation have traditionally been a network of people that occupied the coffee shops, sale barns and court houses, the churches, the juke joints and barber shops. It's not changed all that much. These candidates worked hard to win their elections proving a handshake still stands for something. People still want politicians to ask for their vote and want to believe that their vote makes a difference. Our local Sheriff's race is proof that a single vote can make all the difference. We are lucky we have two men of the quality of character as Sheriff Hudspeth and Lance Bonds to represent the Democratic Party through this process

Local NBC Affiliate Channel 4 interviews Lance

Following the Tuesday night tie, the Stone County Election Commission (SCEC) did a recount. This recount resulted in a reduction of 31 votes giving Todd a 5 vote lead. In due diligence to determine where the missing 31 vote count had happened, the SCEC found that a second precinct ballot box had been overlooked. When it was included the numbers matched election night totals and the tie was reinstated.

After two public meetings, the Stone County Election Commission (SCEC) will likely certify the election as a tie on Friday at 3 pm, a deadline set within the required time frame sufficient to allow for two over seas ballots to come in. Although the SCEC was informed those ballots were not sent in there is a time requirement which must be followed to allow for them to arrive had they of been mailed thus the setting of the Friday deadline. Concerned citizens from both parties filled the courtroom on Monday directing questions to the SCEC Chair Bob Turner, County Clerk Donna Wilson, Deputy Prosecutor Lance Wright, County Atty Daniel Brightwell and Atty for Lance Bonds, William Almand, expert in Arkansas election law.

This race is not fraught with foul play as people are saying. It is in fact a tragedy of human errors. Some might say this is due to Missy Irvin's challenge against Paul White to be the Republican candidate for State Senate which created a highly contested race. In 137 years there has never been a contested Republican primary election in Stone County for State Senate, perhaps even any state office. People have historically been able to go in and just vote in the primary regardless of party affiliation. Because the only contested races were Democratic nobody ever had to say if they were Republican or Democrat. If you came in to vote, you got a Democratic ballot. The fence between a Republican and a Democrat is not very high in this county and we do not wear labels well. We are furiously independent and traditionally vote for the person.

Channel 8 interviewing Lance Bonds

The Republican contested primary race created the confusion for local voters as well as poll workers. A cross over vote which is perfectly legal is when a Republican or Democrat, votes outside their party. In keeping with Stone County tradition more Republicans voted Democratic ballots May 18th and in the June 8th run off than Democrats chose to vote a Republican ballot. The problem arose when people did not know that they could not cross back over in the run off, from Republican to Democrat. I for one was a cross over voter. A staunch Democrat, I voted Republican for the first time in my life in order to vote for Missy because I believed my vote was more important in that race alone than in all the Democratic races combined. I looked at the Democratic candidates who were running for office and I believed them all to be good people that I would be happy to have in service to our county and state. But I knew should there be a run off in any Democratic race that I could not turn around and vote as a Democrat. I gave up that right when I voted as a Republican for Missy. In fact, I can't vote again as a Democrat until our November general election. Nor can the

Republicans who chose to vote as Democrats vote as Republicans until the fall election.

Although solid training was provided the poll workers, I don't know that they fully understood what happens in a run off related to cross over voting, because the cross over voting wasn't isolated to one precinct or one poll worker. Nearly a third of the precincts had one or more persons cross over in the run off switching party lines from what they had voted in the May 18th election. Were they Democrats, like me, who voted Republican to vote for Missy, or were they Republicans who voted their party? It doesn't matter, people voting the Republican ticket May 18th could not vote in the Democratic Primary run off June 8th regardless of their political affiliation.

However, it is the appearance of impropriety, illegality and tampering that most concerns people; who is related to whom and who is counting votes, working the polls, tallying the numbers and who is on the election and party committee's rather than the issue of the tie itself. I looked at the public list of the people who were not eligible to vote and I don't believe any of them voted with mal intent. There were two people who voted in Stone County who are registered in other counties, one person did not register timely and another who had failed to vote in the two previously required federal elections. Two additional voters were determined to be provisional, leaving 24 cross over voters. They voted because they thought they could. It was the poll workers responsibility to ascertain eligibility before giving them the ballot and the SCEC's responsibility to determine any that were ineligible when certifying the vote. The problem that arises here is without compelling those cross over and other ineligible voters to come in, under oath, to disclose how they voted throwing out the vote would not affect the result of the tie. Arkansas chose to do away with the secret numbering that identifies voter to ballot. And then more importantly simply by asking the voters to come in would be an infringement on their right to privacy. While it is a Class A misdemeanor to switch parties in an election the intent of that action will be weighed when considering prosecution. All irregularities that could be a violation of the law have been turned over to the Arkansas State Police for investigation. Even though it is the poll workers responsibility to verify each voter's eligibility to vote, it is also the responsibility of the voter's to know the law. You still get a speeding ticket even if you say, "But Officer, I didn't see the sign that said the speed limit had gone down from 55 to 35." Ignorance of the law is no excuse in any situation. However, it is applicable to intent. There were irregularities that arose, machines not tallying, running out of paper ballots, etc. typical in races across the state and nation and not without resolution.

The people of Stone County have overwhelmingly voiced their desire to have a new election, of which both Todd and Lance agree is the best means of preserving the integrity of the election process. But since a primary tie has never occurred before in this country we are setting legal precedents in how we as the people of Stone County respond. Whatever the outcome of this tied race, it will go down in legal history becoming a requirement in law schools across the nation.

The SCEC will meet on Friday at 3 pm with the intention of certifying the election as a tie. Once the SCEC certifies the election it will then be sent to the Sec. of State for final certification then returned to the Stone County Democratic Committee (SCDC) who has five days in which to request Governor Beebe to allow the SCDC to either hold a special election or to choose a candidate by convention. It was clear at Monday's public SCEC and the required SCDC meeting that followed the people of Stone County believes another election to be the best resolution. The issue becomes is it legal since the laws are non specific to the primary election. Any alternative action considered seems abundantly clear would be struck down if it would disenfranchise voters such as drawing of lots or coin toss. While an action such as a special election would be an effort to support the vote and the voice of the people even if determined illegal under the present general election law guidelines it would likely stand under scrutiny of the courts due to the intent to uphold the right of the individual to vote.

The one thing that echoes in this for me is the voice of so many people who want to do the right thing, who want to preserve the right of the people to vote, to decide. Todd and Lance, they are good men who have worked together, attended church, funerals and weddings, friends, family within this extended community of people who may fight like cats and dogs to win an election, but will also fight to defend each other and the right of the people who cast their votes. This fight is not a fight between Todd and Lance, nor Democrats or Republicans; it is over resolving the tie and selecting a Democratic candidate for Sheriff. It is a fight for the voice of the people.

It is possible that if the Republican Party or any citizen chose to challenge the actions of the SCEC, the Republican candidate for Sheriff could end up on the general election ballot without an opponent. This would disable him, making him a lame duck Sheriff, something no citizen wants. Men and women have laid down their lives, paid in blood for us to have freedom, a choice, for our right to self govern, for our right to vote. I can not imagine any court in this land denying the voters the right to choose a candidate or the irresponsibility of the other party to challenge the right of the people to vote. With over 35 years of politics under my belt, and a life time of living with back room politicking, I know shady when I see it. I am convinced, there was no intentional wrong doing by anyone involved in the Sheriff's election and that a new election is in order so that the people of Stone County will have a viable Democratic candidate in the November election. Stone County continues to make history one day at a time. We are lucky that we have two young men whose character and integrity are the hallmarks of this process. Regardless of the outcome we have every right to be proud of Todd and Lance, native sons and Stone County Citizens.

UPDATE: Lance won in a run off over Todd. The SEC selected Lance officially as the Democratic candidate of choice and he won 4-1 over the Republican candidate.

EIC Crew & The Timber Rattler

Ah Summer time. Sweet summer time. It's officially here along with the heat and humidity. Laughter and sounds of people talking interrupt the usually quiet areas of the creeks and swimming holes, birds chirping and water gurgling. The smell of roasting hot dogs and hamburgers on the grill fill the air. Yes, summer is here along with blackberries and watermelon, ticks, chiggers and snakes. Saturday the crew of Exploring Izard Co (.com) met up for an early morning excursion into what may be the pre-Civil War slave auction site of the Dillard family. A small cave, perhaps 2,000 sq feet partitioned into one large room and four small ones, it is a remarkable location that will now require extensive historical research to document. Will Dillard was one of the largest slave traders in the White River area. The 1837 Dillard Settlement at Round Bottom in Stone Co is on the National Registry of Historic Places. It is a far larger settlement than Wolf House from the same period. Will's sister Lucy Dillard married Henry Harris. Their home built by slaves in 1848, sits at the junction of 5, 9 & 14 at Allison and is presently owned by Guy and Liz Harris.

What may be the underground Dillard Slave Auction House
Denny Elrod (EIC) left, Larry Stroud (EIC-Batesville Guard) right

In spite of the damp air, sandy bottom and deadfall that has washed into the cave, it wasn't here that we encountered our baby Timber Rattler. Larry Stroud from the Batesville Guard who had joined us for this excursion had never seen City Rock Bluff, the large beautiful bluff off Culp Road that overlooks the river bottoms just north of present day Calico Rock. It was named not for the city of Calico Rock seen to the south, but for the bustling community of white people that inhabited the river bottoms on the 'civilized' side of the river (Izard Co) viewed by the Indians atop the bluff on the west side (Stone Co) 200 years ago. Calico Rock was settled long after the name was given the beautiful bluff, which is now part of Stone County's Ozark National Forest.

EIC Crew at City Rock Bluff

A little further down Culp Road lays Table Rock Cemetery. Being this close I wanted to go back by and get a photograph of Josiah "Jody" Rorie's headstone. A remarkable man who deserted the Confederate army, he was found, tried and pardoned then released back home to help his father and brothers make wagons for the cause of the South. Jody had been home only a few months when the Union soldiers attacked and burned Rorie's Mill. Believing the Rorie's also to be the source of the well hidden munitions efforts Absalom and his sons Andrew and Hezekiah were tortured and killed. Their arms were ripped from their bodies by horses pulling against each other. Little is known as to what Jody did to stop the killing, but three days later after burying his father and brothers and moving his entire family to safety near Big Flat, he joined the Union Army. Several of us drove up to the cemetery and walked it, looking through markers and cairns to locate Jody's grave. Recently decorated during Memorial Day weekend, I felt the pride of this small community for its heritage. The older marker was laying flat on the ground with a newer smaller one at the head. Reaching to move the flowers so I could get a better photo, everyone jumped back at the site of a snake curled up there.

True to character, this small baby Timber Rattler remained calm to our wide eyed, rapid back stepping heart beating panic. While I snapped photos one of the men offered to 'stretch him out' so we could see how big he was. This angered the docile little snake who quickly coiled again and began darting his head at me. He was about a foot and a half long. I think. The Timber Rattlesnake is one of the most venomous snakes in Arkansas. Its habitat runs all the way to New Hampshire, where less than 25 are now known to exist. Considered an endangered snake it is protected in most states other than Arkansas and carries a huge penalty if killed. A shy snake they will not generally even move when encountered. Laying on a foot trail, they will remain still and often will not strike even if stepped on.

Their primary food is rodents and birds. There is a balance in our ecosystem as these snakes, like the King and Black snakes, also eat other snakes. The venom of the rattler is meant to disable its prey. Slow to grow many reach as much as 5 ft in length and live 20-25 yrs. The females deliver live birth litters of 8-10 babies. Because these snakes lay motionless as a means of self protection, it also makes them incredibly vulnerable to humans, who in their fear, just want to kill them. Timber Rattlers den in the winter, but don't really hibernate like most people believe. In the spring, they emerge from these underground tunnels, often old animal burrows to begin their basking in the sun and search for food. When out hunting for prey, they may travel as much as three miles. This travel makes them most vulnerable to humans as they are creatures of habit and where clear cutting of timber, construction of new homes and other actions by man change their topography they become confused and may end up in a flower bed near a house, a place normally they would never go. People who kill these and other venomous snakes love to tell tales of how they saved the community from this serpent. As one entomologist says, "The logic of killing one of these snakes is about as reasonable for you to go out and destroy every knife and fork in your community due to the potential danger they hold."

Babies are generally born in the winter in the dens in order to give them a period of growth before emerging into the thick forested, rocky terrains they call home. This baby Timber Rattler is distinguished by his button rattle that as yet can make no noise, and its large head compared to its neck diameter. Often known as the "Gentleman Caller" because they alert you that they are coming, the rattlesnakes are also one of the most feared and misunderstood snakes. Arkansas has a number of other poisonous snakes that unlike the Timber Rattler aren't afraid of people. My niece Josie Phillips nearly died after having been bitten by a copperhead at a picnic table at Blanchard a few summers ago. Although rattlers have the worst reputation, they do not hang out near the water nor play dead. Nor will they open their mouths and lunge without provocation and they rarely even attempt to bite unless startled or harassed. They do not chase people and in fact will retreat quickly if allowed. Any story told of an aggressive rattler without provocation is merely a tale. Now, will they strike and try to defend themselves against a stick, shovel or hoe. This baby rattler was highly irritated at our prodding and efforts to 'stretch him out' to get a better photo. He had remained still when my fingers brushed against him as I removed the flowers. It was me the aggressor that wanted him to show his stuff. I don't know the roll this snake plays in the ever tenuous environmental balance we live in, but I do know, not unlike the lengths to which a man will go seeking freedom when enslaved, this little snake was ready to fight the odds to survive, rather befitting he was warming himself on the head marker of Jody Rorie.

Bill Wallace - Frontiersmen & Ferrymen
1848 Andrew & Lucretia Jeffery Harris Homestead
1852 Miles & Sarah Williams Jeffery Homestead

A ferry man, Billy Joe Wallace is one of the last of the real river men. In fact, in the state of Arkansas he is the last ferryman on the White River. Before they were replaced by bridges, he operated both the Sylamore and Guion ferries. The Guion ferry was to become the last cable ferry in the state, operating until completion of the bridge in 1990. Once the major means of crossing our nation's rivers, today, Peel Ferry at Bull Shoals Lake is the only remaining ferry in Arkansas.

Bill Wallace on right, Stone County background

Bill saw many ebbs and flow in the rise of the river during his years as a ferry man. But in 1982 aboard the Guion Ferry he rode out what remains one of the largest and most significant floods in Arkansas history. He was given a citation for meritus service to the state following the December flood in which he remained on the ferry for over 36 hours. As the river rose to the levels of the cables crossing the river, debris caught and snapped first one then the other of the ferry aprons. Townspeople gathered on both sides of the river anxiously watching the rising river offering prayers for his safety. Ending up on the Izard County side of the river half way to the railroad tracks high upon a pile of sand and debris, Bill was credited with having saved the ferry at great risk to himself. Descended from the first families who settled the White River although rarely witnessed today, this kind of courage and willingness to do what it takes in the face of great odds was characteristic of the early settlers. The Jeffery, Harris and Ward families of whom Bill is

147

descended are rich with stories of survival. The first of the Harris' arriving in the White River Valley around 1820 settled near Kickapoo Bottoms, named for the Kickapoo Indians whose major settlement was there, just north of Jack's Boat Dock. Henry Britton Harris, son of Lucretia Jeffery and husband Andrew Criswell Harris, married Nancy Avey, grand daughter of Chief John Wolf Cornstalk and great niece of Chief Peter Cornstalk/85, a brother to her grandmother. She is the daughter of Peter "Pest"Avey and Mary Jane George. Her grand father Chief John Wolf Cornstalk Avey/92 married his first cousin Nancy Avey/1805 daughter of Peter Cornstalk/55, (sister to Chief Peter Cornstalk 1785), a double lineage of Chief of the 20 Nation Confederacy, Young Hokolesqua Cornstalk 1710-1777.

Lucretia Jeffery Harris 1827-1892

Bill is the gggggg grandson of Jane Mason Jeffery, the Dr. Quinn Medicine Woman of the river valley. Along with her husband and family she arrived in the White River Valley in 1816. She treated whites, blacks and Indians without regard to race or ability to pay. This eventually led to her being thrown out of her home by her husband following a stormy night in which she crossed a swollen White River into the Indian reservation of present day Stone County to treat an Indian woman who was giving birth. Upon her return home, her husband James threw her out. She lived the rest of her life between her son Daniel Jeffery and wife Mary Bowcock, a Native American and her daughter Lavina and her husband Thomas Culp. When she died she was buried on a lone knoll near Daniel's home, "The Old Perrin Place" present day farm of Ken and Sue Coon. The Coon's were vital in the restoration and cleanup of the small cemetery that is the final resting place of Jane Mason Jeffery.

Bill is the ggggg grandson of Jane Mason Jeffery – his father Ray Wallace is descendant of her son of Jehoiada Jeffery through his son Miles Jeffery. Bill's mother Faye Ward is descendant of her son Jehoiada Jeffery through his daughter Lucretia.

The triple pen barn 1852 Miles Jeffery Homestead NRHP
Owned by the Hinkle family

Bill was born in 1949 at the 1852 homestead of Miles Jeffery near Livingston Creek, which is on the National Registry of Historic Places. The triple pen barn one of only a few surviving in our nation received severe damage in the ice and snow storms of 2008 and is seriously in need of repair. It is currently owned by the Hinkle family. The 1848 homestead of Lucretia and Andrew Harris is located in "Forest Home" the original name of Optimus. The home and most of the outbuildings are in remarkable condition owned and cared for by the children and grandchildren of Faye Ward Wallace. Once one of the richest and best homes in the valley, it became a center for preachings, weddings and a place to be cared for when illness hit. Thus many of the major members of this large family have died there, among those Polly, widow of Jehoiada 11/7/1874, Lucretia 1892 and Nancy Avey Harris 1938.

The Ward families are members of the Shawnee tribes who settled Stone County during the 1817 Indian reservation at present day Optimus, descendants from Bryant Ward and Anna Pekowi. Bryant's 2nd wife was his niece, Nancy Ward, daughter of Tame Doe (Catherine Carpenter) and Francis "Chief Fivekiller" Ward, from whom the Chitwoods and Fulks of Stone County are descended. Following the death of her husband Kingfisher, Nancy Ward became the Joan of Arc of the Native Americans, fighting to defend her family and tribe she remains known in U.S. history as The Beloved Woman of the Cherokee.

Bill Wallace on the porch
1848 Lucretia Jeffery & Andrew Harris homestead

Prior to 1830, the east side of the river was "civilization" while the west side, present day Stone County, was Indian Territory extending all the way to the western border of present day Oklahoma. For whites to enter or live in the reservation they had to establish trade with the Indians, marry an Indian or be part Indian themselves. This requirement was met by the most courageous and adventuresome of the early settlers and set in motion a relationship and blending of cultures that created the Ozark culture.

The Jeffery, Wards and Harris families are not only some of the oldest families in the White River valley but also one of the largest and most respected having held numerous positions in the state legislatures, house and senate, and as county clerk's and lawmen they helped birth the Ozark culture. Found in our music, our dance and the way we live our lives, the strength and courage of our people, our willingness to do what is right in the face of great odds, remains. The majority of the descendants remain committed to the preservation of not only their history but the history of the White River Valley which is evidenced in the 1848 Henry & Lucy Dillard Harris House at Sylamore, the 1836 A.C. Jeffery House at Mt. Olive and the 1848 Andrew & Lucretia Jeffery Harris House at Forest Home.

Slave pegs holes are found throughout Stone County in the homes, barns and outbuildings – Miles Jeffery Homestead

But when our historic homes and barns fall into the hands of families and individuals who lack the foresight of preservation and respect for their own families there is little that can be done. The destruction through inattentiveness and intention are clear indications that money does not breed class. A great many of our homes are being bulldozed by local land owners such as the NRHP Noah McCarn Home. I personally hope that outsiders will move in that have the education and foresight to buy up these pieces of land and preserve those places as they are the key to greater individual and regional wealth through historic tourism trails not unlike Lancaster County, PA, Amish Country and the rock walls that are protected and stand as proud testaments to our country in Vermont and Kentucky. History can not be replaced. The 1837 Dillard Settlement and the 1852 Miles Jeffery Homestead are two of the most remarkable places yet to be realized in Stone County, far more significant and larger than Wolf House Settlement.

People move to Stone County, to Mountain View because they love how it feels behind the times. They can't really put their finger on it. They aren't really able to define it, but they know there is something special here. The blending of the Blacks, the Native Americans, the Scots, Irish and British who first settled this valley birthed our culture. The clannish way in which we still live our lives, defend our neighbors and want to know who your people are is ingrained in us from the seeds of who we are, established by the first people who came here it was a necessary skill of survival. As new people come here, move here because they love what we have, they also bring new ways, outside influences of how we can do things differently, like how they did it where they come from. Many are welcomed and seen as a better way of doing things because they embody a respect for our traditions, our

151

heritage and the way we live our lives that brought them here in the first place. They strengthen us and this place we call home. There are also those who just see this place as ripe for change, for development, for festivals that bring crowds that may be short lived and good for a few businesses for a day or two, helping them survive economically but are held without regard to the heritage, to proven means of survival, bringing influences that are like new by passes and super centers that ultimately bring death to the small towns of our nation if not managed correctly. Not unlike Jehoiada Jeffery whose first home on the White River above Sylamore was fashioned as a small fort, with garrison breaks to fend off those that would do him and his family harm, it is perhaps more important today than it was 200 years ago that we know who our neighbors are and if in fact, they are neighborly at all.

Parker Jaynes - Hollandsworth Family Line 1836-2010 & St. James (Jesse James – Cole Younger Gang)

Parker at the Hollandworth Graves at "The Buckhorn"

Parker Jaynes has roots in the White River valley that run deeper than most with multiple sides of his family settling in this valley long before the Civil War. The Lancaster's arrived as early as 1824 when it was still part of the Cherokee Indian reservation. In 1836, Jacob Hollandsworth is first recorded as being in Lawrence County which included everything north of the Arkansas River. The great grandson of Don Dink Lancaster and MaeDell Hollandsworth, Parker Jaynes was born and raised in Stone County. In 2003 he graduated MVHS and in 2006 he received his degree in Business from the University of Central Arkansas in Conway. Hired by Luby's he managed a large restaurant in Little Rock for a year before transferring to College Station, Texas. In July of last year he was presented with an opportunity to purchase Country Time, formerly Joshua's in Mtn View which allowed him to "come home." He has set out to make Country Time the "Cracker Barrel" of Stone County and the unofficial tourist center, with flyers, brochures and photographs depicting the beautiful scenery and celebrating the rich heritage we have. Shortly after opening, Parker joined with the Nikki Lee Atwell Foundation, a non profit supporting Arts, Music and Humanities in Stone, Izard and Independence County, by providing wall space for the Mountain Music Project, a photographic display of past and present musicians which includes many members of his family.

The skies were threatening rain as Parker and I took off down to St. James (The Buckhorn), the first settlement of Stone County and the place where his ancestors entered Heaven. Its one thing to have friends you have known all your life, completely another to have families and a community that know you in that way. Legacies and lives intermingled giving the definition of family and neighbor a deeper meaning. Although not related by blood, as far as we know, our families have known each other and been friends for over 160 years, sharing births, weddings, deaths, droughts and feasts. Stone County is one of those rare places where understanding the family relationships isn't something you can learn in a book, nor is the respect that people have for our ancestors who carved out this place. Many of the early settlers starved to death or died of yellow fever from the mosquito infested swamps. A great number left for the Civil War with many returning wounded unable to care for their families others never coming back all in order to own a piece of ground, to have a home and family. The majority of people in the White River Valley are descendants of white, blacks and Indians (Metis). It is the longevity of the relationships, the blending of these ethnicities found in our dance, music and the way we live our lives that created the Ozark culture and continues to make Stone County unique.

Born in 1792 in Patrick, Virginia, Jacob Hollandsworth married Lydia Fuson Feb 28, 1817 in Wilson, Tenn. They are recorded as living in Wayne Co, TN in 1840 but are also found on land documents dating 1836 in Lawrence County, Arkansas. Shortly after 1840 they were residing at The Buckhorn, present day St. James, Younger Access on the White River. Although much is written regarding the first settlement of Batesville, Independence County and later Izard County by the Lafferty family most of it is inaccurately attributed to Lorenzo Dow Lafferty who would have been a child in 1810. Lorenzo was the youngest son of John Lafferty who first arrived here as early as 1797 and in 1810 applied for the first land patent in what is now Stone County, St. James/Younger Access – "The Buckhorn". Perhaps it is because Stone County has been Lawrence County, Independence and Izard, these counties lay claim to the Lafferty settlement. In 1828 when the reservation ended and the Indians were once again facing having their land taken from them, most chose white names and stayed, assimilating and blending with the other settlers to create the culture that we know today. Between 1820 and 1850 people with land grants from the war of 1812 predominately Irish and Scottish immigrants began making their way west, crossing the Ohio and Mississippi Rivers to settle the White River valley. A great number of those people including the Hollandsworth's came from Wayne County, Tenn.

The 5th grand parents of Parker Jaynes, Jacob Hollandsworth and his wife Lydia had 10 children. Maleatha b 1821 and Alaminta b 1824 both died in July 28, 1854, some stories say the sisters drown in the White River near their home, one trying to save the other. Manerva Hollandsworth b 1825 married James Harvey Collum and had one son James W. Collum in 1850; Margaret b 1828 married Joel A Massey. They lived and raised their six children in the Franklin Township of Stone County in an area that is still known as Massey Hollow east of Guion Road. Joel died during the Civil War in 1864. Margaret then married her brother in law James Harvey Collum after the death of her sister Manerva. They had one son, Robert E Collum. Mahala b 1829 married Richard Summers Decker. Rhoda b 1832 no info; Emarantha b 1834 married Zahariah Ford, home at St. James on NRHP. Isaac born 1837 married Sara E. Lancaster; Tabitha born 1840 no info and Jacob born 1845 married Malinda Decker.

(gggg) Rev. Isaac Hollandsworth served The Buckhorn, St. James as a minister. His son (ggg) Cantrell Bethel Hollandsworth married Martha Pruett from Pruett's Island south of The Buckhorn on the White River. Their son (gg) Harvey Andrew Hollandsworth b 1899 died 1934 married Mytrie Caldone Cannon. Before his death they had their only child, MaeDell Hollandsworth who remembers how her life changed when her daddy died. Living in Oklahoma she and her momma returned home to Arkansas to be near family. "I was born a very long time ago," MaeDell offers. MaeDell was included in Voices of Our People published 2009, available at Country Time. MaeDell's daughter Chloeann Lancaster married Gary Don Stewart, their daughter Shelly Stewart Jaynes is Parker's mother.

Parker is a hard working young man with a history that is richer than the food he serves. During the Civil War after repeated droughts and record winter colds our fore fathers ate roots and bark from the trees still many people starved to death. An agrarian people, we have grown up with gardens, orchards, hunting, fishing and slaughtering our own meat. A way of life that is common to us; smoking and salting meat and canning. We render lard, keep our bacon drippings, fry foods and eat too much starch. We no longer eat bark and roots but we also no longer walk every where we need to go, or labor in the fields from sun up to sun down. Health activists would have us stay away from fast food places like McDonald's, which by the way has brought 60 much needed jobs to our community (and probably the buffet line at Country Time). They would have us eat whole grains, nuts and fruit's, perhaps get out and walk a little more, enjoy a granola bar which many say is a bit like eating sticks and twigs with a little fruit, if you're lucky. But I say, they never tried venison, fried green tomatoes or blackberry cobbler! Our lives have changed, and sometimes, the more we change, the more we remain the same.

St. James – The Story of Jesse James

Local stories say the Younger and Ford families of St. James are "kin" to the Jesse James – Cole Younger Gang, and that St. James was named in honor of Jesse James. From the days of the Lafferty settlement in 1810 through the Civil War, the community was known as Buckhorn, complete with postal delivery and the "Battle of the Buckhorn". The period of time immediately following the Civil War was a difficult time throughout the south with people starving. It was particularly bad in Arkansas which remained under a state militia until 1903, its' first 3 governors, northerners. In order to survive, people made a kind of mash out of the soft meat of trees to have something to eat. But the community of Buckhorn had something other communities didn't have, their own "Robin Hood," brothers, Frank and Jesse James, along with Bob, Cole, John and Jim Younger. They had met serving under Quantrill's guerillas, the Missouri Militia Home Guard.

In June 1862 Henry Younger, father of the Younger brothers was shot and killed while riding in a buggy near Kansas City by Federalists. A young Charlie Pitts found the body. Frank had just joined Quantrill when on May 25, 1862 Union soldiers roughed up his mother, hang his step father who didn't die and beat up his younger brother Jesse. In Aug. 1863 a building in Kansas City where wives and children of Confederate's were being held captive collapsed killing and injuring almost everyone. Aug 21 Quantrill's troops went on a rampage randomly striking Lawrence, Kansas destroying it and killing 183. A young sharp shooter Jesse joins the guerillas. In May 1865 Quantrill and his men are ambushed by Union soldiers. Quantrill is shot and Jim Younger captured. Jesse tries to surrender but is shot by Union soldiers while riding holding a white flag. He escapes and survives avowing revenge. The Civil War ends. The gang sees a ravaged countryside, families starving and a continued Union militia ruling throughout Arkansas and areas in Western Missouri loyal to the South in large part due to the Missouri Home Guard. Over the next 10 years they robbed banks, trains and stagecoaches across the nation.

Rare 1870's photo of Jesse James Gang taken near Wild Haws

On Jan 15, 1874 they rob a stagecoach in Hot Springs, AR then travel back to Missouri through the Buckhorn. A month later in Feb they rob the Craig & Son General Store in Bentonville, then head to Hot Springs where they took up residence. In March in Missouri John Younger is killed by a Pinkerton agent. Jim located Cole and Bob at the Buckhorn. It is believed that the above photo was taken in March 1874 at the Buckhorn, or Wild Haws Landing (now Guion). The men reportedly stayed with a number of people including Zachariah Ford whose house is at St. James is on the National Registry of Historic Places and Wimps Canard, whose home before being torn down sat near the Turner/Mingues Rd on Dugan Stretch, at the location of Johnny Ray Thomas' sawmill and Cagle Canard's house on Guion Road near Roaring River. Stories include how the gang hid horses in barns and caves including the Arnold Hollow Cave off Guion Rd, Ennis Cave (St. James) and a cave near Piney Creek in Izard Co. In April Jesse married Zee Mimms, they headed to Texas again coming through the Buckhorn. On each trip, stories go that Jesse would leave money and goods for the people of the community, whether it was for pay off for their stay, for their silence or true "Robin Hood" conduct, the community was soon referred to as "St. James." Local stories support that when Jesse traveled through he used the names of John Davis Howard and Thomas Howard. On April 2, 1882 Jesse James was killed in his home during breakfast by brothers Bob and Charlie Ford. In the Fall of 82 Frank James is prosecuted by William Wallace for bank robbery and murder. He is acquitted after only 3 and a half hours jury deliberation. Two years later Missouri Gov. Crittenden dismissed all charges against Frank James.

Jesse and Zee had two children who survived to adulthood, Jesse Edward and Mary.

In 1899 Jesse Jr. wrote a book about his father that paints a much different picture than those typically told. Jesse Jr married Stella McGown and they lived out their lives in California where they had four daughters – Jesse m Mervyn Baumal, Lucille m Frank Lewis, Josephine m Ronald Ross and Ethel married Calvin Owens. As a youth Jesse went by the name of Tim Edwards. He became a lawyer in Orange County, California. He died in 1951. His youngest and last living daughter Ethel died in 1991. His grandchildren, the great grand children of Jesse James live primarily in Huntington Beach, California.

Mary Susan James married Henry Barr. They lived their lives in Kansas City, Missouri. They had 4 children, their only daughter died at birth. Their sons, Lawrence m Thelma Duncan, Forrester m Gertie Essary, and Chester married Beatrice Holloway. Both Chester and Lawrence died in 1984. Their mother Mary died in 1935. Mary's grandchildren, the great grand children of Jesse live primarily in the Kansas City metropolitan area, in both Kansas and Missouri.

Frank James married Anna Ralston; they had one son Robert Franklin who died on the James family farm in Kearney, Missouri in 1959. Robert married twice and had only one son.

Whatever the relationship between the Stone County Younger's and the Jesse James – Cole Younger Gang – they will be remembered in the town of "St. James."

Tristin Lancaster - Sylamore Creek Massacre

Tristin Lancaster is the youngest grand daughter of Harold and Freda (Leonard) Lancaster, owners of Pine Wood Cabins along with their son Todd, daughter Tammy and each of their grand children. Tollie Leonard, Freda's dad set a standard for excellence both in the rock masonary in Stone County and as a caller for square dancing, a legacy that continues to be seen and heard throughout our county. In 2009 Tristin graduated MVHS and is currently attending Arkansas Tech. When I caught up with her, she was at work at Pine Wood Cabins, something every grandchild has been required to do. The Lancaster's opened Pine Wood cabins in 1998. Each cabin pays tribute to the history of Stone County by showcasing members of their family and the community. The Lancaster's arrived in Round Bottom long before the Civil War. Tristin is the great grand daughter of Russell Dink Lancaster, gg of Green Dink Lancaster and ggg of Frederick S. Lancaster (1828-1874) whose barn at Round Bottom is on the National Registry of Historic Places. Square nails and slave pegs demonstrate it is a pre-Civil War barn. Lancaster's Hardware opened its doors for business in 1898 and is the oldest remaining family run business in Mtn View.

Pine Wood Cabins office, Tristin seated on steps.
Expositor Newspaper & Stone County Recorder 1800's

We are a people with routines that are simple and predictable, swimming in the same place our parents and grandparents did and church on Sunday. So, it wasn't surprising when J.C. found me Thursday night at Kin Folks BBQ to go with him to hear some folks play music. The Beal family was a special group, people who have been coming here for nearly 25 years making it their destination for their yearly family reunion. The reunion has become so large that family members can no longer all stay in one place. In fact, they have 23 of the Pine Wood Cabins along with additional rooms at local hotels as well as the bed and breakfast. Friends they have made over the years now join them like Brenda Moss from Glenwood, AR (out near Hot Springs). Almost a local, you can buy "Brenda's Old Fashioned Chocolate Gravy Mix", at the Ozark Folk Center and Pine Wood Cabins. This wonderful concoction takes root in a time when we were owned by France and the War of 1812. Anyone who has ever visited France or a French bakery and eaten Pan Au Chocolate' realizes the connection right away. When the French came here, they brought their chocolate but in order to make it last, they diluted it, making it into gravy. Eaten with fresh bread that is dipped, torn or smothered is a personal choice, but when available the soldiers mixed with it a bit of butter in order to supplement their diets with much needed fat. It remains a favorite that 200 years later is distinctively Southern.

As we arrive, the Beal family is singing and dancing on the porch. A slight rain is falling. Some people have taken out their umbrellas. Others stand almost without notice drowning in the music, getting soaked in the rain. Gary Beal wants us to hear a song about the Mingo Swamp Massacre which occurred during the Civil War near their home in Arab (pronounce A–Rab), MO written by his brothers Jimmy and Jesse and put to music by David Garner. An incredibly emotional song sung with deep voices and haunting harmony, it brings tears to the listeners. As 12 year old Jennifer makes her violin cry it is the moans of the dying men you hear.

On Feb 3, 1863 Union Maj. Reeder in pursuit of Confederate Capt. Daniel McGee heard they were in the area of the nearby swamp. With 40 of his best men and horses, they rode to the farm of Simeon Cato, Capt. McGee's uncle, where they found the men. Although the official report by Maj Reeds reports "We took no prisoners amongst them, as I had previously been ordered not to do so," it also says that the whole band was exterminated, "with 9 killed instantly" including Cato and McGee, and "with 20 who fell mortally wounded". Notorious Missouri Bushwhacker Samuel Hildebrand who was not harmed during the massacre told that McGee's men were unarmed, feeding their horses and resting when the Union attacked. They stood over Capt. McGee and shot his body repeatedly until his entire midriff was cut through. Stripped of his clothes, his bloody uniform was hung as a "trophy" and as a warning to other Southern sympathizers at the courthouse in Fredricktown. An investigation confirmed portions of 29 skeletons in a single mass grave with pieces of Confederate uniforms and buttons found.

Not unlike the Mingo Swamp Massacre, the Sylamore Creek Massacre of Stone County ended with 47 young men of the Izard County Peace Society (which included most of present day Stone County) enlisting in the Confederate Army. Arkansas had voted initially not to leave the Union, but later on a vote of 69-1 joined the Southern effort which had more to do with the rights of states than slavery. The issue was economic, cotton in the south and factories in the north. The north did not want the south to have the freedom to sell their cotton to the highest market, which at that time was

Europe. Most people are unaware of the fact that the north did not immediately free their slaves either before or after the Civil War. A system of indenturing was put into place that allowed those born after the Civil War to work in trade to purchase their family members freedom. The Izard County Peace Society (different than the Home Guard) was formed of Union and or anti-War sympathizers. Governor Rector ordered that an investigative committee be put in place to learn the identities of these sympathizers and "put the matter to rest." This is the same Governor that was attorney to notorious Bill Dark, who as Governor got him out of jail with a commission to seek out northern sympathizers in the northern counties including what is now present day Stone County. For the most part, it didn't matter how. Between Nov 18 and 28, 1861 the Izard County Investigative Committee arrested 103 men, mostly boys. On Nov 28, 1861, 47 young men volunteered for duty with the Confederacy. The other 56 men who refused – 3 are recorded as having been hang, the others were shot. Those bodies were not claimed by family members too afraid of being suspected of being Northern sympathizers. They were buried in a mass grave reported to be near the home site of Hale Dobbins. The Harris house, later owned by the Dobbins family, was the most prominent home in the community. It was used by the Confederate officials for such meetings and commandeered by the Union as well on at least two different occasions. The community of Sylamore (present day Allison) was so outraged that Col. J.J. Kemp of the Arkansas Militia was called out less than a month later to contain the people who were threatening an insurrection. Official Confederate records do not list the reasons for this threat of uprising simply that it took 40 to 50 days to gain control. According to several family letters and Mister Ches Beckham, the Sylamore Creek Massacre set the stage for many people in this area to vehemently take sides, turning family and neighbors against each other thus making them easy prey for the likes of Bill Dark, who operated much like an early CIA operative he was allowed extreme measures with little oversight.

When the Civil War started most of the fighting actually occurred in Missouri which was a split state. In 1861 alone of the 157 engagements and battles listed in the Army Register, 66 were in MO, 31 in VA, 28 in West VA, 12 KY and the remaining 19 in NM, FL, TN, SC, MD, NC and TX. Although not as critical to the overall success or loss of sides, not major battles per se, Missouri saw more action than VA and WV combined. North Arkansas in close proximity suffered greatly. Much fighting occurred during the Civil War that was not reported as battles nor even skirmishes due to the fact most of the fighting was done by individuals attacking the Federalists. The numbers of men who were wounded or killed were often inaccurately recorded if recorded at all. In a careful review of Civil War records and death dates, over 256 men were killed in the White River Valley of Stone and Izard County that were not considered soldiers that was 'war' related. Therefore the stories held by the families become a vital part of what we know such as the burning of Rorie's Mill and the torture and murder of Absalom and sons. Just as with any oral history with little written documentation, over time, they can change but are still one of the most reliable means we have of understanding our people and the sacrifices that were made counted in the lives affected by the Civil War. The war had the effect of brutalizing its participants. Men who only months before sat in church pews, singing hymns found themselves capable of unspeakable acts as the war swept people up into its nightmares. Homes were burned, businesses destroyed, livestock slaughtered, once fertile farms overtaken by weeds and saplings. Frequently the women, young boys and old men left behind fled to safer areas moving across state lines between Missouri and Arkansas.

Buddy and John Dink Lancaster (Parker's great grand father)

When people talk of the war here, they still mean The Civil War. And music has remained a vital part of the lives of the people then and now expressing sorrow, heartbreak, grief, love and happiness in song. Will the Circle Be Unbroken is a Civil war song, a blend of the whites and blacks working alongside each other in the fields of the Ozarks. In 1908 it was attributed to Ada Habersham. However, it has been handed down in family bibles of the Ozarks long before Miss Habersham of England was ever born. It is suspected that Miss Habersham received the beautiful words of the song in a letter from a relative here.

Tristin's great uncles, Buddy and John Dink Lancaster, Parker's great grand father, pictured above, brothers to her grandpa Harold were incredible musicians. From just over the state line in Missouri, the Beal family is also incredible. They hold a yearly gospel singing the last Saturday in September on the Beal family farm at Arab, MO not far from the Mingo Swamp site. Grandma Beal, 79, who raised 8 children, prepares all the food. Upwards of 3 or 4 hundred people attend. Every Sunday she cooks dinner for at least 25 of her children and grandchildren. Tonight, in the drizzling rain a soft light illuminates the porch where the men, women and children united in more than their voices transport us to a different place and time. Although no longer traveled by foot, horse or wagon, the distance between here and there, now and then, is not all that much. We sing. We worship. We fight when needed and always we remain family, no mater what side of the fight you are on or in which churches pews you pray.

The Beal Family

THE MINGO SWAMP MASSACRE By Jesse Beal

This tale I tell, it's sad, but true.
These folks are kin to me and you.
They lived, they loved, they worked, they cried.
This tale I tell is how they died.
At the old Mill Dam, they forged across.
The soldiers came, their cause was lost.
To the Mingo Swamp, they made their way…
To hide in a house, that sealed their fate.
In the Mingo Swamp, the sympathizers died.
The soldiers ran into the field to hide.
Blood was spilled on the ground that day …
Of babes and men, and they left them lay.
To Greenbriar Hill, they were carried away.
Twenty-nine souls, to one lonely grave.
Above Cato Slough, their fate was sure…
The Mingo Swamp Massacre.
This tale I tell, it's sad, but true.
These folks are kin to me and you.
They lived, they loved, they worked, they cried.
This tale I tell is how they died.

Carl Gayler – "Gayler"

It's been much too hot this week, rain is forecast and should it drizzle or downpour more than welcome. I took off with my grandson Denali, and father and mother in law, Carl and Naomi (Hedges) Gayler, his great grand parents, down to the old home place on South Sylamore Creek. When I was a kid, Gayler Road was gravel. It ran behind the City Hall all the way past the Drive-In to the creek then up the mountain to the road that came in from Sylamore. The road from Sylamore to Fifity Six was one and a half cars wide. If you met someone, it required that one of the cars pull over. Gayler Road present day Hiway 87 was the preferred road between the forest and Mtn View. In 1974 during the opening of Blanchard Caverns, they completed the bridge over the White River and made a new bigger better road to Fifty Six. When they paved Gayler Road, they eliminated the steep climb after crossing the bridge on the creek just below Gayler Cemetery. The cemetery established in the 1856 sits next to the home of Don and Suzi Mellon. The land was donated by Joe and Mary (Risner) Prichard who had migrated from Wayne Co, TN. They died in a flu epidemic in 1860 and are believed to be among the unmarked graves in Gayler Cemetery.

As we leave the cemetery he points to the rocks down below in the creek, beautiful in the hot summer sun, water cascading over them. He tells Denali about watching his momma and his grandma wash the family clothes in the creek. It was easier to take the clothes to the creek and hang them to dry on lines strung between the trees than it was to haul the water to the top of the hill. "Plus it was probably the best way to keep us kids entertained while work was being done. Then we'd help carry everything back up the hill to the house. I'm sure tuckered out from swimming and working, we were easier to handle."

Following the Civil War, Carl's Grandpa, James Perry Gayler, built his house in the valley there just west of where the road turned steep going up the hill towards Fifty Six. Carl was raised on the hill. He and his siblings would walk down the hill catching up with other kids walking to school or church. "Orbie Stevens lived across the big field" near Carl's grandparent's house, "and Bill Gayler he lived over there, Albert Sands lived up this hollow," Carl tells us pointing to the locations as we drive.

He remembers that the Sands would house the teachers for the school. This one year, "Albert he didn't much like the teacher. So he'd linger a bit and when the teacher had gone off to school Albert, he'd take out a glass of water and pour it in the bed making it look like the teacher was a bed wetter. Now after about 3 weeks of this, a new teacher was brought in," Carl says laughing.

In 1976 Carl and Naomi's son Ivan and I were married at Gayler at the old church/school. We have one daughter, Mariah, who lives in California. With great pride, our daughter chose for her son, Carl and Naomi's only great grand child, to carry the Gayler name.

Stopping at the old home place, all that remains is the old hand dug well. Denali lowers the rope and the coffee can bucket into the well coming up with mostly dredge, mud and muck, but still some water. They look around the well at the hand hewn rocks that after 150 years remains intact capable of providing good water. Carl figures the mud is from the deposits of the spring floods this past couple of years. He remembers flooding on the creek, but not like we've had. There was a lot of logging going on back then and people worked the creeks, keeping the road beds that ran up the creeks solid and maintaining the watering holes. With new roads and without rock movers, the creeks are becoming stagnant and foul. "We need a big rain to wash'em out," Carl says.

Denali & his great grandpa Carl Gayler

Carl is the 10th of 12 children born to Ira Owen and Zadie Dobbins Gayler, on September 16th, 1928 at "Gayler." In 1963 following the challenge of President John F. Kennedy to walk more, "Daddy, Ira Gayler, then 75 and Felix Wallace, 76 (descendant of Solomon Brewer) took the challenge to walk. They started at the Charley Smith store after he accused them of being soft. They walked down the (Gayler) road to where it joined Government (Blanchard) Road, off Government Mountain to Sylamore and back up the hill to Mtn View, 30 miles. They showed old Charley by doing it in 8 hours and 15 minutes, better time than most people could walk it today." I.O. Gayler was Stone County Judge for years, during which time he ordered the new state road signs for the county roads. Gayler Road came in mis-spelled with an "O" instead of an "E". Being the penny pincher he was it didn't matter if it was his dime or the county's, he wasn't returning them which has provided newcomers the ability to argue the spelling is with an O.

The (Calvin & Cassandra) Gayler family homesteaded the land which is now Branson, Missouri long before the Civil War. In an area off Lake Taneycomo high in the Branson Heights Bluff above the White River lays a cave which has become known as "Old Soldiers Cave." Calvin Gayler, 40, being a gun smith was highly sought after by both the North and the South during the war, which resulted in his home being burned on at least two occasions, one reportedly by the North and once by the South. Since they did not own slaves, it is presumed their sentiments may have actually been Northern. After the first burnout, not wishing to join either side, Calvin hid out in a cave not far away. His wife Cassandra Parrish Gayler would bring him food to the cave. Sometimes to an agreed spot due to the presence of soldiers in the area looking for munitions efforts spread out through the hills and caves, along the creeks and rivers between Branson and Sylamore. The Gayler family grew crops in the fields along the river. One of the sons was shot in ambush in an open field. His mother and his sister had to bury him by themselves. It is believed that the grave rests somewhere in those fields, now downtown Branson. The surviving son, James Barney Perry Gayler moved south to the Ozark hills of Stone County, homesteading South Sylamore Creek, known by locals as "Gayler."

The first post office was established at Gayler March 1, 1920 with Leonidas M Gayler as postmaster, followed by his brother David R Gayler. When discontinued the mail was sent to Sylamore. Re-established in 1929 with Ewing Thomas as the postmaster it remained open until 1941 at which time mail was sent to Mountain View. Places here are still known by the people who lived their lives there. Locals prove just how local they are when giving directions that include those old names, with reminders of turn right, where the tree was split by lightning. Carl never knew his grandpa. He died before Carl was born, but he remembers his grandma getting water from this well. As he and Denali return the bucket to the bottom of the well, I realize that as Carl tells Denali and me these stories, he is telling the stories he heard first hand from his grandma of what happened in the Civil War and the settling of this valley to his great grandson. I heard the stories from my great grand father John Chitwood who was born just after the Civil War. The passing of oral history of our families, our heritage is a priceless gift. I don't always find 'official records' to support the things that I write, but I listen and talk to the people who remember the stories that they were told by their grandparents, their great grandparents, of a time in our nation's history that is pre-Civil War. We are a people who understood the necessity to know our neighbors and ask of new comer's "who's your people." I encourage everyone to put down the cell phone, turn off the t.v., take a walk or drive to your neighbors, go for a visit. Sit on the porch and drink sweet tea and listen you'll be amazed what you learn about who you are.

Cassandra Ann Parrish & father Ira Owen Parrish
Cassandra – Mother of James Perry Barney Gayler

I am only able to take the Gayler line back to John, Calvin's father and have identified no Native American's in it. Yet. However on Amanda's line in the Parks family, we find a rich heritage of Native American's. Amanda Parks was 5/8th Metis/Thawikila (Father) and $1/8^{th}$ Chalakatha/Pekowi & Kishpoko/Black/Metis (Mother) making her 2/3

Cherokee. When figured with her husband's bloodline – their 12 children would have been $5/8^{th}$, just slightly over ½ Cherokee: Son Ira Owen Gayler $1/2^{th}$, Ira's son Carl Sevoy Gayler $1/4^{th}$, Carl's son Ivan $1/8^{th}$, Ivan's daughter's Mariah and Angelica $1/16^{nd}$ and our daughter Mariah's son Denali $1/32^{nd}$ Metis/Thawikila/ Chalakatha/Pekowi/ Kishpoko/Black

BLOODLINE of
Amanda Clementine Parks & James Perry Barney Gayler

AMANDA CLEMENTINE PARKS (5/8th Metis Thawikila Father's line
Father Robert H Parks 1810 (3/4 Metis/Thawikila)
Robert's Parents Phillip Parks (1/2 Metis) 1785 & Thawikila Woman 1781
Phillip Parks Father – John Parks 1760 Mother Maria Metis

      Although there are other "Indians" within the parental lines of both Mandy & James Perry the lineage that follows is only of the Parrish line they both share. They were $1/8^{th}$ Cherokee and descendants of the Royal Family of Native Americans in the Parrish line and 3rd cousins.

AMANDA "Mandy" PARKS   JAMES PB "Jim" GAYLER
Mother Rebecca Parrish 1824   Mother Cassandra Parrish 1820
Father George 1780   Father Ira Parrish 1790
Father George 1750   Father Meredith 1763
Parents George Parris 1720   Parents Richard Parris 1725
Cheeke Greenwood 1737   Preachy Greenwood 1735

**George/1720 and Richard/1725 were brothers. They married sisters Cheeke/1737 & Preachy/1735 making their children genetically like brothers and sisters. Their children were full blood Cherokee – bloodline Chalakatha/Pekowi & Kishpoko/Black/Metis, this makes both Mandy and Jim 1/8th Cherokee in the Parrish line. We find variations in the Parrish name as Pearis, Parris and Farris. It is likely that many of the Farris and Parrish's of Stone County are descendants of the same line. In the late 70's we find the "H" added in Census which was likely due to the census taker's own spelling of the name. Additionally sisters, Cheekee & Preachy were the children of John Greenwood and Ahneewakee Muskrat Moytoy (Ahnee Muskrat Moytoy – Royal Family of the Native Americans). John's father, Thomas Greenwood born in Ireland, was part of the 1730 delegation to King George II. The delegations portrait called the Trustee's of Georgia painting hangs in the British Royal Museum in London.

Carl tells great stories about growing up, like the one of his friend Albert. Stories of lives lived on Gayler Creek.

The Wilcox Skunk Farm

It's that time of year when sugar and spice fill the air. Smells like holiday food, pumpkin pie and vanilla cookies that evoke a warm feeling of family and friends. Once I was at my friend Rita's as she was cleaning her chicken house. The smell was sickening. I asked her, "How do you stand that smell?" Laughing she said, "Oh girl, that's the smell of money." Our sense of smell is an incredible thing. It has been linked to how we interpret situations and even fall in love. Most people are only familiar with skunks due to an otherwise pleasant drive being interrupted by the putrid smell of skunk spray emitted when they are frightened or killed, run over by cars. Native to North and South America skunks are distinctive to most people not only for their smell but for the white V striping down their backs. While the stripe can vary in width it can be long or short some skunks are entirely black, white or spotted like a Dalmatian. Constantly chasing after the beautiful kitty cat with whom he is in love Pepe LePew is perhaps the most famous skunk of all. Stone County fundamentally remains a farming and timber community even as we enter into the 21st century. But few people are aware of the variety of animals 'farmed' in the history of Stone County such as the "Wilcox Skunk Farm".

Around 1915, in the U.S. hunting and fishing clubs began to see muffs, caps, capes and collars and soon after ladies hats and gowns glistening with fur as an accessory. Soon skunk fur with its naturally glistening sheen and beautiful white stripe became highly sought after. Within a short time, contrasting furs mimicking the black white contrast of the skunk were being used including raccoon, fox, mink, marmot, ermine, sable, squirrel and others indigenous to the U.S. heightening the fur trade for the American frontiersmen. Modern fur designers continue the color contrasting that began with the use of the skunks. Bordering the National Forest, Stone County has always been a trapper's paradise with its abundant streams and rivers. Through the 1960's raccoon skins locally brought $35-70 dollars each, supplementing many Ozark family incomes. The Daniel Boone fever following the successful television series of the same name made real coonskin caps a must for both the re-enactors and traditionalists. A wave of nostalgia engulfed the nation with the 200 year anniversary of the American Revolution in 1976, which saw another huge burst in traditional furs and skins from the U.S. including skunk.

Stone County was not immune to the national fever of fur farms at the turn of the 20th century. In 1914, almost 100 years ago, George W. Wilcox had a large and successful skunk farm on Sylamore Creek specializing in the all black variety which brought more at the market. The black furs were prized and many farmers attempted to breed their skunks to produce the all black variety in greater abundance. The black furs were used to make the full length coats worn by both men and women accented by the contrasting white. The under fur of skunks which is thick and long wears well but back then had a minor problem that when damp or wet emitted a smell. Nowadays that has been eliminated.

George Wilcox and his family lived on South Sylamore Creek near the present day home of Jack Thomas, son of Jewell Gayler Thomas. Wilcox Drive, named for the family, traverses the ridge into the valley along the creek. The area of the creek remains known as Gayler Creek, settled by Perry Barney Gayler, son of "The Old Solider" Calvin Gayler who settled Branson, Missouri prior to the Civil War. Ewing Gayler and Andy Pitts, George's neighbors on South Sylamore (Gayler Creek), commended him for his special caging of the animals, similar to chicken coops. Most families had a few chickens for both eating and their eggs. The occasional chicken thief, primarily fox and bears, could wreck havoc on a family farm in seconds, but skunks along with weasels and mink, were known to consider the eggs a delicacy and could sneak in and out undetected cracking and eating the entire coop full of eggs in minutes. These days without the balance of natural predators and trappers, skunks, house cats, bob cats and other cats are destroying the quail and turkey populations by consuming the eggs and if missed, the young foul. Although both of my daughters are vegetarians, I like my fur coat, leather soled shoes and meat with my potatoes. I have cow and goat hides on my floors for rugs, leather covered chairs, pillows made of animal hides and skins of pheasants hanging to dry waiting on me to use them in head dresses, mandela's, talking sticks and staff's.

George Wilcox in 1914 sold nearly 1,000 skunk furs to merchant Ray Case who shipped them to New Orleans, with a final destination of Europe. Ray and his father George "Dick" Case ran the mercantile in Mountain View. Dorothy Hinkle of Mtn. View is a niece of Ray Case's. Case reported having bought 1800 local furs which set the area record in any one season. One of Case's shipping lists for the year included 1,175 possom hides, 300 skunk hides, 150 coon hides, 25 grey fox, 35 civit, 8 house cats and 9 mink totaling 1,700 at a value of $1,500. Prior to the Great Depression and the Wall Street Crash between 1910 and 1940, skunk farms were at their heyday.

Born in 1860 in Tennessee to Caleb Wilcox and Elizabeth Shell, George Washington Wilcox married Memma Ozilla Hartley, from North Carolina in 1890, daughter of Jasper Hartley and Nancy Dyer. George and his wife soon moved to South Sylamore (Gayler) Creek. They had 8 children: Alvin, Lillie, James, Martha "Mattie", William Jerry, Frankie, Anna and George Jr. In 1942 Memma died followed by George in 1945. Their son, William Jerry and his wife Margaret had 3 children that died as infants and are buried at Gayler Cemetery. Their children William Glen, Floyd, Grace and Vada were raised on the Gayler Creek in the area now bearing the name Wilcox Drive. William Glen married Eula Pierce of Mtn View. They had Barney, Ivan, Carl, Carolyn, Sue, Karen, Edna and Steve. Karen Wilcox Gilbert, great grand daughter of George and Memma still lives in Mtn View.

Laudis Brewer - Oga, Red Doors & Roastin' Ear Creek

These last few weeks, with record breaking heat, it's not hard to find people at home under the cool breeze of the fan or the creek, taking a dip in hopes of cooling off. Laudis Brewer born October 1925 to Dexter and Ethel Gammill Brewer was home where it was cool. He is the grandson of Solomon and Sarah Branscum Brewer and John and Martha Cooper Gammill. Along with the Steven's and Rorie's from Tennessee, these families arrived in Stone County long before the Civil War, homesteading land between Big Springs and Mill Creek.

Solomon Brewer Family
Solomon, Sarah, Dexter and Floyd, Willie and Oscar in back

Laudis was raised in the old log home that was known as the 'Jimmy George house'. Laudis begins his story; "During the Civil War it was the home of notorious Confederate outlaw Bill Dark and Addie George Dark. Now, think about it, I'm 85 years old this year, as a boy when my grandpa and grandma told me stories they were from 1935 back to 1850 before the Civil War. Aunt Sarah Rorie she lived to be over a hundred. She was born before the Civil War, died in the 1940's. Well the house was mostly a falling down log home by the time us kids came along. When daddy built the new house, he tore it down. Now they had been telling stories, I believe Uncle Floyd told it best I recall, about how the jawhawkers buried treasure somewhere near the Jimmy George house and just after the Civil War ended the law came searching for it. They looked in the caves, cut outs, overhangs and big holes, but they didn't find nothing. Us kids we looked all around, up and down and under as daddy tore it down, thinking we just might find some treasure. We didn't. But another time daddy had decided that we needed

171

more crop ground so we were out clearing for a field when I took the bucket down the hill to the creek to get water. I saw this little path through the woods that I'd never seen before. I got the water and went back up to where daddy was. He went back with me to see the path. We followed it through the woods away from the creek. We come upon this big hole in the ground. Now us boys we thought that we had found the treasure hole at the end of that path, so daddy he let us go get some digging tools. Of course, we didn't find nothing either. But when metal detectors came out, I was one of the first, along with Edwin Luther to have one. I went out to that hole and I passed it over and over and then, "Ting", off it went and my heart was a racin'. I thought I'd found me the treasure. I dug and dug and finally several feet down I come on a big log chain." Laudis laughs as he puts his hand over his chest holding his racing heart just as he might have over 70 years ago.

"Now are you talking about Big Springs or Onia," I ask. "No, Oga, O-G-A. It was the community closest to Big Springs, about a mile or two from Onia, take the first dirt road to the left past the church building at Big Springs." Laudis showed me a picture of the old building at Oga before it was torn down and explained right where it sat and that they had a post office. "Now one of them Union General's rode through here looking for Dark and his men, searching for the munitions that was being made in the caves on the creek, "Gunner Pool" now. He gathered everyone up and was a standing on the bank of Panther Creek at Oga. Mill Creek is a bit removed from there and wasn't no Roastin' Ear Creek until after the Civil War. This general was a tellin' everybody how they was gonna protect them from the likes of Bill Dark and his men and the other bad boys, when Bill Dark rode up as he was talking. Wasn't no one in that crowd about to say it was him because they knew that if they did, they might not be waking up from sleep the next morning. Bill Dark, he'd kill them so everyone stayed hush. Our families settled here long before the Civil War. Absolom Rorie had built a big two story saw mill and a grist mill on the creek so people started a calling it Mill Creek. In the war, the Union men tortured and killed Absolom and two of his boys, burning down both mills. Later on there was other mills around, Cooper's, Richardson's, so Mill Creek was a good name. People they feared both Bill Dark and the Federalists. Aaron Stevens he had the place on the other side of the mountain from Rorie's across Mill Creek. Sometime after the Civil War was over there was a huge flood, it opened up the side of the mountain over on the Stevens farm, flowed right through great Grandpa Jonas Brewers place carrying all of the roasting ears from both farms with it. That's what give Roastin' Ear Creek its name. Sad story, Joe Ward was a Confederate soldier married to Martha Snellgrove from over Big Flat way. Jody Rorie was married to her sister. He'd been let out of the army, wounded. He had traveled by train to Little Rock walking the rest of the way home in a pouring rain. He got to Mill Creek and it was surging, much too high to cross. So he sat down under a tree, leaned his gun up and they found him there, dead, probably not more than a stone's throw from home."

"What about Red Doors name," I inquire. "Now there are a couple different stories but the one that's repeated as the truth most often has two men, probably tipsy, making a challenge of the other one that they would kill the next man that come along. Well, that next man was my grandpa, George Cooper. They knifed him to death and then it's said that they rubbed the blood off their hands on the doors of the church. I reckon though that it was school house back then as the school's allowed circuit rider preachers to hold church in'em on Sunday. This was Blue Mountain district, so I reckon that the building that this happened at was most likely the school house, but everybody kept on a callin' it Red Doors Church and in 1881 about 5 or 6 years after Grandpa Cooper died, they officially named it Red Doors and joined the church association. Don't reckon anybody wanted any schoolin' there."

I listen to Laudis' stories, remembering that many lives have passed on but among us are people who hold first hand stories from the Civil War in their hearts and minds, words spoken to them by their grand parents, great grand parents. These stories passed down are the roots of who we are as a people, that which we find in us today that causes feet to tap to the music, voices unite in praise and rifles aimed with every intention of killing what's at the other end, man or beast. People that move here that take offense being recognized or labeled from "off" simply don't understand the heritage that defines the generations of people who arrived here carving out this place that so many now take for granted believing somehow that it just happened. The people who arrived here are important to our nation's history. Although their stories are not found in history books, it the lives of these pioneer families who gave us the values we hold sacred. It is their lives that birthed the Ozark culture. Their lives are felt in the way we live our lives, praise God, call our elders Mister and Miss and honor story tellers, the keepers of our history. In the tradition of our forefathers, Mister Laudis welcomes anyone to get out of this heat, turn off the t.v. and come sit a spell.

Laudis & Gladys - Sons & Daughters Sylamore Creek

As the 1800's approached, many of the leaders of the Native Americans understood the narrowing chances of survival as a culture. The Cornstalks and Moytoys were the last of the free natives east of the Mississippi to try to stop the encroachment of the whites. Many if not the majority of the Shawnee, Creek and Cherokee simply faded into the pioneer communities of the late 1700's early 1800's. The intermarriages of the whites with the royal families of the native American's, gave Stone County, the Avey's, Ward's, Logan's, Watt's, Fulks', Adam's, Park's, Parris/Parrish', Gayler's, Brewer's, Bean's, Harris' and many others who chose to settle the White River Valley. Along with the arriving immigrants, most Native Americans spoke broken English which provided a mutual ground as they all fought to survive. In Arkansas until 1956 when the last great 'relocation' occurred, it was illegal for Native Americans' to own land. For more than the

Native Americans denying ancestry was a way of life here in the Ozarks. Many of the British who had fought in the American Revolution did not want to return to England told they were Scot-Irish. The people who settled here are a clannish people who for over 200 years have survived in this place by knowing who people are.

Laudis with his only daughter Gladys "Punkin" Brewer Wallis

Laudis Brewer's great grand parents Jonas Brewer and Margret Brewer married in 1834. Jonas was the son of George and Jane Butler Brewer and Margret was the daughter of Solomon and Sarah Cockman Brewer. Margret died in 1875 and is buried in the Ward cemetery on the banks of Roasting Ear Creek. An old cemetery with only a few graves it signifies the relationships between the people who arrived here to settle this valley. Solomon (b. 1786) and George (b. 1775) were the sons of Lanier Brewer, Jr. (b. 1746) who is reported to have had 30 sons and 3 daughters, with at least two wives and a concubine (although likely the concubine was a nice way of saying she was black and Indian mix).

We learn through George that he was half Indian of Tuckey Ho Indian descent. The term Tuckahoe means Wild Potato Clan, or Root Diggers and was associated with the nomadic people within the Chickamauga Cherokee, Lenape (Delaware), Creek and Algonquin. The Wild Potato Clan was within the seven tribes recognized by the Cherokee Nation. Lanier Jr. lived in Moore County, North Carolina where sons Wiley and Julius were born. Comparing the birth dates of the known children of Lanier strongly supports that he did not have children with three consecutive women/wives, but rather concurrently. Polygamy was widely practiced by many of the Native American tribes, including the Moytoy's and Cornstalk's of the Shawnee. It seems more than probable that Lanier had sons George, Henry,

Wiley, Julius and Solomon with his Indian maiden, listed as his concubine wife, one of his three polygamous wives. By most accounts of the Stone County descendants of Lanier, the mother of George and Solomon is said to be Rebecca Narcises, a Tellico Cherokee. Some support that she was the daughter of Oconostota "Stalking Turkey" of the Moytoy's and Ooloosta of the Paint Clan. Ooloosta was of the Red Paint Clan however Oconostata and Stalking Turkey are two different people, nephew and uncle. Oconostota was the son of the Elder Sister of Old Hop "Standing Turkey". Old Hop, Attakullakulla, Oconostota and Francis Fivekiller Ward were the principal leaders of the Shawnee and Cherokee, the Royal Family of the Native Americans and members of the 1730 delegation to King George II. After the death of Old Hop in 1761, Oconostota and his brother in law Francis Ward - "Chief Fivekiller" Kiteguesta Kollanah Rainmaker, shared the responsibilities as Principal Chiefs of the Cherokee. They were largely responsible for the decision to begin moving the Shawnee out of the Ohio River Valley into the area of present day Cape Girardeau, Missouri then to White River Valley including what is now Stone County.

The most concentrated push to settle and assimilate followed the death of Tecumseh in 1813 lead by his adopted brothers Stephen and Abraham Ruddell, among the first settlers of Batesville, Arkansas, the oldest surviving city in the state. Stephen, 12 and Abraham, 6 had been captured along with over 200 others, in 1780 at Ruddells' Station, KY. They lived with the Shawnee for almost 20 years. Oconostota's #3 wife was Lucy Ward sister of Francis, Bryant and James Ward, cousin to Joseph Ward who was killed in battle with Tecumseh. His 5th wife was White Wing Cornstalk, grand daughter of Hokolesqua Cornstalk, Principal Chief of the 20 tribe northern confederacy until his death in 1777. White Wing, daughter of Young Cornstalk, was a first cousin to Chief Peter Cornstalk/b 1785, son of Peter/b 55 and Mary Avey. Peter's/b 85 village, known as Sequatchie, was in north Searcy County. In 1826 at Wolf House, Chief Peter's/b 85 #3 wife was a young Mary Adams. He was killed in 1841 in Kansas by Peter A Tyler (Tyler's Bend Hiway 65 North out of Marshall). Chief Peter Cornstalks'/85 first cousin was John Cornstalk/92, son of his uncle John Cornstalk/b 1750. John/92 after taking his #2 wife, Nancy Jane Avey, daughter of Chief Peter/b 55 (sister to Peter/85), John Cornstalk/92 took the name John Avey. With his first wife a Shawnee from Shawneetown (present day Yellville), he had Andrew Avey Cornstalk/1819, John Avey Cornstalk/1822, and Daniel Avey Cornstalk/1824 all born in Kentucky and or Tennessee during the movement of the Shawnee. With his second wife, Nancy Jane Cornstalk Avey/b 1805, he had Peter Avey/1829 (his daughter Nancy/b 1852 married Henry Harris, of whom Faye Ward Wallace, Von and Fred Ward of Stone Co are descended), Jake/34 (Martha Roper Blackwell's forefather), Elizabeth/43 and Mary/45. John's/92 first cousin was Chief John Black Wiley, of Wiley's Cove, present day Leslie, Arkansas, the son of Black Wolf Cornstalk and Jenny Sellard Wiley.

In 1858, Jonas and Margret Brewer, husband and wife, and first cousins, grand children of Lanier Brewer and his Indian wife, moved to land on the Upper South Sylamore. The Mill Creek/Big Springs area that was part of the former settlement of John Cornstalk Avey of whom they may have been related. During the 1817-1828 Indian Reservation this area was heavily populated by the Creeks members of the five civilized tribes of the Cherokee. They had nine families who moved to this region including The Wild Potato Clan or the Tuckahoe and the Isyllamo's from whom the name Sylamore is derived which suggest that Lanier's wife may have been Creek, rather than Cherokee. When reviewing the languages of the Algonquin and Old Norse, we get Isy = Jesus, all = all and Lam = pure, o everywhere. Present day Sylamore comes from Isyllamo translates "Jesus ever pure everywhere."

So although it is unclear who Rebecca Narcises was, the relationship created because of her provided the Brewers a unique place within the Native American dynasty and a significant role in the birth of the Ozark culture. It has been said that over half the 1840 census of Wayne and Hardin County, Tennessee found themselves here by 1850. So, why did the Brewer's pick up stakes in Wayne County, along with so many other families and move here?

Perhaps they were seeking a peaceful place in the Isyllamo Valley of the Lord to begin a new life. A place where they knew they already had friends and family who would welcome them. A cultural historian seeks out the stories of our people and our places, and then looks for the documents to support the stories. I have contacted the Chief of the Appalachian Shawnee to help confirm who Narcises was. But all I need to do is look at Gladys "Punkin" Brewer Wallis, Laudis daughter and the beautiful eyes and skin that reveal her lineage or marvel at the quilts, handiwork of her skilled hands, or watch her feet as she dances and I know all I need to know about who her people are.

Punkin and her husband Floyd Wallis organize an impromptu square dance in front of the Music Shop on Mountain View's historic court square, where music is found almost any night of the week – weather permitting and sometimes when it doesn't.

Founding Families - 56 Missionary Baptist Church

Tom and America Teague, Paradine Teague, Frank and Mary Teague, Zack and Tennessee Southard, Lizzie Holt, Tim and Callie Sartin, Cuba Ward, William and Effie Allen and William and Lillie Shipman.

While sorting through old family photos with my sister Robbie and first cousins Francis, Linda and Junior, stories are told on each other. Frances tells about stopping at our house on their way home from someone's funeral and Robbie running out to the fence asking "Well Aunt Alpha did you have fun at the funeral?" We laughed remembering as children the events that brought out food and fellowship included funerals, marriages, anniversaries events in a small town that become community reunions as everyone turns out. Sunday August 15th was that kind of event as a little church in the hills above Blanchard Springs Caverns at Fifty Six, Arkansas celebrated its 75th anniversary by honoring the 15 founding members. Shortly before Sunday school ended people started arriving to join in the celebration then stayed for church service and of course followed by dinner on the grounds and gospel music. The bluegrass gospel group, Hard to Get, yearly campers at Blanchard, drove in from Texas to share in the event. The small church currently has just over 200 members with many generational descendants of the original founding members. This Sunday as the sanctuary filled to capacity folding chairs had to be brought in to accommodate everyone.

"The church was organized in 1935 when Franklin D. Roosevelt was President," Michael Cartwright tells the audience. "A postage stamp cost 3 cents. It was the year that the Hoover dam was completed and Ma Barker was killed in a shootout with the FBI. Babe Ruth hit the last of his 714 home runs, Arkansas beat Texas 28-13 and Elvis Presley was born." Fifty Six was a growing community with a post office, two stores and a school and since 1908 they had the Ozark National Forest in their back yard. It would be almost another 40 years before Blanchard Caverns would be discovered and made ready for public viewing. Fifteen individuals organized the church then began meeting in the school building. In 1950 Arvil and Verna Balentine donated land for the church, but it takes more than land to build a church. Construction money was raised with pie suppers and selling chances on hand made quilts. Men and community boys donated their time to work and in 1952 the doors were opened to the church which continues to serve the community today.

A granite plaque was placed out front of the church designating the 15 founding members (FM): Tom and America Teague, Paradine Teague, Frank and Mary Teague, Zack and Tennessee Southard, Lizzie Holt, Tim and Callie Sartin, Cuba Ward, William and Effie Allen and William and Lillie Shipman.

Zack and Tennessee (Qualls) Southard were founding members (FM). Zack was the nephew of Tom Teague. Paradine Teague was the wife of Price Teague, a brother to Tom and a sister to his wife America. Frank was Tom's son. Price and Tom were the sons of Isaac Teague who settled the majority of the land in and around Blanchard in the 1840's, over sixty years before John Blanchard from whom it takes its name arrived. Isaac Teague homesteaded the area including Blanchard Springs under the Choctaw Indian Patents of 1842, shortly after the Cherokee Indian reservation of 1817-1828 ended. Sometime later he sold the springs to a member of the Teague family who put in a mill. It was then sold to Blanchard who got the first "white" patent on the land in 1904. Although we know Blanchard was a prisoner of war during the Civil War, little else is known about him. Isaac's home place sits just above the amphitheatre at Blanchard with the family cemetery located nearby.

As (FM) Tom Teague aged he looked remarkably like his famous cousin Samuel Leghorne Clemens, author "Mark Twain." Clemons' grandmother was Margaret Peggy Casey, a cousin of Rhoda Casey, wife of Thomas Riggs who settled Riggsville, first site of Mountain View in 1819. Isaac Teague's mother, Martha Elizabeth Clemons was a cousin to Samuel's father. Rhoda was born in 1802 and Peggy in 1803. Peggy married Ben Lampton, their daughter Jane married John Marshall Clemons in 1823. Samuel was one of 7 children born to them before John's death in 1847 of pneumonia. Samuel was a young boy of only 11 when his daddy died. Stories go that he was sent to Arkansas to stay with family for awhile. That family included the Clemens, (Casey) Riggs and Teague's.

Raised at Hannibal, MO a port on the Mississippi, it is likely that Samuel Clemens traveled by steamer from his family home to Riggsville, docking at Sylamore met by William or John Riggs, sons of Thomas and Rhoda Casey Riggs. This was during the days when steam boats plied the waters with horns whistling and bands playing. Samuel Clemens and his cousins undoubtedly spent time at Sylamore Landing watching the fancy boats and merriment aboard them. Taking Mark Twain as his name is not lost on people who have been raised along the rivers. The depth of the river was sung in a sing song cadence by men who stood at the bow of the boat. Measured not in feet but in terms that were understood in the wind, hail and storms by the cadence of the songs as shallow depths were short while the deeper the river the more prolonged and drawn out the cadence. A depth of 12 feet was a mark 'twain', mark three pronounced as a long thi-ree, was the call for 18 feet and mark four was 24 feet. All water deeper than 24 feet was called a "no bottom."

Samuel Clemens – author "Mark Twain"

It has also been told that Samuel Clemens may in fact not have 'lived out' many of the childhood stories he wrote about rather they may have possibly been the adventures of his childhood friends in Hannibal and his cousins Isaac Teague, the Riggs or Clemens who lived in what is now Stone County. They may have stayed in the Lucy Dillard Harris home at Sylamore, or the Lucretia Jeffery Harris home at Optimus. When Samuel Clemens died, his estate was sold to a college in New York. A photograph of Tom and America Teague on their front porch taken by Clemens was among his belongings. The Teague family discovered this when the photo was used in a brochure by the college with the image of America captioned "Grandma Goes to College".

Cuba Ward (FM) was born at O'Neal Landing on the White River across from Marcella. She married Carl Ward, a descendant of the Lucretia

Jeffery (Harris) the first white settlers in 1814 of the White River at Mt. Olive across the river from Optimus and Nancy Avey (Harris), grand daughter of Chief John Cornstalk Avey whose tribal land was near Big Springs, Mill and Roastin' Ear Creeks. Built in the 1850's the 160 year old home of Lucretia Jeffery Harris still stands today, an amazing testament to the wealth and influence of the Harris and Ward families.

Photo of America and Tom taken at their home in the Ozark National Forest at Blanchard by Samuel L Clemens was found in Clemens belongings

Tim and Callie (Brewer) Sartin (FM) are buried at Stevens Cemetery on Roasting Ear Creek. Tim was born at Mt. Olive the third site of the county seat of Izard County. Callie, a descendant of Jonas and Margret Brewer, grand children of the Royal Family of the Shawnee, the Moytoys was born on Roasting Ear Creek.

Effie (Thomas) Allen, wife of William, (FM) was the grand daughter of Amanda Clementine Parks (see Gayler story). Amanda was the wife of

James Perry Barney Gayler son of Calvin. Although some believe that Stone County is named for the rocks here, or for the Stone's on the 1817 Census, many other's believe it took its name from Stone County, Missouri where the Gayler's had lived. Calvin Gayler, the Old Soldier, homesteaded Branson, MO. Following the Civil War they settled South Sylamore creek, still known as Gayler. Effie and her husband are buried at Gayler Cemetery.

William and Lillie (Balentine) Shipman (FM) were both born in Stone County and were members of the church at Roasting Ear Creek, when the decision to organize a new church was made. Lizzie (Vickery) Holt (FM) was also born in Stone County. She married Joe Holt also a descendant of Solomon Brewer, grandson of the Royal Family of Shawnee, the Moytoys.

Only recently have we been able to translate from Algonquin the meaning of the name Isyllamo, the Creek family who had the first trading post at what is now Allison, formerly Sylamore, Stone County, from which the creek takes its name. Isyllamo translates "Jesus, everyone pure everywhere". Isy=Jesus, all=all, Lam=pure, o everywhere. The 56 Missionary Baptist Church which sits in the Sylamore District of the Ozark National Forest, just up the road from Blanchard, where Sylamore Creek flows, didn't happen by accident, nor do the traditions, honor and devoutness the generations of families who attended this celebration share. The Fifty Six Missionary Baptist Church remains the only church in the small town serving an extended community of friends and family. The dedication was a day of celebration and praise to our Lord honoring the founding members who held the promise of God within their hearts just as the early Native Americans did 1,000 years before the first white settlers arrived here.

Descendants of Founding Members - Teague Cemetery

Historic cemeteries dot the Virginia landscape around Richmond, markers denoting the burial places of key figures in the birth of our nation, the American Revolution and the Civil War. Fall colors are overtaking the green in the trees, mornings are crisp and afternoons warm. This state is preparing for the 150 year commemoration of the Civil War. It is every where, every day. No one escapes it and all are bathed in it.

Born in 1825 in Kentucky, to Joshua Teague and Martha Elizabeth Clemons, Isacc Teague was homesteading the areas around what is now known as Blanchard in the 1840's. Men of that time traveled long distances searching out new land with how long they were gone marked in the space between the births of their children. Isaac Teague married Margaret Miller from SC in AL and their first 3 children were born there. It was here Isaac Teague likely met Thomas Riggs whose wife, Rhoda Casey b 1802, was from AL. Riggs was settling another area of what was to become Stone County, just outside of present day Mtn. View lays Riggsville with its historic dam and remains of perhaps the first mill. It had a blacksmith, livery, tavern, school and where the Methodist Church and later Flatwoods began. Riggs wife, Rhoda Casey was a cousin to Isaac's wife, Martha Elizabeth Clemons b

1800 and Margaret Peggy Casey b 1783, grandmother of Samuel Leghorne Clemons aka Mark Twain. After the death of Twain's father, Marshall Clemons in 1847 of pneumonia, Twain was sent to Sylamore to spend time with family, the Casey/Riggs and Teague's where he returned throughout his life.

Alvie Green, Danny Stewart, Wilma Teague Wolfe, Billy Wolfe
Kevin Mitchell, Hinkle Decker
Jimmy Mitchell, Dean Teague, Jap Holt

It was a beautiful crisp fall morning as we gathered at Blanchard for the trek to Teague Cemetery. The leaves were beginning to turn and the chill in the air was a welcomed relief as we hiked to the top of the ridge. Although some people not familiar with the history of the cemetery have dubbed it North Sylamore Creek Cemetery, it was never called that. But it is where it is located, on the North Sylamore which flows through the Ozark National Forest on a hill overlooking the creek. The Teague cemetery has four distinct families within its boundaries with as many as 100 graves; 38 are known. Some family members have replaced or restored markers. Jap Holt and Danny Stewart brought in a new carved sandstone marker for William S Holt born 1848 died 1924. Today they restore the headstone of Miss Dannie Holt carving out the letters with a small specialty drill.

Miss Wilma Teague Wolfe searches for the graves of Isaac Teague and his wife finding them at the top of the hill, the oldest part of the cemetery. Located in the Ozark National Forest, Sylamore District, Kevin Mitchell with the USFS, son of Jim Mitchell accompanies the group and helps with the cleaning. The Mitchell's are buried slightly down hill from Isaac, with the Holt's and Sexton's nearby.

Jap Holt, Wilma Teague Wolfe & Alvie Green wading creek

Danny Stewart & Jap Holt

.   These are family members, born of the same bloodlines, inter-marrying and rearing their children here in the early days of the settlement of Stone County.   Teague's, Mitchell's, Harris', Coyle's, Southard's and Sexton's, brothers and sisters intermarrying as brothers and sisters married into other families strengthening the ties between them that made survival possible.

In 1910, Alvie Green's family of whom Green Tower is named served along with the Wards as the first rangers, fire fighters and refuge keepers. Steve Mitchell, son of Malinda Mitchell, built the mill that operated between 1900 and 1928, at the base of Mirror Lake. Mitchell Mill provided the nearby community with ginned cotton and ground corn. In the 1940's the CCC workers began the process of tearing down and restoring the mill, but when WWII broke out the project was abandoned. Almost nothing remains of the incredible work done by the CCC, torn down by the early administration of the USFS throughout the nation. Not unlike the possibilities of Stone County's rock walls, log homes and historic locations falling to ruin, being bulldozed, it is often difficult to see how our actions today, although made with what we believe to be good judgment end up being not only to our economic demise but to the town, county, region and state in which we live. Like the household items of yesterday now treasured items, some costing thousands of dollars, these homes, cemeteries, outposts, barns and rock walls are the future of Stone County's revitalization. It is the Jamestown, VA of the Ozarks, where three distinct people, white, black and Indians merged creating the Ozark culture.

Mirror Lake Dam above Mitchell Mill

Malinda Mitchell's son, Steve sold the land to John Blanchard, who secured the 1906 land patent 60 years after Isaac Teague had homesteaded it. It would be another 60 years before serious exploration of the big hole would open up to become Blanchard Caverns.

Sarah Teague, second daughter of Isaac married Thomas Clark, who rode to Texas in March 1859 from Riggsville (Mtn View), along with Thomas Riggs Jr and Walter Clark to bring back the surviving children of John Riggs to their grandparents, Thomas and Rhoda, after John and his wife Jane

Johnson Riggs were murdered in the last great Indian Massacre in Texas (historical marker Comanche Gap, Texas).

John Joshua Teague married Sarah Harris. The Harris land lay north from Sylamore (Alison, Stone Co) and remains known as Harris Bottoms. The historic home of Henry Harris and Lucy Dillard built in 1848 is the home of Guy and Liz Harris who own and operate the campgrounds at the mouth of Sylamore Creek across from their home.

Because of the Green's, Holt's, Sexton's, Mitchell's and Teague's, Stone County is rich with people who believe in the Lord's laws. A people who holding God close to their breast honor the mother's and father's who rest high on this beautiful mountain above Sylamore Creek. While others refuse to extend the boundaries of historic cemeteries, bulldoze down historic barns and homes, or simply let them fall to ruin, there are those that honor our heritage and the people who gave us this place by trudging through the forest, wading the creek, on a chilly morning to clean a place deep in the woods. Because honoring thy mother and father is more than just who a particular family is. It is God's commandment.

Gennive Beach - Aaron Stevens Place on Roastin' Ear

On the Stevens side Gennive Beach is the daughter of Grover Beach and Bessie Stevens, the grand daughter of Aaron Stevens and Viola Alexander. Both Aaron and Viola are descendants of the Royal Family of the Shawnee, 20 Tribe Northern Confederacy of the Cherokee. Aaron was the son of John Stevens and Nancy Brewer. Nancy was the daughter of Jonas and Margret Brewer, children of brothers George and Solomon Brewer, sons of Lanier (lineage in Sons & Daughters of Sylamore Creek Laudis Brewer) descendants of the Royal Family of the Shawnee, Chief Onoconstota Rainmaker Moytoy. Up until the early 20th century it remained common for royal bloodlines to marry within the family in order to maintain those lines, especially in European aristocracy (Wards) with whom the Shawnee were allied with in 1730 under King George II. The Jonas Brewer family arrived in the area of Newnata, Big Springs and Mill Creek on the South Sylamore of present day Stone County in the 1850's. They settled land that was the former tribal land of Chief John Cornstalk b/1792 (John Avey).

Viola was the daughter of Mary Ward and William Alexander. Viola's mother, Mary, was the daughter of Joseph O. Ward, who died on the banks of Mill Creek during the Civil War. Wounded he rode a train to Little Rock, then walked in the pouring rain home, but with his home in sight was unable to cross the flooded Mill Creek. His family found him after the water receded, leaning against a tree gun in hand dead. Joseph O. was the son of David Ward b 1810 d 1902 buried at Alco, grandson Joseph Ward b1762 who in 1781 fought with Joseph Brant and George Girty in the Blue Jacket War. He was killed in 1793 in Kentucky along with his father, John "White Wolf"

b 1741, during a raid with Tecumseh. Joseph Ward's/62 children were raised by his uncle John Jack Ward, sons of Bryant Ward and Anna Pekowi.

Gennive has recently refurbished the Stevens family home including landscaping which unearthed remains of the former Shawnee occupation. Gennive tells me, "As kids we would play in the dirt, work the gardens and swim in the creeks, arrowheads were everywhere. Someone in the family told that this was a former Indian battlefield. With some of the things we have found over the years, including the arrowhead I found just planting that little sapling over there a couple months ago, it certainly seems to be the case."

Gennive remembers a family story about her grandpa Aaron Stevens a twin to Fanny Stevens Balentine. "They lived on Roastin Ear Creek all of their lives. Each year on their birthdays they would get together. A favorite family story is how the creek was up one year and could not be crossed to unite them for their birthdays. So, Fanny stood on one side and Grandpa (Aaron) on the other waving as they each wished the other one Happy Birthday. The creek got its name shortly after the Civil War when a record flood made an entirely new opening in the mountain pushing water down through the cornfields of the Brewer's and my great grand dad's John Stevens. It remains known as "Roastin' Ear Creek" because of the ears of roasting corn that filled the water."

Aaron was always a business man, beyond the required family chores his first job was making marbles which he sold to his classmates. At age 18 he began work at his first public job on the railroad between Sylamore and Batesville. He was paid $1.50 a day for ten hours of work. He learned the rail road needed cross ties so he returned to his farm and began producing them for the rail road. The rail road tracks are laid onto the cross ties, a spike is then driven into the cross ties to hold them in place. A great many of the salvaged cross ties from the tracks along the White River Valley now in flower beds and shoring up banks were likely produced by Aaron Stevens and the hands that worked his mill. He and his wife had seven children which required a large family run farm be raised in order to feed everyone. Aaron began fitting and shoeing horse and mule teams in their family run blacksmith shop along with repairing wagons, sharpening plows and grubbing hoes. As his work grew so did the newly formed Stone County. He worked for H.S. Mabry at his stave mill where he made two stave buckers. He would then buck the staves, haul them to the river at Sylamore for shipping and then bring freight back to the mills, as well as he continued doing all the blacksmithing for the horses and mules used in the timber business. Many of the animals were a bit wild requiring that they be tipped and hog tied with a stick put in their mouths to keep them from biting in order to be fitted and shoed. Although many folks from off think it a tale associated only with pushing over sleeping cows, the tipping of animals remains an often necessary act to subdue an animal for vaccinations, shoeing, etc. If you want to understand something about how this is done, visit the vet when he's working with animals or the rodeo arena and watch some of Stone County's most beautiful and petite young girls rope and tie a calf often picking them up waist high in the process, knee dropping them onto the ground. Aaron Stevens was paid 5 cents per shoe whether he had to tip them or not. Maybe this is where the practice of "tipping for extra service" came from as some farmers and especially city folks would pay a little extra if animals were difficult requiring more effort or added service.

The Stevens family raised corn, hay, cotton, sorghum cane and vegetables for family use which lead to his putting in a sorghum mill where they made molasses for both family use and public sale. He later bought a saw mill and grist mill where he made cross ties, sawed lumber and ground meal for the public. Both mills were run by the same big steam engine. He ran those mills for nearly 30 years providing work for his family as well as his son in laws and the extended community.

Roastin' Ear Creek was almost dry as Gennive and I forded it to go to the Ward Cemetery. Located deep in the hollow near the creek is has been unattended for some time. There are a number of graves there most are marked with only stones. Margret Brewer, Indian Princess, wife of Jonas, grand daughter of Lanier and Rebecca Narcises from whom Gennive is descended is buried here. The Ward family was part of the Shawnee move into the White River Valley, a decision made by Chief's Frances "Fivekiller" Ward, Onocostota and Black Fish Cornstalk. David Ward and his son Joe Ward were among the first Ward's arriving in present day Stone County, settling the upper valley of present day Roastin' Ear Creek and Forest Home now known as Optimus. The failure of the Shawnee, the last great tribe of Native Americans east of the Mississippi, to stop the encroachment of the whites, along with the deaths of their primary leaders and chiefs in the late 1700's clearly influenced the decision to move the Shawnee into the White

River Valley. Here, the families of the immigrants, Scots-Irish, British and Native Americans intermarried forging out a new people and culture, the Ozarks. It is still felt and seen today in the way we celebrate the birth and death of our people, sing our hymns and play music, in the vernacular of our speech and the clannish way in which we live our lives. In the traditions set before him, Aaron Stevens provided not only for his family but for the extended family of his community. There are some who will never understand the gift that one life so lived offers to all those that come after. But for those of us who know Gennive and the hundreds of other Stevens, Brewer, Ward, Alexander, Avey and Wallace descendants, we know they are living testaments to a proud ancestry of people who consider all of us family.

Alfred Via & Bickles Cove

During high school at Mountain View, Alfred Via lived next door to my mother Ima Fulks. She graduated in 1946 a year before he did and then while she attended Arkansas College (now Lyon) like most of the young men, Alfred joined the service. He hands me a photo of a beautiful young woman pictured with him in uniform delighting in telling how he and his buddy snuck into town and met these two girls who also had snuck out for the evening. They danced the night away but as dawn approached they needed to get back. They all had had such a great time and knew no one would believe them so they found this little machine that took photos and wah lah they had their proof. "We had never met before and never met again, but I've pulled that picture out more than a few times when telling the story," he says with a smile on his face some 60 years later.

Jerry Sutton and sister Dorothy Sutton Craig
at old home place in Bickles Cove

Alfred was born in Bickles Cove. A gravel road that connects Hiway 5 South and Hiway 14 East traverses the cove, but once it was a thriving community that lay in direct line to the river landing at Rocky Bayou and Wild Haws. The Bickles family migrated from Germany before the Revolutionary War. John Michael Bickle and Elizabeth Wytzel (Whitesell) married and had 12 children, around 1840 four made their way to what is still known as Bickles Cove east of Mtn View. Stories handed down tell how when Henry born 1811 first arrived he set about building a log home near the spring that feeds the creek. While working on the home he was chased to the roof by a pack of wolves. It has been reported that he had to haul his logs more than 75 miles from the nearest sawmill and his one room house in the 1840's had to grow in size with the addition of 16 children by 1856. Elizabeth married (m) Alex Mackey, John m. Margarite Kaufman, Isabelle m. Napoleon Turner, Eliza m. Gallaway Anderson, Rachel m. Ben Reynolds, Nancy m. John Dale, James m. Emily O'Neal, Henry m. Katherine McIntire, Joesph m. Nancy Haynes, Sarah m. Noah Haynes, William m. Nancy Baker, Daniel m. Mary Yeager, Amanda m. John Baker, those not listed died as children. After John died, Elizabeth moved to Bickles Cove with her daughter Lydia, a sister to Henry, who had married John Freeze (Freeze Mountain is known for the family, not because it freeze's over so easily as many believe). She is buried in Bickles Cove Cemetery. The children of the families who lived in Bickles Cove attended school at Riggsville. The first mail route ran weekly by horse from Bradford, through Bickles Cove and Riggsville to Blue Mtn (Timbo) on to Wiley's Cove (Leslie). A post office was established in 1880 at Bickle's Cove but was discontinued then reopened as Anvil. Billy Daum carried the mail from Mtn View to Kahoka on a mule through 1930 when Clarence Anderson, County Judge got the W.P.A. to turn what was nothing more than a wagon trail into a road from Mtn View to Kahoka bringing traffic into Bickle's Cove this was the first time many of the residents saw their first vehicle.

Alfred is the son of Thomas Frank Via, born 1880 died 1972, and Angeline Parrish. The same family as Cassandra Parrish who married Calvin Gayler, mother to James Barney Perry Gayler, husband of Amanda Clementine Parks. Cassandra was living in the Cove when she died and Meredith Parrish is listed as her grand father. This lineage places Alfred Via in the Royal Family of Native American's. Alfred's momma's parents were Meredith Washington Parrish (it's not certain if this a brother to Ira Owen Parrish, Cassandra's father, or a son) and Effie McIntire, daughter of John A. McIntire and Mary Elliot. John's parents were John C. McIntire and Nancy Wall. Their home still stands on Hiway 5 South on the Gary McClung place, just west of the Bickles Cove cemetery. A once magnificent structure it has suffered in the ice storms and tornado that have ravaged our county in the last few years. The nearby Noah McCarn double dog trot home on the National Registry of Historic Places has recently been torn down and now is nothing more than a piece of land with highway frontage. These historic homes and structures are unique to the White River Valley, the oldest surviving section of the state. Stone County has the potential to become the Jamestown (VA) of Arkansas. Our rock walls are as beautiful as anything CT, VT, Pennsylvania, England and Scotland have that are their mainstays of tourisms and increased property values. It's unfortunate that the current landowners of the Noah McCarn place and others don't have the economic means or foresight to see the long term value financially and historically that preservation of these sites would mean to not only their pocket books but the county and state as a whole.

Alfred, Pauline Mitchell and Jerry Sutton are the gg grand children of Nancy Wall and John C. McIntire. Pauline Mitchell is the daughter of

Charlie Guy Mitchell and Gladys McIntire. She is the gggg grand daughter of Solomon Hess of Marcella, formerly Hesstown, one of the oldest settlements in Stone County. Jerry is the son of James Edward Sutton and Rosalee Collins. He recalls the road coming by their house as he was a kid growing up in the cove. As we climb the stairs into the second story, the hand hewn logs remain intact, the home sturdy. The tornado and ice storms of the last few years have compromised the roof on one corner otherwise the chimney is sound and with minimal work the restoration of this home would be of incredible historical value not only to the family but to Stone County and the White River Valley.

Jerry Sutton, Pauline Mitchell Via & Alfred Via

Alfred continues his stories of growing up in Bickles Cove as we ride about Cove Road taking in the historic places of our ancestors. "When I was a kid, 1942 I think, I was 13 years old, me and J.T. McIntire was asked by the Agri teacher, U.S. Buckley if we wanted to go work at the CC Camp. Now we were just boys, kids, not old enough but they promised to pay us $1.00 a day. They took us to Batesville and put us on the bus. Now us boys we went straight to the back so we could see out the big window. The black folks on the bus thought it was funny, us two white boys clearly never been to town. Now, S.D. Mitchell with the U.S.D.A. was expecting us to call him when we got to Camp Catherine. Well, I'd never used a phone before, come to think of it, I may have never even seen a phone before then. I went up to the ticket lady and told her that I needed to make a call. I think she read it all over me and J.T. that we didn't have a clue what we were doing, probably because we were hanging onto every word she said, watching her every move. When Mr. Mitchell drove up he was in one of those battleship gray military cars. He took us to the camp. We worked from 4 or 5 in the morning to 10 at night to make that $1.00 a day. Now this little cabin they put us in had running water in it, something else we'd never seen. But more than that, it had an indoor toilet that when you sat down it flushed. That was pretty upsetting to a 13 year old boy who'd never seen anything like that! When it come time for us to go home we had to find our way home. We wrapped ourselves in sheets and sat on the headlights of a car. We had about 4 flats in that all day trip to get home. I bought myself a wrist watch with the money I made."

Born Dec 29, 1928, Alfred will be 82 this year. His father was born following the Civil War, in 1880, 130 years ago. He heard the stories of his father, Thomas G. Via first hand, stories that spanned into the late 1700's. Stone County is an incredible place with incredible people who have lived incredible lives. The Hess house of Marcella, Miles Jeffery Barn at Livingston Creek, the Orvil Gammill Barn at Newnata, Mabry Barn at Richwood's and the McIntire house, Noah McCarn house (now gone), the Elliot house and Sutton's of Bickle's Cove, and a majority of historic Marcella provide an opportunity to preserve and celebrate the people who lived the lives that birthed the Ozark Culture, here in the White River Valley of Stone County.

John & Mary Evelyn Ridgley - 50th Anniversary

     "It doesn't take a lifetime to know when you've done something right," John says as he smiles at Mary Evelyn, his wife of 50 years. They are surrounded by over 200 friends and family who have come to share in their celebration at the Foothills Baptist Church on this beautiful Saturday. "We got married on my birthday," Mary Evelyn says, "I'm not sure that was a good idea, since it eliminated a second celebration each year." "Rather like being born on Christmas," a nearby friend adds smiling. "You'll have to come out to talk to us, we have a great story about how we met," John declares. A few weeks later sitting at their kitchen counter the smile on my face broadens as Mary Evelyn and John interrupt each other, one finishing the sentence of the other as they tell the story of how they met.

     "I was 18 years old," Mary Evelyn begins. "I had tested positive for T.B. a year before and had been admitted to the sanatorium in Booneville for treatment." "I think it's now defunct, no longer there or possibly they've turned it into a center for special needs individuals," John says. "My daddy was there for treatment at the same time Mary Evelyn was." "He was working as a cook for $90.00 a month just to be near his dad," "when I met this beautiful woman," they say. "Just a young girl then," Mary Evelyn adds. The smile that passes between them still as coy and loving as one might suspect it was all those years ago. Mary Evelyn retrieves a framed collage of photos from the wall of their families and childhood, with one of them taken on their wedding day. "We had only known each other two weeks when we got married. I had been there a year and had earned myself a reputation of being a troublemaker." "She was bored," John says. "I would wander into the areas that were forbidden, talk with people sneaking a smoke," Mary Evelyn continues. "Well his momma come to me and said, 'John wants you to meet him around back of the building. He's got something to say to you.' I went to where he was and he asked me right then and there after only two weeks to marry him. A few years ago I got in my medical records and right there in black and white it said that 'Patient had left AMA – Against Medical Advice. Information was that patient had run off with the worthless Johnny Ridgley to Mexico.' I couldn't believe it. I was the troublemaker because I wouldn't stay put on the assigned floor and he was there working just so he could visit with his daddy. Can you imagine?" Mary Evelyn and John clearly delight in the fact that this declared trouble maker and worthless man have had a wonderful committed relationship for 50 years raising incredible children and delighting now in grandchildren. They were married by John Balentine in a house that sat where the Bank of Mtn View later built, "not Mexico," Mary Evelyn says smiling. They are members of Red Doors Baptist Church. John provided well for his family as a Union Ironworker near Chicago. Their daughter Vickie is the first woman to join the UIA.

John & Mary Evelyn as Newlyweds 1960

Mary Evelyn, the daughter of Herbert Jones and Pauline Wallace, descended from the Jeffery's who settled the area of Mt. Olive across from Optimus/Boswell in 1814. Her daddy died of T.B. when she was only four. She is the great grand daughter of Atlantic Jeffery and William Jackson Wallace, great grandson of Col. Samuel Wallace and Rebecca Anderson. William Jackson's father was William Wallace, son of James Wallace b 1778 son of Col Samuel and Rebecca. Following the death of her husband Col. Samuel Wallace, Rebecca married James Grigsby. Her daughter Elizabeth Wallace married James' brother Charles. Charles and Elizabeth's son James married Margaret Houston, cousin of General Sam Houston and John Paxton

Houston, first clerk of Izard County. The Grigsby's purchased the Hardin ferry at Marcella (See story on Martha Grigsby Hinesley). Wallace Township in Batesville is named for Elizabeth Wallace. After his father's death, Mary E. Martin came to Arkansas with her young son, William Jackson Wallace hoping for a new start. Perhaps she returned to her maiden name or remarried a man named Martin. The lineage of Mary Martin has not yet unfolded nor has a clear relationship between the Wallis and Wallace families. They have traditionally been reported as being two separate families with no relationship may have seen a change of spelling sometime around the time of the American Revolution. With incredible baroque dialects it was difficult to understand many immigrants compounded by the fact they often did not read or write therefore leaving both the census takers and military personnel trying to figure out how to spell individual and family names. They may yet prove to be related or unrelated, which if unrelated, here in the White River Valley, would be remarkable.

Pauline and daughter Mary Wallace Ridley 2010

People often ask where I find my information, how I know what I know. Tidbits come at the least expected time. In researching the Hess family with Pauline Mitchell Via on an 1850 census there was "Wallace township". From this I learned that James "Pawnee Berry" Trimble was married to Elizabeth Wallace Stewart. Although little is found on her as well, they named one of their children "Wallace". James was born in Augusta, Orange Co, Virginia in 1774, which records in England say he was born in "New Colonies, England" because this land belonged to England in 1774. Many people who believe their forefathers were born in England are finding out that they were born on American soil while it belonged to England. Elizabeth Wallace Stewart was born in 1782 Culpepper Co, VA. They both died in Batesville, 1841 and

1836 respectively. James Trimble was the son of Robert Trimble and Hannah Moffett who moved to Batesville between 1816 and 1821. He was a surveyor and helped lay out the town of Batesville. Therefore as surveyor he named the township which is the lower portion of Stone County around Marcella/Melrose "Wallace Township." What is the relationship between these Wallace's? Certainly something as that is where the Grigsby's settled and where Mary Martin and her young son came to be with family. More research is needed.

Pauline Wallace and her younger brother Walter circa 1925
with their dad Dickie Wallace, Livingston Creek

John's family is rich with Native Americans of undocumented lineage. His great grand father James Ridgley was married to two different women, both named Sarah and both of whom likely was Native American, of Cherokee, Shawnee or Chickamauga heritage. A photograph of Joseph Ridgley, John's grandfather, born 1864 with his wife and children show him wearing a beaded choker something clearly indicative of his ancestry as well as the baby, Tom Davis Ridgley, John's father has on leather moccasins'. John has a bit of confusion within the family from a story that has been told. In the 1800's his great grandmother admitted that the older children were not Ridgley's but were Delahiets (sic). She had killed her husband, their father who was a very mean man and buried him in the basement of the house. She then moved to Arkansas and did not tell the story until she was on her death bed. It is told that she was a full blooded Indian, likely Cherokee from the Upper Missouri Territories. People who moved to the Ozarks between 1800 and 1850 were looking for a better life. The promise of land to Scots, Irish and British escaping serfdom who could never expect to own land in their own countries and Native Americans who were increasingly losing their land due to the encroachment of the whites found common ground here in the White River Valley. They worked and lived together against odds creating a new culture. Taking untold risks for the promise of land and a better life many hid their true heritage readily taking on the new names of colonists, frontiersmen and settlers to become the first Americans. John and Mary Evelyn are like the first frontiersmen who forged ahead on faith blindly taking a chance believing they were making the right choice for a better life and like their forefathers, time has proven them right.

John's father is the baby in moccasins

Ward Family

Summer is the time for family, school and community reunions. A time when people remember with laughter pranks and antics, deaths and births, love and tears that sharing a person's life brings. The Ward family has gathered at Blanchard, one after the other stands telling who they are, from whom they are descended, naming off their kids and grand kids. Some weeks back, following the 56 Missionary Baptist Church 75th anniversary, Fred, Von, their sister Billie and I drove down to Gunner Pool.

Fred, Billie and Von Ward

We talked about their brother Kenneth Carl Ward, born June 5, 1930, a U.S. Army Corporal who went missing in the Korean War. He and his siblings were raised at Gunner Pool, where their father Carl Ward was one of the first refuge keepers of the forest. They lived in the buildings that had been vacated by CCC Camp Hedges. They have placed a memorial there for their brother, a place where memories flow in the clear clean water and laughter of young children is still heard. Family reunions are bittersweet, places where people look to see who wasn't able to make it this year, mourn the loss of those that have passed on and celebrate births. We are celebrating a history that is remarkable not only to the White River region of Stone County, of the Ozarks, of Arkansas, but to our nation.

The Ward family is an incredible family, full of teachers that first began with Lucy Ward in the 1700's, when she aided Sequoyah in developing the Cherokee syllabi. Sequoyah along with many Ward's was on the 1817 Indian Census of Arkansas. He took at least 3 wives here, including Sally Waters (Kahoka). In 1730, an alliance of the Cherokee with the British was formed through the marriage of the Wards from England to what King George II dubbed, the Royal Family of Native Peoples. This was common practice during this time, the child of the King and Queen of one country would be married to the child of another creating an alliance. The Cherokee-British alliance was formed to fight the French and Shawnee in the French Indian Wars. After 1755, the Cherokee and Shawnee formed the 20 Tribe Northern Confederacy of the Cherokee aligning with the British against the "Colonists". Chief Hokolesqua Cornstalk (Shawnee) was the first Principal Chief of the Northern Confederacy of the Cherokee, 1757-1777. Frances "Chief Fivekiller" Ward was the War Chief of the Shawnee and Pucksinwah, father of Tecumseh was the War Chief of the Cherokee. In 1780, Abraham Ruddell, 6, one of the first settlers of Batesville, AR and his brother Stephen, 12, were taken in the raid on Ruddell's Station, KY. They remained living within the Confederacy for over 15 years, marrying and having children prior to their return to the whites. Adopted into the tribe of Pucksinwah they were raised as brothers of Tecumseh. Tecumseh's 5th wife was White Wing Cornstalk, daughter of Young Hokolesqua, grand daughter of Hokolesqua, further uniting the Cherokee and Shawnee.

In 1789 following the end of the American Revolution as the America's selected their first President, the Royal Family of the Native Americans as well as the British who did not want to return to England had to hide their identities. They began a massive migration north into the Ohio River Valley, Canada and then into Cape Girardeau, MO. Following the death of Tecumseh in 1813, many moved further into the White River Valley into present day Stone County.

Many families in Stone County are descended from two lines of the Royal Family of the Native Americans', the Cornstalks and Moytoys. At the time of her death in 2010, Faye Willie Ward b 1915 (pictured below with her youngest son Bill Wallace) was the oldest living descendant of Chief Hokolesqua Cornstalk. She is double descended from the Royal Family of the Native Americans in both the Avey - Cornstalk line and the Ward - Moytoy line.

Bryant Ward, white b in England, had at least two wives Anna Pekowi and his niece Nancy Ward (daughter of his brother Francis "Fivekiller" Ward and Tame Doe Catherine Carpenter Moytoy – it is the children of Chief Fivekiller and Tame Doe that the Fulks and Chitwood's of Stone Co are descendants.)

Faye Ward Wallace with son, Bill Wallace 2010

BRYANT WARD - Children with Anna Pekowi - Lucy 1736, Bryant (2) 1738, Unknown child, John "White Wolf" Ward 1741, 2 other children and John Jack 1750 ½ Pekowi

SON - John "White Wolf" Ward/1741 m Chalakatha Woman/1744 – Children 3/4th Pekowi/Chalakatha - John Jr "Young White Wolf"/58, Sutawanee/60 and Joseph/1762; John "White Wolf"/41 and his son Joseph/62 were killed in battle fighting alongside Tecumseh in 1793;

John "White Wolf's SON – Joseph/1762-1793 m Kissie Kannachee (Kishpoko) John Jack took in his nephew's wife and raised Joseph/1762's children: 7/8th Kishpoko/Chalakatha/Pekowi George/1779, James/81 and Joseph/83, possibly others. They are found along with their mother Kissie Kannachee (Kishpoko) on the 1817 Indian Census of Arkansas.

Joseph/62's SON 7/8th JOSEPH (Jr II)/1783 m Lizbet, a Shawnee; they had Squire/1803, John/1806 (KY/Ohio), George/1808 (Oklahoma Indian Territories), David/ 1810, and James 1812 (m Millie), possibly other children. James and David are believed to have been born in the Missouri Territories near Paducah, KY 7/8th Shawnee/Chalakatha /Kishpoko & Metis they were considered "full blood" Shawnee

Joseph/1783's SON DAVID WARD b 1810 KY d 1902 buried at Alco Cemetery, Horton Hill m Susannah Gholsten – Children ½ Shawnee (Chalakatha/Kishpoko & Metis)   William 1829, Martha 1830, Malinda "Lindy" 1832 (m. Henry Snellgrove), Thomas 1832, Joseph Oconastota 1834-1864 (m Martha Snellgrove), James Lafayette 1835-1922, Sarah 1841, John 1844, Jane 1847 1/4th Chalakatha/ Kishpoko /Shawnee & Metis

Grand Children of Anna Lou Harris and Joseph Ward
1/8th Chalakatha/ Kishpoko/Shawnee, Cherokee & Metis

David's SON JOSEPH O WARD 1/2 Shawnee b 1834-1863 m M. Snellgrove –Children: Mary Jane 1854 (m. William Alexander), William Henry 1857 (m. Martha Rebecca Rorie), Rebecca 1858 (m J.M. Tice), Thomas J. 1861 (m Sarah Alexander), Joseph S. Ward March 8, 1862-1945 (m Anna Lou Harris).   All 1/8th Chalakatha/Pekowi/Kishpoko/Shawnee & Metis.

Joseph O/'s SON, JOSEPH S WARD b 1862 d 1945 (1/4th) m (1/4th) Anna Lou Harris (1872-1949) Children 1/4th Chalakatha/ Kishpoko/Shawnee, Cherokee & Metis - Della May 1889, Ewing 1892, Joe H 1894, Zelpha 1897, Baby 1899, Junious 1901, Hazel killed by a mule kicking her – 2 years and 8 months, Carl 1903, Lois 1905, Marie 1909, Hazel 1913 and Faye 1915 (Joseph's wife, ANNA LOU HARRIS (1/4 Cherokee /Shawnee /Metis) is the daughter of Nancy Jane Avey, grand daughter of Pest Avey, b 1829. See Cornstalk Story)

CARL WARD married Cuba Lynch their children are 1/8th Shawnee (Chalakatha/ Kishpoko/Shawnee, Cherokee & Metis)

Fred's DAUGHER Becky 1/16th Shawnee

Becky's CHILDREN Brad & Amber 1/32nd Shawnee

The birth of the Ozark culture occurred here in the White River Valley as the descendants of the Royal Family of Native Americans along with the British, and many others, migrated here, into this beautiful and isolated region to begin a new life. That migration began in 1790 and continued heavily through 1840. It is that period of time and the blending of these cultures that gave us the music, dance, speech and the clannish way in which we live our lives that distinguishes the Ozarks from other regions in the U.S.

MIA In Memorium

Thanksgiving is a time for remembering, for families and friends to have that occasion to get together and share a meal. It is a time when people set aside their differences, put up with attitudes and indulge in food, friends and family. Coming on the heels of Veterans' Day, Thanksgiving is often a time when people celebrate the freedoms we have that were hard fought, won through untold sacrifices worse than dying. Death can mean the end of pain, illness, suffering and the portal to life everlasting. But for the family left behind, it often is the beginning of suffering, of life without that loved one in it, a future not shared, forever changed.

A large group of local veterans, along with the Ward family, honored Stone County's only Missing In Action veteran, Kenneth Carl Ward, on Saturday following Thanksgiving. Born in Stone County June 5, 1930, to Carl and Cuba Lynch Ward, Kenneth was a U.S. Army Corporal. He was a member of Company D. 9th Infantry Regiment, 2nd Infantry Division serving in the Korean War when he was seriously wounded by the enemy in South Korea on Sept 7, 1950 and returned to duty on Oct. 27, 1950. He was listed as Missing in Action while fighting during the Battle of Ch'ongch'on River, North Korea on Nov. 27, 1950, Thanksgiving, 60 years ago. He was pronounced dead Dec. 31, 1953 and posthumously awarded the Purple Heart. He and his siblings were raised at Gunner Pool, where their father Carl Ward was one of the first refuge keepers of the forest. They lived in the buildings that had been vacated by CCC Camp Hedges. After Kenneth's death, the Ward family placed a memorial here for their brother and son. Gunner Pool at Camp Hedges is a place that in the brilliant sun of this Ozark Fall warms the soul as it transports this family and these men and women who fought for our freedoms, people whose lives were forever changed back to a time when their laughter as young children echoed along the valley.

Francis Burns Brightwell Gammill, Betty Ward,
Siblings Von, Fred & Billie Ward, Bill Rosa next to flag

Carl's baby sister, Faye Willie Ward Wallace born 1915, the youngest and last remaining sibling of the children of Joe S. Ward and Anna Lou Harris Ward died at the end of 2010 at age 95. We are all children, babies to our parents until they are gone and we become that next generation standing alone. We are prepared for the loss of our parents, but never our children. The recent vehicular deaths of local young people poignantly remind us of the difficulty of losing a young life by any means, but not knowing what happened is always worse, haunting us for the rest of our lives, relief brought only in our own death. When someone passes, we often bemoan with regret what we last said, didn't say or should have said, made all the worse for the survivors whose lives must go on without that person in it, our futures forever altered. As we sit and watch a loved one die from illness, old age or injuries, we bargain with God to relieve their pain, to make them whole and well, to bring them back to us, or take them quickly. But when our children are taken from us we reckon how much sin we can live with, what indignities, hypocrisies and self righteousness of others we are to stand without reaction, without some kind of self defense or withdrawal. Often we too sin with stupid mistakes or a sharpness of our tongue that no "I'm sorry" can fix with that person. We, the family, become members of a group that no one wants to be a member of and of which we invite no one, not even our worst enemy to join. No matter how we try to be more loving, less needy, forgiving, unforgiving, critical or kind, we are changed and often only God knows us as he is the only one we allow close to our hearts.

In 1975, at 17, with just the doctor and nurse present, my only son died in my arms, minutes after his birth. Alone and telling no one, I buried him in a shoebox wrapped in my baby blanket. In 2002, when my 19 year old daughter died, I finally told my mother about my son. Two years later, in 2004, I buried my momma. In 2006, I told a neighbor that I couldn't talk to God as I stood watching my house burn. She told me that was okay she would talk to him for me. I continue to be thankful for Carol Miller. Recently someone told me that the reason I keep having bad things happen to me is because I am not right with God. I replied, "Maybe you're not praying hard enough for me." I have withstood human cruelties of being called the worst unkind and unholy things people can attribute to another human being, and maybe in their eyes, their words true. Although I have often had to play the devil's advocate and take the low road, I was saved in April 1971 and it is that 40 year relationship with God that continues to see me through.

Psalms 88 describes someone who has suffered a great loss, a tragedy, perhaps a parent who has lost a child. For me, it describes a relationship with God that is real. One that is solitary, angry, pained and sorrowful, beseeching and yet devout not forsaking. I know God and he knows me well. In the 22 years that I have been 'back home' after leaving at 17, only one pastor actively tried to get me to return to church, Wayne Harper at Flatwoods, where I was saved all those years before. Wayne accompanied me on several occasions to the cemetery, praying with me and drying my tears. I know I am still in Lorinda's prayers. And in those 22 years, only 4 people invited me to come to church; John Sherrard, Jehovah's Witness, I went twice; Dorothy Hinkle, First United Methodist Church, my family and I attended for nearly 8 years; Lori Dobbins, Flatwoods, I couldn't do it for Wayne knowing they were tearing down the one place I felt safe, "the old chapel", I certainly couldn't go now, but as I told Lori, I was touched and grateful; and Bill Wallace, Sylamore Baptist Church, where I have joined. After a life time of joy and celebrations of lives lived and the deaths of both my parents, two of my children, Wayne Harper and my friend Bob in May, with no one any longer in my life that I could call in the middle of the night, no one I call friend, I have returned to a church family through the love of God and the unlikely efforts of one good man. More than God watches us. I can stand naked in front of my church, in front of God, without shame, can you? This is still a county that expects a politician to ask for their vote. I encourage you this holiday season to pause when you ask someone "how are you?" rather than simply expect "fine, how are you" in return as you move on. Ask someone into your life. Ask someone to church. Faye Ward Wallace, a veteran of life and her nephew Kenneth, MIA Korea, are missing in the lives of their families, but their life everlasting continues not only sitting at the feet of God but in the lives they touched and continue to touch.

Terry Reece – McPhearson

It's a hot morning in August as Terry and I begin the journey from Big Flat, through Bluff Springs to Cold Water, ending up at McPhearson at the once magnificent home of William Josiah "Bill" Rorie where Terry Reece was born. Built around 1900 it is located near the site of the home of Jody Rorie, son of Absalom. It was here on the banks of the White River that Terry Reece spent the first few years of his life.

Terry on porch of 1900 Rorie House at McPhearson where he was born

Among the first settlers here, the Reece and Rorie families are rich with White River Valley history. Jody had first been conscripted to the Confederacy. He deserted, was pardoned and returned home to help his father and brothers build wagons for the cause of the South. He had been home only a few months when the Union soldiers came through in Jan 1864 burning the mills, torturing, dismembering and killing his father Absalom and brothers Hezekiah and Andrew. It can only be imagined what it was that Jody Rorie said but clearly he used his desertion as a maneuver to stop the killing and torture of his family. He was allowed three days to bury his family near Big Flat then he joined the Federalists. Following the Civil War, he built the largest and most competitive sawmill in the region at McPhearson, supplying the Missouri Land and Title Company with raw timber. The port of Sylamore is said to have exported more raw timber than any other port in the South. The 110 year old home that Terry Reece was born in still stands a testament to the wealth and influence of the Rorie family.

McPhearson is found on early territorial maps. Its first known residents were James McPhearson Jr and John Beck, both found on the 1817

Cherokee Indian Census of Arkansas. James McPhearson Jr was the eldest son of James McPhearson aka Skwalakalee or Red Faced Man who was born around 1770 and died after 1830 and Mekoche Woman. The 'town' of McPhearson had a number of post offices in the general area and once called Sneeds Creek after two brothers who lived there, followed by Table Rock (1835) and Morton (1877) before taking the name of McPhearson around 1888 after E.C. McPhearson. Culp, Table Rock, Cold Water and McPhearson are different places in close proximity to each other, located just over the county line from Stone in Baxter County just up river from Calico Rock. Table Rock's first post office was established in 1854 with John A. Beck, son of John Beck, as the first postmaster. Many of the Native American's, primarily Shawnee and Cherokee, who arrived in the White River Valley after 1800 but before 1830 did not leave. The majority were former members of the 20 Tribe Northern Confederacy of the Cherokee belonging to one of the five families, Chalakatha, Thawikila, Mekoche, Kishpoko or Pekowi of Shawnee, the largest tribe within the Confederacy, who had voluntarily chosen to relocate here to the White River Valley. A number of Native Americans whose descendants remain in the White River Valley arrived here by choice, 20 years before the Trail of Tears, including John Brown Jr, son of John Brown (1) Drowning Bear and Quatisis Fox, Head Chief of the Arkansas Cherokee 1839; John's brother Robert Brown b 1749 who refused to move, died in 1835 on the Trail of Tears.

Tustennuccee Emathla "Jimboy" a Creek Chief of the Chalaka b 1773 in Alabama witnessed the Fort Mims Massacre and in 1836 raised a party of more than 700 warriors to fight the Seminoles in Florida under Gen. Andrew Jackson. This was during the period of Creek removal and Chief Jimboy was assured that his family would be cared for during his absence. However, his property was destroyed and four of his nine children were among the 236 Creeks who perished when then steamboat Monmouth sank. Martha Chalaka married John Reece. More than one story says that Timbo was originally called "Jimboy" after Chief Jimboy and over time through strong dialects and a majority of people neither reading or writing, like Isyllamo now Sylamore, became Timbo.

Terry Reece is descended from John Reece of Welch ancestry. John fought in the American Revolution (1776-1789). In 1823, the Reece family moved from GA to IN, from there to Rolla and later Hartville, MO before settling Arkansas in 1846. Terry Reece was born 101 years later in 1947 at McPhearson, one of 14 children born to Aldrun Prevo Reece and Cora Elizabeth Baker. Terry's older siblings attended school at Cold Water, walking or riding a mule the distance from the river to school, about 3 miles. When Terry was a young boy, Aldrun moved his family back to Big Flat where his children attended Bluff Springs School down the hill from the family farm. Continuously held in the Reece family for over 160 years, Henry Reece bought the land from Chief John Wolf Cornstalk Avey (b1794). Terry like many other young men in the Ozarks left for work but his roots run deep in the White River Valley.

Mary Treat Hollow & Round Mtn

As Terry and I traveled across the hills and valleys of Round Mountain and Big Flat, descending the mountain into the river valley of McPhearson, Table Rock and Culp, the beauty of the Ozark Mountains was everywhere. The majestic views where roads cut through opening up the trees are breathtaking. A person can see for miles, far into Izard County to the east, across the river into Baxter to the north and west. Most of the land belongs to the Ozark National Forest, Sylamore District and remains virtually uninhabited. It is a slow arduous trip through these hills today, we marvel at what our forefathers had to endure as they eked out a living. Small communities burst forth everywhere, near springs for water, the rivers were the roads of the day. Few people made an overland trip, cattle were as often moved on keelboats as they were herded when families made their way from TN, GA, AL, KY and OH into the Missouri Territories and present day Stone County.

Communication remained limited almost halting during the Civil War when steamboats who had previously vied for the coveted mail routes and the guaranteed income became targets. Snipers easily disrupted mail routes and supplies on the lower White River virtually cutting off the Middle and Upper White. A system of hollering was put in place from mountain top to mountain top wherein news could travel many times faster than the traveler. The families, most often old men, young boys and women left behind at home had to defend against Southern bushwhackers and Northern jayhawkers as much as they had to defend against both Confederate and Federalist soldiers all of whom would simply take what they needed. There were skirmishes that resulted in unaccounted deaths in the toll of lives lost in the Civil War as these people were not 'soldiers'. As the war neared its end, the escapades of the renegades escalated with killing, raping and robbing starving families, wives, widows and orphans. Northern Arkansas and Southern Missouri was hardest hit, mostly because of the munitions effort in present day Stone County that supplied much of the Confederacy. One such skirmish took place at Big Flat when a group of jayhawkers drove some livestock into a widow's pasture, took over the house and consumed what little food was on hand. When they began gathering up their livestock, one of the children, a 14 year old girl, slipped out of the house running and walking five miles to reach the Henry Reece house. Henry and his sons James, Samuel and Bryce along with Dave and John Morrison hid in the woods at the edge of the widow's field. When the jayhawkers began herding the cattle preparing to move them, the men let loose with the ball and powder. The story alive in the Reece family today has only one variance, which man fired the first shot, James Reece or John Morrison. James Reece maintained that he had hit the leader of the jayhawkers "right where his gallouses crossed." Five of the robbers were killed on the field. One of them dressed in women's clothing escaped. It was reported that word of the skirmish was 'hollered' along the route he traveled. He was caught and hung near Gilbert on the

Buffalo River. The livestock was turned loose and found their way home. The jayhawkers were buried near the present day county line between Baxter and Stone County on the road between Timbo and Big Flat. The markers have long since rotted and the graves are no longer visible, except one. While hand digging and rocking a fall out shelter in the 1950's, over 60 years ago, Harry Tilley built a rock monument atop one of the graves located closest to the road that ran in front of the Tilley store.

The creeks, springs, hills and hollers of Stone County still carry the time honored names of the families who settled them. Many take on names like Bull Pen Holler, the place where the Indians herded the buffalo into for slaughter and then there's Mary Treat Hollow. The lives of the families who first settled here became intertwined and interdependent as siblings married siblings of another family, children becoming double first cousins, genetically the same as brothers and sisters. The Reece, Treat, Rose and Bratton families are much like this. Mary Reece Treat, daughter of Henry and Elizabeth Wood Reece was born in 1836 in Hartville, MO. She married John Treat at the age of 19. They had at least four children, perhaps others. John is believed to be the oldest son of Stephen Treat, who had 3 wives and 23 children. John was 'shanghied' into military service May 21, 1862 at Locust Grove, Company F. He deserted in Jan 1864 and was believed to have joined the Union Army. He was discharged in Ohio at the end of the war. The family legacy is that John Treat survived the war and made his way home. But Mary had heard that he had died and remarried. When he got near home he learned of her marriage and left. She learned of his return and understandably did not deal with it well. She lived the remainder of her life in the holler in which they had lived, rarely leaving. The family says that her children buried her near the spring at her home in the holler. It is a place that is now covered with moss and rocks, returned to the earth and undiscoverable lending more to the Legacy of Mary Treat Hollow. The home in which Terry Reece lived with his family after moving from McPhearson still stands. It is a short walk from the place where Mary Reece Treat lived and died, a beautiful spring fed valley that once heard the laughter of children and tears of sorrow.

House in Mary Treat Hollow

The history of the White River Valley is rich. We live in a place that is unique to the history of the U.S. and where the Ozark culture was birthed. A place where different cultures and ethnicities came together with a common purpose, to find a place, a piece of land that was theirs and make it home. Most of these people, British, Native Americans and mulattos had something to hide. In order to survive, to hold onto their land, knowing who your neighbor was and being wary of people from off was a necessary act of survival. The music, speech, dance and food that we delight in today was first shared among these people who created the Ozark Culture. With over 85% of the land in Stone County still held by the families who homesteaded it, there is a high degree of familial relationships that newcomers do not understand. Although blacks could own land after 1880, it was before laws were changed allowing Native Americans to own land in the state of Arkansas. White

Supremist Harold Sherman brought racism to Stone County in the 1950's. We are still recovering from the damage done promoting Stone County as an all white enclave and his efforts to make Blanchard a white's only retreat. Only in the last 50 years with discrimination laws, have people begun to disclose the wonderful mulit-cultural ancestry that birthed the Ozarks, here in the White River Valley. The majority of our people share Indian, white and black ancestry, we are a people who survival brought together and like Mary Reece Treat, we are sometimes reclusive and misunderstood, but overwhelmingly survival and maintaining our way of life continues to guide us.

Stacey Avey - Newnata & Big Springs

Through family journals, bibles and letters such as the message sent Sept 23, 1823, by Acting Gov of the AR Territories, Robert Crittenden, to John C. Calhoun, Secretary of War, that there were "at least 10,000 Indians gathered at the mouth of the Big North Fork" (Wolf House settlement, Norfork, Arkansas) we confirm the massive migration here to the White River Valley. Many believe that when the 1817 reservation ended that "the Indians left." This is far from the truth. Many of the Indians who arrived here were part of a planned and intentional migration 20 years before the Trail of Tears. The Northern Confederacy of the Cherokee under Chief Hokolesqua Cornstalk (1710-1777) aligned with the British in the American Revolution on the promise of land west of the Mississippi should the British win the war, with the British maintaining what lay east of the Mississippi. Sensing the looming defeat by the Colonists, the Confederacy, a 20 tribe nation, began the last great migration from throughout present day TN, KY, VA, GA and AL into the Ohio River Valley and Canada. By the close of the war in 1789 and the election of the first President it was clear that the children and grand children of the Royal Families of the Native Americans had to be sequestered away to ensure their safety. Just as many of the British who chose to remain in the colonies had to hide their identities and thus claimed to be Irish, Scots, etc, so did the Native Americans. These new settlers, including many of the children and grand children of Chief Hokolesqua, made their way across the great rivers of the Ohio, the Cumberland and Mississippi to the Missouri Territories settling from Paducah, KY and Cape Girardeau, MO to Batesville. Not unlike Jamestown, Virginia where the blending of the cultures and races birthed our nation; the blending of the 'settlers', the blacks, whites and native Americans birthed the people and traditions of the Ozarks seen in our music, our speech, our dance and the clannish way in which we live our lives. We are a strong furiously independent people who do not look for outside help nor influence. We remain cautious of newcomers.

Chief Hokolesqua b 1710 had at least 5 wives. Although Shawnee, he was the Principal Chief of the 20 Tribe Northern Confederacy of the Cherokee formed in 1757 until his death in 1777. His second wife, Ounacona Moytoy Rainmaker, sister to Oconastota who was part of the 1730 delegation to King George II are most significant to the White River Valley due to the marriages within the Cornstalks, Moytoys and Wards. Faye Ward Wallace, b 1915 of Optimus, the oldest living descendant of Chief Hokoloesqua, her grand mother was Nancy Avey Harris, daughter of Peter "Pest" Avey, youngest son of Chief John Cornstalk Avey, died in December 2010 leaving behind a proud legacy of family.

Hokolesqua's sons with Ounacona - Black Wolf b 1740, John (1)/50 and Peter (1)/55 gave us: Chief John Black Wiley of Wiley's Cove, Leslie, Arkansas son of Black Wolf and Jenny Sellard Wiley; Chief John Cornstalk Avey b/92 settled Stone County and Chief Peter (2) Cornstalk Avey/85 Searcy Co, son of Peter (1)/55 and Mary Avery. A half brother to Peter

(1)/55, Young Hokolesqua (2) Cornstalk, son of Hokolesqua and 1st wife Helizikinopo was the father in law of Tecumseh. Abraham Ruddell one of the first settlers of Batesville in 1814, was raised as an adopted brother of Tecumseh. Paukeesa, Tecumseh's daughter, moved north of Mtn Home with his brother the Prophet, present town of Tecumseh, Missouri. Sequoyah (white name George Gist/Guess) who created the Cherokee syllabi with Lucy Ward, 3rd wife of Oconastota, husband of Sally Waters of Kahoka and half brother to Jacob Watts who settled at Sylamore and Arkansas Chief John Jolly, adopted brother of Sam Houston arrived here in 1815. John Houston, Sam's brother was the first clerk of Izard County and is buried at Athens, south of Calico Rock. Their cousin, Margaret Houston, married James Grigsby. The Grigsby's bought the Hardin Ferry at Marcella in 1856. Their son ran it until 1902 (aka Hardin, O'Neal, Grigsby and Hess ferry).

In the above photo at Big Springs Cemetery, Stacy and cousin Jr. Avey are standing at the grave of James Epson Avey, brother of Nancy who married Henry Harris, children of Peter "Pest" Avey, grand children of Chief John Cornstalk Avey of Newnata of whom Jr. is descended. Stacy is descended from James' first cousin John, sons of brothers, Peter "Pest" and Daniel. Behind them are unmarked family graves believed to include Chief John Wolf Cornstalk Avey and his wife Nancy Avey, sister to Chief Peter Cornstalk/85, grand children of Chief Hokolesqua Cornstalk.

Peter Cornstalk (2)/b1785, son of Peter (1)/55 and Mary Avery, grandson of Chief Hokolesqua settled in present day Searcy Co. Robert Adams, the first white settler was allowed into the reservation after the marriage of Chief Peter/85, a War Chief, to his 3rd and young wife, Mary Adams, sister to Robert. After Mary's cousin, Peter A. Tyler killed her husband Chief Peter/85 in 1841 in Kansas, his nephew Peter (3) born 1794 became Chief over the now heavily assimilated and disbanding tribe in Searcy Co. Peter/94's brother, Chief John Wolf Cornstalk Avey/92, who took the last name of his wife and dropped the 'r' (perhaps as a result of speech or census takers) held rule over a much larger constituency of people and a far greater amount of land. Stone County Judge Stacy Avey, 1/8th Pekowi, Mekoche, Shawnee & Cherokee, is the ggg grandson of Chief John Cornstalk Avey b 1792 and the ggggg grandson of Chief Hokolesqua Cornstalk, Principal Chief of the 20 Tribe Northern Confederacy of the Cherokee (1710-1777) and Ounacona Moytoy Rainmaker of the Royal Family of the Native Americans.

Stacy points to a still visible path leading up to the Avey house above where a pulley was installed that allowed the family to lower a bucket to the spring for water. Stacy's home sits on the former land of Chief John Wolf Cornstalk Avey at Newnata which means "My Big Spring there."

Hokokesqua/Rainmaker's son John Wolf Cornstalk's b 1750, son John Cornstalk (2) Avey b 1792 1st wife Shawnee woman – Andrew, John Jr. and Daniel Avey b 1824, 2nd wife Nancy Jane Avery, sister of Chief Peter Cornstalk/b1785 children of Peter b 1755 and Mary Avery.

Daniel Avey, full blooded Shawnee married Tennessee Nancy Jane born 1833 d 1892, full blooded Cherokee. Their son (a first cousin to James Epson Avey) John Lee Avey 1864-1929 (full blood, ½ Shawnee, ½ Cherokee) married Martha Jane Rorie. Martha was the daughter of Hezekiah Columbus Rorie and Louisa Ticer. Hezekiah, his younger brother Andrew and father Absalom were tortured during the Civil War by Union soldiers. Their arms were tied to opposing horses, dismembering and killing them. They refused to tell where the ammunitions were being made for the cause of the South (nearby Gunner Pool). Their mills and homes at Mill Creek and

Bear Pen Holler, just a few miles from Big Springs, were burned. Martha and John's son, James Marvin Avey 1889-1973 (½ Shawnee/Cherokee) is the father of Erstle Avey (1/4th Shawnee/Cherokee) father of Stone County Judge Stacy Avey (1/8th). The primary settlement of Peace Chief John Cornstalk Avey over 200 years ago included Round Mountain, Big Flat, Jimboy (Timbo), Newnata, Big Springs and the fields where Stacy Avey built his home.

In 1836 during the Seminole Wars under General Andrew Jackson, Creek Chief Jimboy Chalaka (Chalakatha) took over 700 warriors to fight the Seminole. The government had begun what became known as The Trail of Tears, the forced relocation of tribes east of the Mississippi. Chief Jimboy was assured his family would be safely relocated from Alabama. However, four of his nine children were among the 236 Creeks who perished when the steamboat Monmouth sank. Cleda Morris, wife of Jimmy Driftwood, and third grade teacher, taught us that Timbo was originally called Jimbo. The Creek settlement that was near present day Timbo was named Jimboy by Chief John Avey to honor those that died from Chief Jimboy's tribe and family offering a new home to those that survived. Martha Chalaka, a descendant of Chief Jimboy, married John Reece. The Reece's bought their original homestead at Round Mountain from Chief John Avey. Stacy Avey, 1/8th Shawnee and Cherokee, Stone County Judge, is descended from a long line of people who have sat in counsel making decisions that protect our way of life and has given us all this place we call home.

Zelda Gammill Bullard - Onia & Pordue

Zelda with her sons Jim and Truman – Pordue Cemetery

      Lunch at Country Time with Zelda Bullard and her sons, Jim and Truman is like old home reunion. People coming by, making well wishes and how are you's add to the fact its election time and both men running for office. Born in 1919 Zelda is the oldest living grand child of John James Balentine and Malinda Branscum. John was born in 1868 in Wayne County, Tennessee to Ben Simmons Balentine and Melissa Sport. It has been said that Melissa was a full blooded Cherokee Indian Princess. Her father James Sport and her mother Catherine Baxter would have both had to have been full blooded and no official records are available to support the extent of

Melissa's blood line. However, her grandmother Elizabeth 1774-1810, wife of William Sport is more likely of Indian ancestry based on when and where she was born in North Carolina and her last name is not recorded. It is more than likely John Balentine's mother Melissa "Lizzie" Sport was at least ¼ to ½ Indian. Being an Indian Princess requires that you be at least the grand daughter of a shaman, medicine man or woman, wise man, or chief and at least ¼ Indian, Lizzie may be the legendary Indian Princess buried at Farris Cemetery near their home at Onia. Her husband Ben is buried at Pordue.

In 1870, as the country was trying to heal from the wounds of the Civil War, Ben and Lizzie with five year old John, moved from Wayne County, TN to Hickory Grove, located between Onia and Big Flat. Lizzie was reported to have cared for a number of people in the community, always tending to the sick and dying, which supports the premise that her mother was a medicine woman. This family story suggests that Melissa Sport's grandmother Elizabeth was full blood Native American and likely a medicine woman within the tribe. John married Malinda Branscum in 1895. Malinda died in child birth in 1913 with Jessie Balentine, her fourteenth child. John later married Jane Woody who had 5 children in the home to John's seven. Together he and Jane had 3 more children.

When it came time due to the growth in the community in which they lived to warrant a post office names were considered. Finally Ona was selected in honor of one of John's younger daughter's. Now, we all know just like in Boston where everything seems to have an "r" added to it, such as Eddie becomes Edder, every locale lends some of itself in the way things are spoken. In the White River Valley, just as the naming traditions of the Native American's and white settler's alike were to signify bloodlines by giving your children your momma's last name as a first name, here, many names are pronounced with a "y", "e", "ia" or "ie" which is what happened when they sent in Ona as the selected name – after all wasn't she O- nee? It is presumed whoever sent in the name spelled it as it was spoken.

When 21 year old Roscoe Lee asked John for his 14 year old daughter Lizzie's hand in marriage, John asked only that he not move her far from home. Promising that, Roscoe purchased the land adjoining John's at present day Onia. A portion of their land was donated to the community for the Pordue Cemetery because it was worthless, not much you could do with it. It would be a "poor man's due" trying to work worthless land hence the phrase, "That's a Pordue" which means working at something that isn't likely to yield much.

John's oldest child Claudia married George Gammill. Their oldest daughter, Zelda, like the other children were born at home or at Grandma's house, at Fairview, a couple miles north of Timbo near where the Caston Farm is. Zelda married Clyde Bullard. As a young woman she carried the mail for over 30 years on a route by mule and horseback that took her from Timbo, to Fairview, Oga, Onia and back to Timbo, along Dark Holler and Panther Branch, pronounced Painter the Creek word for Panther. The area of Onia was inhabited by Creek and Shawnee 200 years ago, hundreds of Native

American descendants continue to reside in Stone County including a great many in the family of John Balentine's. Zelda takes a lot of pride in the fact that she never once lost a piece of mail. She explains that people would leave money in the mail box for stamps and sometimes there might be a sweet tea for her or a piece of pie. If a letter was sealed she couldn't take it without the required stamp, however if it was open it was not considered a letter, just a note for the family down the way and she'd take it and leave it in their box. Letters going outside her route had to have a stamp whether they were sealed or not. Both her boys, Truman and Jim ask her to tell how old Dan took a bite out of her. "Dan was my horse and he had a mean way about him," Zelda begins. "He was so onery. He liked to bite and I had to keep a watchful out for him most all the time. Well, one day he took a notion rearing that head around and took a big bite out of my side. I bout couldn't get around it hurt so bad. Well, I learnt him. I run him until he was tuckered bad out for several days. We got mail out in record time," she says laughing. "Toward the end we got an old truck to deliver mail in. Even though there weren't much of any kind of roads we just pushed along the old trails and soon they came to be roads. It might have been a pig trail or Indian trail but it was my mail route and likely was shared by a few wild hogs and deer. I'd start out at one place and by the time I got back to the startin place I might have had several hanger on's. People sometimes would need a ride over to a family members' and sometimes they just wanted to ride. Motor cars were still a novelty," she said grinning from ear to ear.

"Now my Grandpa John was a devout preacher becoming so passionate in the heat of the summer he would repeatedly have to wipe his forehead, neck and face of sweat. He'd wring out his trade mark red hankie throughout the sermon. He worked hard all of his life and required that his family do so as well. Hoeing cotton, corn and truck patch gardens were every day work and visiting family was expected to pitch in, Grandpa didn't raise no idlers. He'd say, "The Lord didn't intend on people being idle." He come in from plowing in the fields, ready himself up for church but onest he forgot to change his shoes before beginning the sermon. He noticed them and was perturbed but was soon given over to the heat of the sermon," Zelda recalls clearly remembering. After the death of Lizzie, John and his second wife Jane Woody moved over near Fifty Six, the farm now owned by grandson R.C. Alexander.

At the time of John Balentine's death in 1957, he had 16 living children, 84 grand children, 132 great grand children and 32 great great grand children. Exploring who is who in the extended Balentine family requires an extensive mapping of Stone County including Burns, Fletcher, Shipman, Bullard, Gammill's, Kendrick, George and others. Many people in Stone County found their salvation in the churches and arbors where John Balentine preached. He raised 5 sons who became preachers and had 3 daughters marry preachers. Five of his grandson's Earl Gammill, John Lee, Charlie Lee, Thurlo Lee and E.G. Balentine became preachers. Nine of his great grand children and five of his great great grand children also are in the ministry. He left a proud legacy not only in his descendants, honest, hardworking, reverent people who serve the Lord but both his and their continued influence and service within our community, and the House of the Lord.

I had the opportunity to work with Richard Avedon in the late 1970's early 1980's during his work on *In the American West*. When it was completed it was met with harsh critical unfavorable reviews. The show almost didn't happen. It wouldn't of happened if it hadn't of been for Laura Cunningham Wilson (mother of now successful actors Andrew, Owen and Luke Wison then just little boys). The show opened in Dallas, where she lived. The rest, is as they say, history. During the work on that project I learned that the manner in which I looked at people, how I saw beauty and character was an art, "something that should be treasured", he said. It has taken me a lifetime to understand the full weight of that, but when I see the life that has been lived on the face of Zelda Gammill Bullard, I understand completely. I see an incredibly beautiful woman who has touched the lives of so many people, she is "life everlasting" because like John Balentine, she will live on in the lives and hearts of those she leaves behind. If it's a gift for me to see that, it is a greater gift to know someone like Miss Zelda.

Sister's Mary & Linda Jessen - Brewer House

Brewer House 2010
Wayne Jackson, Linda Jessen Jackson and sister Mary Jessen Edwards

Situated in the midst of 22 acres of gentle rolling terrain, with a pond and weeping willows The Brewer House is a magnificent example of homes of the late 1800's. Sisters, Mary Jessen Edwards and Linda Jessen Jackson along with their siblings, have worked to keep the home as true to when they were children growing up there as they can. As we walk through the home, I think we all hear our momma's calling out to us, executing a scolding for running and sliding on the slick polished wooden floors in sock feet or a stern second reminder that it's time to get washed up for dinner. The Brewer house is a home complete with the lives lived there and the memories that make it so. Pots and pans our momma's and granny's used, small bottles for the home made concoctions, medicines, the ironing board, coffee tables and beds smaller than what most know as a double bed, but bigger than a twin are still in their places. If these walls could talk, the stories would rival Shakespeare, tears of joy and grief, marriages and deaths, love stories, children needing prayer and whoppin's. Once an opulent two story structure it has been remodeled by its various occupants who have closed off the fireplace, stairs to the attic and 'cold' house. Covered by decking, the cold house was a hole in the ground outside the kitchen door where fresh spring water kept milk, eggs, butter and other items as cold as any modern day refrigerator. Both Linda and Mary recall the ice cold milk on the hottest of days, with sweet cake. They point out where walls now cover the double fireplace that once stood that as children they warmed themselves by before running to jump into cold beds where they slept three together. And areas of the walls that are still original leading to the attic that is now a loft bedroom.

Adam Brewer house with its second story

The Brewer House was built in 1892 by Adam Brewer and his wife Mary Moffitt Brewer but the story begins long before they arrived here. The relationships between families in Stone County are as evident today as it was nearly 200 years ago. People here know from what part of the county you come from by your last name. The Ward's, Fulk's, Brewer's and Avey's of Stone County are descendents of the Royal Family of Native American's who settled the White River Valley prior to the Civil War. Lanier Brewer, born 1746 is said to have had three wives and 30 children of whom only one was a girl. George, Henry, Wiley, Julius and Solomon are his sons with Rebecca Narcises, a Tellico Cherokee, daughter of Oconostota of the Moytoy's and Ooloosta of the Paint Clan. Along with Francis Fivekiller Ward, Oconostota was the principal leader of the Shawnee and Cherokee, the Royal Families of the Native Americans and members of the 1730 delegation to King George II. Lanier's grandchildren moved here to the White River Valley along with many other grandchildren of the Royal Family of the Native Americans aligned with the British in the American Revolution.

Christian Jessen born in 1812 in Denmark arrived in the Ozarks just prior to the Civil War along with the Anderson's. Peter Anderson would marry Christian's oldest daughter Anna. His son Christian would marry Bodel Anderson. Jordan would marry Mary A. Brewer of Mtn View a sister to Adam Brewer. Their sister Elizabeth married Nancy's brother Silas Moffitt. Mary, Adam and Elizabeth are believed to be the children of Wiley Jackson Brewer and Ceila Daniel, grand son of Wiley Brewer (a grandson of Lanier Brewer) and Mary Cockman. Wiley's brother Solomon married Mary's sister, Sarah Cockman. Several of the Adam Brewer family contacted me regarding a DNA project that has shown they are not the descendants of Lanier Brewer as previously believed. Since the Shawnee were polygamist and accepted the children of their wives and husband's as their own, it is likely that they are not actually the descendants of Lanier Brewer by blood but rather the children of one of his wives who took the Brewer name. For all intents within the Shawnee/Cherokee Adam would have been considered his son. After Christian Jessen's first wife Anne died in 1865, he married Elizabeth Sands, widow of Matthew Sands and mother of 10 children. They first made their home at the Red Doors Community of Stone County before moving to Sylamore (Albert Sands family). A small cemetery there tended for years by Sarah Kendrick, a grand daughter, is believed to be where Christian and Elizabeth Sands Jessen are buried.

William Henry Jessen, their grandson, son of Peter and Lucinda Williams Jessen was born on Sylamore Creek in 1888. He married Minnie Ellen Smith. After spending a year farming corn on Roastin' Ear Creek with cousin's through his Aunt Mary Brewer Jessen, they moved to Oklahoma. Minnie was five months pregnant as they made the trek by wagon. In Feb 1920 she gave birth to Juanita Lorene then 9 months later died. Henry brought her home on the train for burial at Flatwoods. After spending four years as a single father, he married Mae Robbins in a shoe store. They returned to Stone County in 1924, accompanied by Silas and Roscoe Tinkle and their families. The wagon train had five wagons and took 18 days to arrive from Okemah at the home of Henry's sister Cora, wife of Johnny Anderson in Newnata. Henry and Mae moved into a small farmhouse owned by his sister Ada and husband John Dodson which they purchased along with 280 acres in 1925 for $2,500. They raised their family here on the banks of the South Sylamore creek. The children walked to Red Doors to school and on Sunday the family attended church services there. Coming to town was a 9 mile walk and meant not only conducting business but visiting with family including an overnight stay at "The Brewer House."

Adam and Nancy Brewer had William, 1845, Alfred 1847, Mary 1849, and Stephen, 1852 born in North Carolina. Just prior to the Civil War they moved to Ripley, Missouri where James was born in 1857, Joseph M 1860 and Robert 1864. After the Civil War, they moved to Stone County where their youngest child Nancy was born at Roastin' Ear Creek in 1867 on land settled by his great uncles Solomon and Jonas, brothers to his grandpa Wiley. Little is known about the lives of Nancy and Adam between 1867 and

Dec 17, 1892 when during the construction of the Brewer House, 68 year old Adam died, leaving his widow Nancy alone. She died in the house six years later on Oct 17, 1898 at the age of 70. The house and 22 acres was maintained by their son Joseph M. Brewer and his wife Cora until 1937. During the infamous 1929 murder trial of Connie Franklin the population of Mtn View swelled. The Dew Drop Inn, Commerical and Case Hotels were filled. Stagecoaches ran multiple routes daily to Sylamore to the railroad and steamboat landing. The Brewer House hosted prominent lawyers and statesmen. Beds were let out by the hour for rest. The term "Politics Make Strange Bedfellows" comes from a time in our nation when this practice was common. One might find themselves sleeping next to the opposing party or candidate. In 1937 the house was sold to Daniel and Birdie Bickle Martin for $1,500. The transaction shows Willie Austin, son of Solomon and Sarah, and Dick Brewer, son of Jonas, as witnesses, along with Joseph (son of Adam), great grandson's of Lanier Brewer. William Moffitt Brewer who died in 1962 in Mtn View, was the great grandson of Adam and Nancy Moffitt Brewer.

In 1939, the Brewer House was sold to Henry Jessen for $1,600. He and his wife remodeled the house including removing the second story. In 1941 they moved in. With its gentle terrain, weeping willows on the pond, and the beautifully maintained home, "The Brewer House" has witnessed the development of Mountain View and is a special landmark within our city limits. The land and home has been split among the children of Henry and Mae Jessen. Linda Jessen was born in 1943, just after her parents and siblings moved into the Brewer House. With Linda and her husband Wayne Jackson becoming the proud owners of the historic home, they are ensuring the family ownership of a home that is a symbol of over 170 years of Jessen's and Brewer's in Stone County.

Martha Grigsby Hinesley - Grigsby Ferry 1856-1901

"Beautiful, serene, delightful," are words that describe Martha Grigsby Hinesley who always greets everyone with a smile, whether at Woods Pharmacy where she works or passing in the grocery. She is the daughter of Edd Jr and Irma Olmstead, grand daughter of Edd Grigsby, youngest son of Charles Grigsby and the gg grand daughter of James and Margaret Houston Grigsby.

Her great grand father Charles Grigsby from 1856 until his death in 1901 owned and operated what is now remembered as the "O'Neal Ferry" at Marcella. It may be the first ferry on the White River. Local stories support that the "O'Neal Ferry" is the same ferry as the one established sometime between 1814 and 1816 by Nathaniel and James Shield. Although many people think that ferries simply crossed the river, the truth is like keelboats, they would often run the river for miles, navigating the current as they traveled to various landings. In 1816 Joab Hardin bought the Shield's farm and in 1817 licensed the ferry. He lived in a log hut near the water's edge. It is believed this is the ferry and hut that Schoolcraft writes of in 1819 and the same one Thomas Riggs writes of crossing into the Buckhorn around 1819 as he found the place that would be first known as Riggsville and later in 1873 Mountain View. The ferry was described as two small canoes tied together with boards laid across them. The Hardin, Lafferty, O'Neal, Penter, Fulks, Grigsby, Houston and Hess families all arrived in the area before the Civil War, many of them among the first families to arrive prior to the 1817 Indian Reservation. John Lafferty arrived in 1797 and applied for the first land patent in Stone County in 1810, 200 years ago. His daughter married one of Joab Hardin's sons. Martin Hess and his sister Elvy Jane would marry sister and brother. Martin married Elvy Jane O'Neal and his sister Elvy Jane Hess married Charles O'Neal, children of Abijah O'Neal, causing considerable confusion. Redmond Penter (Penter's Bluff) married Polly Hess. Emily Hess married George Fulks. George's parents were Elias Fulks and Martha Houston Grigsby, a sister to Charles Grigsby, ferry operator.

Although Solomon Hess was a chimney builder by trade he was known to run the river. It is believed that Solomon Hess and his family operated the ferry following Hardin. After Solomon's death in the 1840's, his daughter Elvy Jane's husband Charles O'Neal took on operations thus establishing it as the O'Neal Ferry. In 1856 they sold it to Charles Grigsby, son of James and Margaret Houston Grigsby. It was a major route of travel which brought the Grigsby family a great deal of prosperity. During the Civil War it was commandeered by the Union troops on more than one occasion. Only one action, considered an 'accident' as recorded by General Curtis May 12, 1862, was noted in the river bottom land; the sinking of the Grigsby Ferry which took the lives of 11 Union soldiers including Capt Thomas B McClelland. Determined to be a vital means of transportation for the war effort, the Union helped put the ferry back into operation at no cost to the Grigsby's. Some suggest the ferry was sank by the "White River Monster," but that's another story.

Charles Grigsby ran the ferry for 50 years, until his death in 1901. At this time William T. "Tobe" Grigsby, Charles son, having no interest in being a ferryman, sold it to Thomas Marion Hess. Although owned by the Hess', it remained known as Grigsby Ferry until 1905 when the eastern terminal of the ferry and rail road station at O'Neal became permanently attached to the ferry. Began as Sheid's Ferry, it became Hardin's, O'Neal and Grigsby Ferry but due to the O'Neal railroad station on the east banks of the river, it is remembered as the O'Neal Ferry.

The relationship between the Grigsby, Houston, Martin, Ivy, Younger, Fulks, Hess', Wall, Greenway, O'Neal, Wallace and Hardin families began long before they arrived in the White River Valley. In 1782 James Grigsby/b1748 ran a hotel in Rockbridge Co, VA, not far from Fulk's Run and Martinville. In that year he was visited by Marquis de Chastellux, a touring French general who left us with solid documentation as to the wealth and culture of the family. It would be 7 more years before this country would have its first president. James's wife died shortly after the visit and he married Rebecca Anderson Wallace, widow of well to do Col. Samuel Wallace owner of Rockbridge Plantation. Rebecca's daughter Elizabeth Wallace/b1772, four years later married James' younger brother Charles Grigsby/b1755. In the 1840's within 3 years of each other, both Rebecca's son James/b1778 and grandson William Wallace/b1810 died. William's son, Rebecca's great grandson, William Jackson Wallace b 1839 came to Arkansas with his mother, Mary Polly Martin to the home of James' Wallace's nephew James Grigsby/1791 (and wife Margaret Houston), son of his sister, Elizabeth Wallace Grigsby/72 on the White River Valley near Batesville. William J. Wallace's great grandson Phillip Ray Wallace married Faye Ward b 1915. Marcella was originally called Hesstown and was part of Wallace Township.

The Avery Blair family crossing the Grigsby Ferry at O'Neal (Marcella)

When Elizabeth Wallace/1772 married Charles Grigsby/55, it was Rev. Samuel Houston, a first cousin to Gen. Sam Houston and Charles Grigsby who officiated. Charles and Elizabeth had 13 children with two of them marrying Greenways and Houston's. Charles son James served with Sam Houston in the Creek Wars in Alabama under Gen. Andrew Jackson, along with Chief Jimboy Chalakatha. Chief John Wolf Cornstalk Avey named the community now known as Timbo, Jimboy after the death of four of Chief Jimboy's children during the Trail of Tears. After military services, James (the younger) would marry Sam's cousin, Margaret Houston. (Gen.) Sam's father had died when he was 12. Although he lived with his mother, he frequently ran off to spend lengthy periods of time in both the home of his cousins and the Indians later becoming the adopted brother of Chief John Jolly of the Arkansas Cherokee. Sam's brother John Paxton Houston was the first clerk of Izard County and is buried at Athens, 3 miles south of Calico Rock, site of the second territorial courthouse of Izard county.

Charles Grigsby, grandson of the elder Charles Grigsby, prospered greatly as a ferryman building a huge dog trot home on the hills above O'Neal Creek in Independence County. The Grigsby's were considered culture bearers as they knew how to store ice from the winter and how to can. The dog trot home of Charles Grigsby, ferryman and great grand father of Martha Grigsby Hinesley, built in the Barrens over looking O'Neal Creek has been relocated to the campus of Lyon College and although it clearly hosted some of the most important people of not only our nation, but of the White River Valley, it is simply known as "The Grigsby House."

Pauline Mitchell Via - Hess & Wall's Ferries

Pauline Mitchell is the daughter of Charlie Guy Mitchell and Gladys McIntire, the gg grand daughter of Nancy Wall, sister to Grandison Wall, ferryman and gggg grand daughter of Solomon Hess, ferryman.

Born in 1760 in Germany, Jacob Hess, believed to be the father of Solomon came to the United States with General Rochambeau a French General who came to the aid of this country during the American Revolution. Hess served two years in the revolution and declared that he preferred this country to that of his birth. Little else is known about the Hess family until the arrival of brothers, Solomon, Samuel and William in the White River Valley following the War of 1812.

In 1810, the first ferry operations began on the White River in present day Stone County through the efforts of John Lafferty who was operating a keel boat company at the Arkansas Post with his future son in law Charles Kelly, who later became the first sheriff of Independence County. Lafferty had first traveled into the Buckhorn in 1797. He established the first trading post and likely the 'first' ferry just north of what is now Lock and Dam #3, site of the original Lafferty settlement that both Izard and Independence County lay claim to as the history of our county includes being part of each of those. The Lafferty Ferry and extension of his keelboat operations was abandoned after Lafferty's death in 1816. His widow Sarah Lindsey Lafferty continued to run the trading post with her youngest son, Lorenzo Dow Lafferty. The establishment of the 1817-1828 Indian Reservation required their older children and families to move across the river into present day Izard and Independence County. Stone County would not be established until 1873 and was considered the hinterlands of the established counties of Independence (1820) Izard (1825) and later Searcy (1836) and Van Buren (1839). The site of Lafferty's first ferry became the location of the lower landing of the Wall's ferry around 1860, situated between the O'Neal (Grigsby) Ferry to the south near Wallace Creek and the north landing of Walls ferry across from East Lafferty Creek. It would be run for a short time by the McClelland family but the exact time frame seems unclear. It may have been during peak ferry use when Grandison operated landings across from both East and West Lafferty Creek, or may have followed Grandison's death. There are no documents to support anyone other than the Wall family actually owning and operating the ferry at what remains known as Wall's Bottoms at Younger Access.

According to McCulloch's Universal Gazetteer: Independence County, Arkansas : "contained in 1840, 6998 meat cattle, 1928 sheep, 19329 swine' and produced 9151 bushels of wheat, 219,635 of Indian Corn 8702 of oats, 5878 of potatoes, 19,595 of tobacco, 18,932 of cotton. It had eight stores, eight grist miles, three sawmills, two tanneries, two distilleries, one printing office, two weekly newspapers, one academy, 55 students, two schools, 45 scholars. Pop.; whites, 3146, slaves 514, free colored 9, total 3669." Most "free colored" were Metis, a combination of black, white and

Indian as simply being simply 'mulatto' of white and black heritage did not gain an individual their freedom. The Hess family had one of the two very profitable liquor operations. It necessitated use of a ferry and lay across the river from Martin Mines (Izard County), north and east of present day Martin Access. Stories go that when there was suspected trouble for the Hess's, the ferryman would hold up travelers until the liquor could be safely transported and stored. On one occasion the Wall's boy were reported to have hid the whiskey under the pilings of the ferry. The Hess ferry was located near present day Martin Access and Davis Island just below Lock and Dam #3. The Earnhart family owned the Hotel Earnhart (Main and Central in Batesville) and the Earnhart Distillery which had a production capacity of 100 gallons of whiskey per day on the opposite banks of the river (from Marcella) south of O'Neal, near present day Earnhart and Lock and Dam #2, 10 miles down stream from the Hess'. Thomas Marion Hess had built a log home, store and distillery in what was became known as Hesstown on the ridge above the riverport. His son, Thomas E "Terk", b 1873 died 1974, inherited the family distillery business and expanded it to include a riverport and ferry operation (at Davis Island/Martin Access), cotton gin and warehouse, retail and wholesale businesses as well as increasing land holdings to include most of the river bottoms.

Kent Brewer uses the old ferry to transport farming equipment to and from Davis Island at Martin Access, location of former Hess Ferry. The Thomas E "Terk" Hess house on the NRHP at one time had ten outbuildings including two storage sheds, two barns, a corncrib, two chicken coops, a garage, pumphouse and storm cellar. He was the gg grandson of Solomon Hess. Around 1860 Grandison Wall put in one of the first cable ferries on the White River near Lock & Dam #3 with west bank landings at the north and south end of the bluff about a mile apart at West and East Lafferty Creek, operating it until 1908. The license to operate the ferry cost Wall five dollars. Grandison served in the Confederate army as a private, enlisting at the older Hess ferry down river.

Terk Hess House NRHP Marcella, formerly Hesstown

During the Civil War in the winter of 1864, the O'Neal (Grigsby), Hess and Wall ferries were commandeered for up to two weeks by the Union troops as they moved in and out of Stone County including the burning of Rorie's Mill and the torture and killing of Absalom Rorie and his sons. At the north end of Wall's Bottoms a mile long almost perfect rampart wall (on private land) still stands. It was built by slaves prior to the onset of the Civil War, as a first line of defense as the people on the west side of the river knew Batesville, the oldest surviving city in the state would be one of the first to fall to Union troops.

Grandison son's were said to have hand walked the cables across the ferry entertaining waiting crowds. Stories go that he lost his ferry because as he was continuously having to 'bail out' his bunch of wild boys. With the completion of the railroad in 1902 at the base of Penter's Bluff (named so for the Penter family, one of whom married into the Hess family) the ferries were in top demand bringing cattle, crops and timber for transport. Many locals recall continued use of the O'Neal Ferry up through the 1940's and the onset of WWII to move loads of timber and staves across the river to the railroad station there. Began around 1799 with Lafferty's keelboat and ferry operation many ferries operated for well over 100 years. In 1899 there were as many as a dozen ferries between Batesville and Sylamore. Today, three bridges, Batesville built in the 1930's, Sylamore opened in 1974 and Guion opened in 1990, provide access across the river. The once bustling communities, ferries and steamboat landings with thriving river ports along the White River that provided economic growth to the area are now mostly memories.

Sampson's Big Adventure – Or was it Ours?

My friend Beau's dog, Sampson, went missing. Neighbors saw him swim out to people who were river rafting near Lander's Island. Beau was stunned. Not his dog, he wouldn't go out in the river unless he was tempted by the kids in the raft. Worried and unfamiliar with the territory I drove him to Norm and Gail's house above Sylamore. The only place Sampson might have emerged at if he hadn't drown. I was really worried he'd drowned. They would keep an eye out. Knowing the river the way I do, I went through the terrain in my mind, envisioning every possibility of where and how this dog might have made it to. The "old Perrin Place" was closest but there were no houses, just farmland. I could see the steep bluffs in my mind and realized he had either managed to get to the other shore directly across from Lander's Island emerging at Mt Olive or he had in fact drowned. I truly thought this dog had drowned. It was dark and Beau who was convinced he'd made it to the other side, didn't want to get a boat from his friend Chris at Angler's to see if he was stranded. I knew there were no houses on the east bank of the river until you got to Norm and Gail, across from Hale Hayden's, at least 3 miles down river from Lander's Island. And it was not a normal reaction to turn back, to turn north, unless it's going to get you home. I decided we needed to go to Mt. Olive. Only a stones throw from Beau's house it was 30 miles by today's road.

After knocking on several doors, it was clear that although this was news to us, this was not the first time this dog had swam the river. They didn't know him by name, but they knew him, his red and sometimes blue collars, red for Razorbacks and blue for University of Memphis, Beau's alma mater and the scar on his tail. "He's a lover, not a fighter," one said. "Oh, he plays with my grandkids," another lady told us. But the one that took the cake was Shane Linn telling us he'd seen him riding around with the neighbor in his gator earlier in the day. Beau was stunned that his dog had not only swam the river but had done so many times. "Kinda like finding out your kid isn't as angelic as you thought," I told him as he eyed me. We went down a road that Beau didn't think was a road at all and at the end there was really nice cabin with a bevy of dogs. And among them was Sampson. "Oh, at a party are you," Beau said clearly not happy but relieved. As we loaded an over eager wet Sampson into my four-runner to head back to Lander's Island, a gentleman emerged to tell us he'd fed him already. I quietly remembered my trips across the river at Guion on the ferry and thought about what I would give now to be able to cross here at Lander's. What I would pay to ride a ferry. At $3.50 a gallon, 20 mpg, Sampson's little adventure cost $10.50 in gas alone, not to mention the stress. I'd gladly pay $10 for a ride across, not just saving wear and tear on my vehicle but for the smell of the water and the memories but mostly to save the time it took me on those "scenic" roads from Mt. Olive access, down #9 back to Sylamore.

On a cold winter day, Beau watches as Sampson dives in at Boswell Landing. I think back on this and realize how foolish we were for going to get the dog. We should have known he was use to this. "Next time, dog, you swim home."

Bud Cooper - Boswell Shoals

Bud Cooper, a life long resident of the river bottoms of Stone and Izard counties is a wealth of information and always a delight to spend time with. "Boswell Shoals is a series of three shoals starting just below where Wideman Creek flows into the White with the upper end across from Pine Bayou as the French named it in 1790, but locally known as Piney Creek. In 1902-1910 a U.S. Post Office was established called Hoyden, but most likely it was a spelling error and should have been "Hayden." The Hayden family grew and canned the Optimus tomato which gave the area its name. Under the RR bridge on Wideman Creek is a very cold spring emptying into the river, then south are 2 more springs between the creeks, and between the Shoal's, then a creek "Huff Branch". These are cold springs and the rainbow trout like this cold water. Below Huff Creek is Soldiers Rock Bluff. A Confederate Soldier jumped his horse off this bluff into the river, swam it and got away from the Yankees that were after him. Up stream to Piney Creek; this is a big creek and it has a swift chute down from it. When the river is up there is a slough on the Izard side. My grand father S. C. Smith b 1893 said there were a lot of steamboat wrecks in Piney Chute. Remember the rock pile we have to watch for near the middle of the river.

Rail Road Bridge at Boswell

Grand father said he saw the steamboat men putting this rock wing there. It was put at the Stone Co bank. Up stream a little from Piney Creek is Watkins Slough on the Stone co side; a turtle, and brim heaven. The PO at Hoyden was in the NW 1/4 Section 6, Township 16 North, Range 10 West, in Stone co. Ar. It was on a mail route from Optimus to Jumbo in Izard Co. James N. Craig was Post Master at Optimus and got the PO at Hoyden started. Hoyden PO was removed around 1910. The Hayden's owned large parcels of land where they grew peaches and tomatoes. Along with other residents they shipped out cattle at the rail yard on the opposite banks of the river. The Hayden's operated a ferry between Boswell and Optimus for years, long after the last steamboat landed in 1906. The big bend in the river was known as Hayden's Bend."

"The shoals were put in by the U.S. Government in the 1890's to turn the river water to the west side (Stone County) of the river at numerous places along the White. The steamboats needed water 4 feet deep and 25 feet wide to move upstream. The shoals were established along with the building of the lock and dams in order to provide access into the Upper White River, north of Batesville. The steamboats aided in their own demise as they hauled in the supplies to put in the rail road which was completed around 1902."

Sylamore, Mt. Olive, Boswell, Round Bottom and Guion (Wild Haws) were once booming river port settlements. The steamers brought in goods from New Orleans and Memphis. The steamer records show transactions with Chief Johnny Cake of the Delaware, Chiefs Cornstalk, Owl, Lewis and other tribes for bear fat, meat and furs, including buffalo hides.

Remains of Steamboat Landing Tie Down

The river towns were much like the interstate cities of today, each one had standard establishments such as a livery, tavern, hotel, trading post or dry goods store and at least one church. The stories surrounding the drunken brawls along the river towns continued well into the early 1940's including

Ma Cook's at Swinging Bridge at Sylamore. Stories of the days of steam boat travel invariably include river men, fiddles, banjos, dice and cards. It's estimated that by 1835 there were 250 riverboats and 2,000 professional gamblers working the rivers and settlements. In the 1840's one of the most famous gamblers was George H. Devol. It is said by the time he was 13 he had learned to play "Seven-Up", was a master at the art of bluffing and could deal seconds, palm cards and recover the cut. Serving in the Mexican War he put his skills to use in swindling the other soldiers. After which he returned to New Orleans and by the age of 17 had headed back home with almost $3,000. He continued to hone his skills and by the time the Civil War broke out he had made hundreds of thousands of dollars working the steamboats of the South. Steamboats were the gamblers playground with cotton buyers, plantation owners, merchants, slave traders and regular folks relying on the rivers for both travel and a means to economic survival. The riverboat gambler is a uniquely American icon with an image as a charming, courageous gentleman who was a shrewd competitor. The truth is most were frauds and hustlers. Although it is estimated that Devol won over two million dollars in his 40 years of gambling he died penniless in Hot Springs in 1903. Devol wrote in his autobiography in 1892, "Forty Years a Gambler on the Mississippi," he was joined by many other card sharps including playing with Wild Bill Hickok, Bill Jones, Bill Rollins and Big Alexander and of lesser known fame river gambler Jesse Ward. Buried at Optimus Cemetery on the west side of the river near Boswell Shoals Landing, it is said Jesse Ward was laid to rest with a deck of cards in each hand, a whisky bottle in each pocket and a pistol on his breast. Local residents remember the grave of the "river gambler" as being surrounded by 52 white palings about 4 inches wide. The tops were in the shape of a diamond with a spade carved out in center, with the other palings having hearts and clubs painted onto them. Faye Ward Wallace recalls told that her father Joe Ward said that the gambler's name was Jesse Ward, but was of no relation to them he thought. One of Jesse Ward's gambling buddies had the palings made to fence in the grave. One morning after having been out drinking, the friend woke up in the cemetery having fallen asleep in the saddle to find the reins of his horse safely hitched to the palings surrounding his friend's grave. By the 1970's the palings were gone, likely removed during a cemetery cleaning by someone who tore down the weathered and fading fencing without knowing the story of Jesse Ward, the river gambler.

Boswell Shoals River Access lays at the end of Optimus River Road half way between Mountain View and Calico Rock. Established to provide more navigable waters for the keelboats, flatboats and steamboats the shoals have become a favorite spot for fly fishermen. Boswell Shoals is a hold out of the wild frontier. Although you will no longer hear the magical whistle of the steamboat, it remains a bit of a gamble surrounded by the Ozark National Forest, farms, fields, cane breaks, wild hogs and an occasional bear. So deal me in for the beauty and freedom as Boswell Shoals is the last free place on the White River to camp.

Garilyn Partee Green & Jim Partee - Partee Springs

It was an incredibly beautiful fall day as Bill Wallace and I forded the sparkling water of upper Livingston Creek carefully driving along what was once Hiway 5 north before it was re-routed and paved. The old road narrowed becoming only a trail of the Syllamo Bike Trails in the Ozark National Forest, Sylamore District. Bill was born and raised here, just down stream. He is the son of Phillip Ray Wallace, grandson of Arthur Wallace, great grandson of William Jackson Wallace and Atlantic Jeffery, who are buried in Livingston Creek Cemetery. His family lived in the home built in 1852 (NRHP) by his gg grand father Miles Jeffery son of Jehoiada, one of the first settlers of the White River Valley near Mt. Olive, just down stream from where Partee Springs feeds into the Livingston Creek. Delivered at home in 1949, Bill's father rode on horseback to Calico Rock to get Doc Copp who forded the now raging creek on his horse holding on only to his hat in order to deliver Bill, the youngest child of Ray and Faye Ward Wallace.

James Coleman "Jim" Partee – March 2011 – son of Fred

As I was preparing the final edit on Places of Our People, Bill called me that Jim Partee was in town from Nashville and was trying to find the springs, could I take him? Jim is the son of Fred and Regine Johnston Partee. Not only did we make it out there on this cold spring rainy day, but we found where beavers were attempting to build a dam in front of the main opening and were able to at least deter them a little by removing it. Jim got him a perfect nature made walking stick out of the deal. The wall along the north side of the creek was more visible today as well as the foundation rocks of the grist mill that once operated there, providing for the families who called this home.

Partee family left to right: The father holding baby Richard Partee, baby Grover, mother Martha Elizabeth Hively Partee, holding Lillian Partee. L to R back row: Irene Wallace Partee holding Myrtle Partee, Samuel John Partee, Mason R. Partee (holding onto the tree), the blonde boy in front Clarence Oscar Partee, behind him Harriet Partee Fitzhugh, next to Clarence is Grover Partee, behind him Lydia Partee, behind the mother James Partee, Mr Mason, a cousin wearing a cap standing in the back, lastly Sarah Reynolds Partee holding baby David Partee.

Children of William Jackson Wallace, grandson of Col. Samuel Wallace and Rebecca Anderson, he arrived with his mother, Mary Martin living out his youth in the Marcella area of Stone County. After the death of Williams' father James, his mother came here where the Grigsby/Wallace family had moved to. The Grigsby Ferry ran the ferry at Marcella/O'Neal (Wallace Township) from 1856-1902. Arthur married Mary Sullivan, Irene Wallace married Samuel Partee (son Fred), Richard Wallace married Leona Stevens (son Syd), descendant of Lanier Brewer. Leona's sister Viola married Mason Partee (1881-1957) (son Neil). Their children, first cousins, Ray and Syd Wallace and Fred and Neil Partee were raised here in what is now the edge of the Ozark National Forest, on Livingston Creek. The Partee family arrived in the Ozarks around 1814 from Livingston, Kentucky. They called the original settlement Livingston on the Creek. They walked or rode horses and mules to Optimus to church; Ray married Faye Ward; Syd, Deloris Wallis; Neil, Pauline Sutton and Fred, Regine Johnston. Garilyn Partee Green is Neil and Pauline's daughter. Jim is Fred and Regine's son. Garilyn is the grand daughter of Mason Partee and Viola Stevens, great grand daughter of Richard Partee (1844-1921) and Martha Hively and great great grand daughter of Lewis Partee from Livingston, Kentucky. In 1793, Lewis served in the Kentucky militia in Capt. James Lanier's Co. of Volunteers from Bourbon Co. Lewis arrived here some time around 1814 when this area was still the Arkansas Territories. Second cousins to Garilyn Partee Green, Syd's daughters, Liz Wallace Hutson and Rebecca Wallace Ford and Ray's son, Bill Wallace all live in Stone County.

Bill Wallace - Fall 2010 – Son of Ray Wallace

Although they arrived and settled in what is now Stone County around 1820 during the time is was part of the Indian Reservation, the earliest homesteads for the Partee family are found in Izard County in 1857 and 1860 by Richard's brothers James and Alfred. Richard would later homestead in what would become Stone County in 1873, then Izard County. The Partee land is located just upstream from the Miles Jeffery homestead, about 11 miles from Mountain View on Hiway 5 north.

Although no records have yet been provided or found in preparing for this piece, family information is that Richard's 67.9 acres of land was left to the Ozark National Forest, in 1921 with the stipulation that it would remain named Partee Forest Preserve for 99 years. Others says it was lost due to back taxes in 1908 when under Roosevelt the National Forest was formed. The name Partee Springs still appears on the Arkansas Gazetteer and until the early 1970's you could find "Partee Spring and Hunter's Camp" on U.S.F.S. maps. In the 1960's during the re-routing and initial paving of Hiway 5 north, the Arkansas Hiway Department or the U.S. Forestry Service removed the official signs which were never replaced. Some of the signs are in the possession of family members.

A slow and steady hike up the hillside to the north leads to Littleton Gap. The creek on Littleton Gap disappears into the underground. Neil, Ray and Syd told stories of putting saw dust into the creek and a week later it would come out of the spring. Once their grandmother figured out they were the culprits, needless to say, they didn't do it again. The foundation to the old house still remains but you have to know what you are looking at to discover the hand hewn rocks that were once part of the chimney, door step and corner rocks. Today the water levels are low after little rain fall but is still freezing cold. Both Bill and Garilyn can recall their father's telling of keeping milk cold in the spring water along with fishing, swimming, washing clothes, and hauling drinking water and the dutiful Saturday night bath water for Sunday church.

In 1968, Garilyn Partee graduated MVHS and married Roy Green. They have two sons Mike and Chris. Garilyn has been the owner of H & R Block in Mtn View for 40 years and for 35 years with her husband, has owned Green and Partee Real Estate. Her office is located on Hiway 5 South, across from Wilson's Town and Country and the home where Syd Wallace raised his daughters and his wife Deloris continues to live. Garilyn is the gg grand daughter of James Partee who was born in 1811 200 years ago in Livingston County KY and died in 1853 in Izard County Arkansas present day Stone County. Partee Springs is located near the Syllamo Bike Trails where the U.S.F.S. has put up signs marking the path along the lower portion of the stream. But there are no signs indicating the name of this place, or the springs. There are no signs indicating the once heavily traveled portion of the old road that ran along the creek where as young boys Ray, Syd, Fred and Neil played and hunted and as young men married and began their families. Where Ray Wallace rode his horse to get Doc Copp, where they traveled through a pouring rain crossing a surging creek to deliver his son Bill Wallace, or they walked to church at Optimus; or where this once thriving community of extended family members lived and died.

The White River Valley is rich with history. The U.S.F.S. and Stone County could increase the tourist industry through the recognition of the families who arrived here settling this valley, blending with the Native Americans and slaves to create the Ozark Culture, evident in our speech, our dance, our music and the way we live our lives even 200 years later.

About the Author

Freda Cruse Phillips was born at Dr. Burton's Clinic on Main Street in Mountain View, Arkansas, and raised in Stone County. Her forefathers arrived between 1817 during the time it was the Cherokee Indian Reservation and the Civil War in 1861. It has been said that no single person knows more about the White River Valley as a whole. She disagrees on that point stating that "with every interview, with each place I visit, I learn something I didn't know." More specifically she defines that most of her knowledge is limited to the west side of the White River, what was the 1817-1828 Indian Reservation.

Both her parent's families are in the direct line of the "Royal Family of Native American's" created in the 1730 alliance between King George II and the Moytoy's. The delegation is represented in the Trustee's of Georgia Painting which hangs in the British Royal Museum in London, descendant of Francis "Chief Fivekiller" Ward a white man from England and Tame Doe Catherine Carpenter of the Moytoy's. Blended through marriages of Elizabeth Wallace, daughter of Col. Samuel Wallace and wife Rebecca Anderson, to Charles Grigsby, and their son to Margaret Houston of the same family as General Sam Houston and brother John Paxton Houston who became the first clerk of Izard County, and Old John Fulk, a half Indian half white trader whose son married Katy Walker, of Walker Plantation in Georgia and another line of Houston's, cousins to Sam and John and Andrew Ross, brother to Chief John Ross, whose daughter Harriet married James Chitwood. Chief Ross' daughter Emily married Jacob Watts brother, cousin and nephew to Sequoyah, Chief John Jolly, Chief John Benge, Chief Bowles and Chief John Wolf Cornstalk Avey – all who lived in Arkansas prior to the Trail of Tears, who willingly re-located blending with the whites and blacks and in doing so created a new culture – that of the Ozarks. Phillips maintains that the birth of the Ozark culture occurred here in the White River Valley in the years 1797-1847.

Phillips graduated high school in Mtn. View, Arkansas and completed her college eduation at the University of California, San Diego. In the 1970's she worked with two American greats, photographer Richard Avedon and Dr. Jack D. Douglas (UCSD Sociology Department). She worked on *In the American West,* with Avedon and *Creative Interviewing* (Sage Publications), and other publications with Dr. Douglas becoming his co-author on *Love, Intimacy and Sex* in 1988 (Sage Publications). She is a contributing photographer and writer for a number of newspapers, periodicals and magazines including the Stone County Citizen, White River Current, Arkansas Democrat Gazette, Ozark Regional Magazine and Eye on Independence magazine. In 2009 she completed *Voices of Our People*, 52 interviews of local Stone County citizens, the first in the series "The Vanishing Ozarks." Phillips is currently working on Music of Our People for a 2012 release.

She has continued work in photography over the last 35 years with her main focus fashion, politicians and musicians. Her work includes a number of music videos and documentaries including assisting Dave Anderson on his debut piece for *Oxford American's* So Lost series which featured Mountain View. Phillips has a continuing photographic exhibit *The Mountain Music Project* on permanent display at Country Time Restaurant in Mtn. View, Arkansas, a project documenting local musicians and the music history of Stone County. It has been said there are more musicians per square foot there than any other place in the U.S. Any given day, weather permitting, the court square and pickin park is the place to find, join or listen to impromptu music, mostly bluegrass, country and gospel.

Phillips welcomes unsolicited input regarding the history of the White River Valley and acknowledges, "Our history doesn't change but our ability to understand and interpret it, does."

Order Photographs and Books
Nikki Atwell Foundation – a non profit organization – www.nlaf.org or
NLAF P O Box 2133, Mountain View, Arkansas 72560